LIFE SKILLS:
KEYS TO
EFFECTIVE LIVING

JILL RAIGUEL

MARSHALL EDUCATIONAL HEALTH SOLUTIONS, INC.
P.O. BOX 1727 MINDEN, NV 89423

Published in the United States by Marshall Educational Health Solutions, Inc.
P.O. Box 1727, Minden, Nevada, 89423
(800) 428-8321

Designed by Paperweight

Typeset by Falcon Graphic Art, Wallington, Surrey

Printed in the United States of America

ISBN 1-893897-00-1

Dedication

I dedicate this book to all the abused people
I have seen over the years.
Your courage has moved me. Your strength has empowered me.
Your healing has shown me that miracles are possible.
You inspired me to write this book.
My life will never be the same because of you.
And you are in my heart forever.

Acknowledgements

To Catherine Boyer, friend and colleague, who read every chapter tirelessly and returned it the next morning with loving and incisive comments.

To Gene Martineau, Deborah Herr, Bill Lawry, Debbie Woods and Roger Lewis who invested in this dream long before it looked possible.

To Anne White and David Rosen who not only believed in the project but enthusiastically helped bring it about.

To Dr Fred Covan, Judy Fox, Hannah Woods, Dr Sheila Jackman, Randa Mayers, Jeanne Le Blanc, Daniel Sexton, Linda Thurman and Rosemary Cunningham who gave their expertise, advice and generous support.

To my teachers Lynn Bieber, Dr Fred Heslet, Ethel Lombardi, Anne Cooper, Walter Blair, Judith Yellin and The Successful Writing Group, Laurel Sheaf, Werner Erhard who helped me become the person, the writer and the healer I am today.

To Dr Merle Sprinzen who volunteered her time and helped me develop the *Raiguel Life Skills Inventory (TM)*.

To Tracy Smith, who gave this book its missing ingredient and her love. To Beverly Trainer, for her meticulous editing.

To David Cunningham, my brother, who gave his constant inspiration, love and partnership.

To my mom and dad, who taught me how to love and that anything is possible.

And to the many clients and survivors who read drafts and gave me their valuable feedback.

I wrote this book with these magnificent people behind me. I could not have done it without them.

Contents

Introduction

May these words give you comfort,
May they heal your heart.
May these stories lift you up,
May you find peace.

Everyone needs some *life skills* Training. This book is no longer just for people recovering from child abuse, alcohol or drugs. As I have shared this work with therapists, students and professionals of all kinds, many see they are missing certain skills. Most people, not just survivors*, need to recognize blind spots and overcome them. Recent random acts of violence confirm that many need to find appropriate and safe ways to express anger and not indulge their rage. In their 1997 report, the National Committee for the Prevention of Child Abuse states that reported child abuse is up.

Even though Americans vacation, party and recreate, we can still find ourselves emotionally unsatisfied. Many need to discover and practice what does nurture and satisfy them. People who have moved frequently and isolated themselves from family and friends need assistance in systemically creating new supportive friends. Dr. Dean Ornish states in **Love and Survival** that people who experience love and support in their lives are less likely to have a severe illness and are more likely to recover from one. We must practice emotional maturity, as Daniel Goleman calls it in his book **Emotional Intelligence**.

Although America has focused on training people to be productive, now we need to include other life skills: including having fun, building positive relationships, and expressing emotions appropriately. Twenty life skills are discussed in this book as well as exercises to strengthen them. I still have not seen another program that gives people the specific instruction available in this book.

*Throughout the book, I use the term 'survivor,' 'victim,' and 'adult who was abused as a child' interchangeably. The individual cases are based on true stories. I have changed the names and other identifying factors to protect their privacy.

How did I start life skills training? My clients taught me. Even though I had counseled thousands of people who were abused, I began to see that something was missing. In addition to helping people release their pain and resolve the past, something was needed, but what? During a workshop I was leading, I suggested to one survivor that she have some fun. She replied, "I don't know how to have fun."

How in the world do I teach a concept like fun? I walked over to my white wire basket in my closet and pulled out two kazoos. I handed one to her and asked, "Do you know how to hum?" She nodded. "Do you know *Row, Row, Row, Your Boat*?" She nodded again. "Let's go." And we both hummed a wonderfully crazy duet. After a few choruses we were both laughing. I gave her the kazoo to remind her that she can have fun anytime she chooses. That was my first life skills lesson.

Another client did not know how to make friends; still another had no idea how to set goals. I began to see that many survivors did not learn basic life skills as youngsters. My clients were smart people, but no one had helped them identify missing skills or shown them how to learn them. Whenever I named a skill and broke it down into small steps, my clients could, and did, learn quickly.

So, in 1985, I worked with Harvard trained Dr. Merle Sprinzen to design the *Raiguel Life Skills Inventory* ™. Together we found a way to measure 20 skills. Then I created the *Life Skills* workshop so people could not only find out what skills were missing, but also learn those skills. Soon, colleagues and clients asked me to write a book so more people could use the *Life Skills* work. So I have revised the *Life Skills Inventory* and compressed the workshop into a self-study program.

Life skills training really needs to start in elementary school and continue through adulthood. Incorporating mastery of these skills into our culture will not only break the abuse cycle, but bring people more personal satisfaction and mastery. Certainly life skills training will reduce child abuse and help adult survivors maintain recovery. With these new skills you can stand up for yourself and not allow people to abuse you. The cycle of abuse is broken. And, then, we are closer to ending abuse in this generation and as new research indicates, it may even help people become stress and disease resistant.

PART I

Understanding What Happened

CHAPTER 1

Who This Book is For

Professionals estimate that as many as 64 million people in America alone were abused as children. That means one out of every four women and one in every seven men. If you were not abuses, you almost certainly know a friend, family member, lover or co-worker who has been. Abuse is a problem that affects all of us; it colors our relationships, has an impact on our child rearing, and reaches into the workplace. Many individuals were physically or sexually abused, but the vas majority of abuse survivors were abused emotionally and are still suffering silently. *Life Skills* is a book for all those adults who suffered any kind of abuse - physical, mental, sexual or emotional - during their lifetime. This book is intended to help all survivors work toward complete recovery.

If you survived abuse or suspect you might have; if you have never found a satisfactory answer to your question, 'What's wrong?' – then this book is for you. I have written this book for any adult who was abused as a child. You may remember the times you were abused, but minimize their impact on you. Or you may not consciously remember at all, yet you experience recurring nightmares. Or you may not even realize that what happened to you really was abuse.

Like many other survivors, you may have grown up to abuse others. Or you may have abused alcohol, drugs, sex, or food; or you may engage in abusive relationships. You may be an adult child of an alcoholic, or perhaps your role model was a drug addict, overeater, compulsive gambler, or other type of addict. Although researchers cannot provide a definite figure, studies estimate that alcohol abuse or other addictive behavior is a factor in 50 to 90 percent of all abusive families.[1]

The bottom line, if you grew up in a household where you suffered any kind of abuse whatsoever, is that you suffered psychological abuse. Whether your abuse was overt or subtle, whether your scars are invisible or etched on your soul, you are a survivor in need of healing, and having read this far, you are already on your way.

WHERE THIS BOOK BEGINS

When treating people who have suffered abuse, I use the term Trauma Therapy to describe the four phases of recovery:

Phase 1 — Managing Crises

Phase 2 — Re-experiencing and Releasing Feelings

Phase 3 — Recognizing Abusive Patterns and Taking a Stand

Phase 4 — Learning Missing Life Skills

Phase 1 — Managing the Crisis

Hotlines, crisis centers, shelters, and Twelve-Step Programs assist people in the Crisis Phase. By 'crisis' I mean situations in which people require immediate and constant help to live their lives. A newly sober alcoholic who needs to attend AA meetings daily to stay sober is in the crisis phase. So is a person who is emotionally unstable or suicidal or who is actively dealing with addictive behavior. If you are in crisis, you should not read this book right now. Give yourself three to six months, or until you are no longer handling these issues on a daily basis.

If you should discover you have a serious addiction while reading this book, stop wherever you are and deal with that first. I strongly recommend the Twelve-Step Programs – Alcoholics Anonymous, Overeaters Anonymous, Debtors Anonymous, Narcotics Anonymous, to name a few – all of which are listed in the phone book. Get sober or clean, and then come back. If you discover that your abuse was far more profound than you had remembered and you need support, seek therapy before resuming your work in this book. Reading it while you are handling crisis may overload and disorganize you to the point where you sabotage your recovery. If that starts to happen, seek professional help.

Phase 2 — Re-experiencing and Releasing Feelings

When a person has returned to normal daily activities, work can begin on Phase 2. In the adult survivor's case, releasing the pain of abuse can begin many years after the actual trauma. Good therapy can assist you with this phase. The Life Skills program does not pretend to be a substitute for therapy or for healing the past.

Phase 3 and 4 - Recognizing Abusive patterns and Taking a Stand, and Learning Missing Life Skills

Crisis counseling and competent therapy are designed to help people is Phases 1 and 2. However, I have not seen any other method designed to treat Phases 3 and 4. This is where *Life Skills* begins. It offers tools which enable readers to recognize abusive patterns, and then shows them how to live abuse-free lives by mastering missing Life Skills. One Life Skills participant said: 'I no longer think something is wrong with me. I have learned to recognize my patterns and I've taken a stand to lead a non-violent life. I know I'm missing certain skills. But I can learn them. That sounds so simple, but it's very freeing."

ASSESSING YOUR LIFE SKILLS

Whether you are an adult survivor or not, you can assess your own Life Skills by taking the following quiz. Just answer each question honestly and spontaneously. Don't 'agonize' or spend time deliberating over your responses. And relax. There are no 'right' or 'wrong' answers, just ones which give you insights and serve as helpful guides for new learning.

CHAPTER 2

The Life Skills Quiz

YES/NO **1 BUILDING TRUST**

☐ ☐ Do you often find yourself suspicious of people's motives and behavior?

☐ ☐ Do you avoid getting to know people because you don't trust them?

☐ ☐ Do you get into relationships quickly and find out later that you should have been more cautious?

☐ ☐ Do you trust people instantly without questioning their qualifications or letting trust develop over time?

☐ ☐ Do you follow other people's advice when you know you should trust your own intuition?

2 NOT DISSOCIATING

☐ ☐ Do you often feel a sense of separateness or alienation from other people?

☐ ☐ When something upsetting happens, are you surprised by your lack of response?

☐ ☐ When others are terrified by events such as earthquakes or turbulent airplane flights, do you find yourself sort of 'anesthetized'?

☐ ☐ Do you find yourself constantly fantasizing instead of dealing with real situations?

YES/NO Have people told you or do you see that your face looks
☐ ☐ frozen or wooden or lacks expression?

3   EXPRESSING EMOTIONS APPROPRIATELY

Do you question whether you are feeling the right emotion
— happy, sad, excited — at weddings, funerals, football
☐ ☐ games or other significant occasions?

When a person asks you what you are feeling do you have a
☐ ☐ hard time knowing what to say?

When you cry or are angry, do you sometimes worry that
your emotions will overwhelm you to the point where you
☐ ☐ will lose control?

Did your family ever put you down for being 'in the dumps'
or 'on cloud nine' or simply too emotional? Were you
☐ ☐ ridiculed when you expressed genuine feelings?

Do you regularly find yourself getting very upset at little
things — a friend being ten minutes late or the garbage
☐ ☐ disposal breaking down?

4   HAVING FUN

After you schedule a leisure activity, does it become an
☐ ☐ obligation rather than a pleasure?

Is fun something you will get around to when all your work is
☐ ☐ done?

Do you have productive hobbies such as running, reading or
gardening, but find things like jokes, singing or blowing
☐ ☐ bubbles silly or 'beneath you'?

At a party or when out with friends, do you often feel you are
☐ ☐ the only one not having a good time?

☐ ☐ Does the thought of taking a vacation make you feel guilty?

5   EXPRESSING NEEDS

When a friend asks you what you want to do on an evening
☐ ☐ out, do you usually say, 'I don't know'?

THE LIFE SKILLS QUIZ

YES/NO Do you have a hard time deciding what to do with a free moment?

When someone asks your opinion, do you often struggle for an answer?

Do you generally defer to the person you are with?

When you spend time with friends or family, do you put your needs last?

6 DEVELOPING SELF-NURTURING

Is it hard for you to treat yourself as well as you treat your best friend?

Do you rarely take leisure time just for yourself?

Are you secretly jealous when friends treat themselves to vacations, theater tickets, massages or restaurant dinners?

Does being good to yourself — taking a long bath, sleeping late, getting a massage — sound indulgent?

Is it hard for you to buy things for yourself?

7 OVERCOMING BLIND SPOTS

When a person pays you a compliment, do you have a hard time understanding what he or she is talking about?

Have you been in a relationship with a problem-drinker more than once?

When fellow workers discuss office politics, do you not quite see what they are talking about?

Are you able to zero in on what is really happening with people or situations, but then choose to ignore the facts?

Have you ever lost money because you were 'conned'?

8 EXPRESSING ANGER SAFELY

Is it hard for you to recognize when you are angry?

When you get mad, do you throw things or hit people?

THE LIFE SKILLS QUIZ

YES/NO Is your anger often out-of-proportion to the incident? (For example, when another driver cuts in front of you, do you feel like you want to kill him or her?)

☐ ☐

When someone around you loses his temper, do you become anxious and fearful?

☐ ☐

Do you get headaches, stomach aches, or tight muscles because you hold your anger inside?

☐ ☐

9 NOT LETTING PEOPLE USE YOU
When friends use you, do you notice it only after the fact?

☐ ☐

Are you afraid to speak up when a friend takes advantage of you? (For example, when a friend borrows something and does not return it, are you afraid to ask for it back?)

☐ ☐

Do friends ever tell you that you were used, but you just don't understand what they are talking about?

☐ ☐

Do you have trouble saying 'no'?

☐ ☐

Do you let people use you to gain their acceptance?

10 ENDING SELF-BLAME
Do you take on other people's problems as if they were your own? If your spouse comes home in a bad mood do you wonder what you have done?

☐ ☐

When a friend of yours is rude to someone else, do you apologize for him or her?

☐ ☐

If it rains on the day you planned a picnic, do you feel you are to blame?

☐ ☐

When you were growing up, did you feel as though you parented your parents?

☐ ☐

Did you feel your being abused was somehow your fault?

11 NOT SABOTAGING YOURSELF
Before a job interview or important presentation, do you frequently stay out late and get less than optimum sleep and rest?

☐ ☐

THE LIFE SKILLS QUIZ

YES/NO Just as you start becoming successful, does 'something' happen to stop you?

☐ ☐ Do you ever find yourself being rude or inconsiderate to friends when you really want to be nice to them?

☐ ☐ Do you sometimes hide your competence in important situations? (For example, do you minimize your experience at a job interview when you know you are fully qualified?)

☐ ☐ Do you ever show up late on the first day of work even though you know the importance of making a good impression?

12   NOT OVERHELPING

☐ ☐ Do you help others at your own expense? (For example, when a friend calls at 2 a.m. just to talk, do you listen even though you are losing valuable sleep?)

☐ ☐ Are you usually the 'giver' in your relationships?

☐ ☐ If a friend gave you a gift for no particular reason, would it make you uneasy?

☐ ☐ Do you try too hard to solve other people's problems?

☐ ☐ Do you give your help or advice without being asked?

13   NOT NEEDING TO BE PERFECT

☐ ☐ Do you feel you have to be immaculately groomed at all times and keep your home so it would pass 'white-glove inspection'?

☐ ☐ Do you feel that organizing your life to perfection is the only way to live?

☐ ☐ Have you ever worked to make something perfect even if the effort made you exhausted or sick?

☐ ☐ Did your parents tell you that you had to set a perfect example to others?

☐ ☐ Do you try to be perfect because you are afraid of criticism or of making a mistake?

THE LIFE SKILLS QUIZ

YES/NO **14　MANAGING YOUR ADDICTIVE NATURE**

☐ ☐ Are you or have you been addicted to alcohol, drugs, sex, gambling, food or some other substance?

☐ ☐ Are you addicted to sugar, work, danger, coffee and/or another 'soft addiction'?

☐ ☐ Do you or have you binged on your emotions such as anger, sadness, depression or fear?

☐ ☐ Now that you are in recovery, do you find yourself obsessing about getting better, 12-Step Programs, your improvement or your spiritual life?

☐ ☐ Does one or more of your immediate family have an addiction?

15　TELLING THE TRUTH

☐ ☐ When a person is yelling at you, is it hard for you to tell the truth?

☐ ☐ If a sales clerk gave you extra change by mistake, would you keep it?

☐ ☐ Knowing your spouse is sensitive about certain issues, do you omit important details to avoid giving him or her the whole picture?

☐ ☐ Do you lie to get out of traffic tickets?

☐ ☐ Do you make up stories about exciting things you have done just to impress people?

16　MAKING FRIENDS

☐ ☐ If you are at a gathering, do you find it hard to talk to strangers?

☐ ☐ Do you spend more time alone than you'd prefer?

☐ ☐ When you do see a person you'd like to talk to, do you have trouble knowing what to say?

☐ ☐ Do you automatically think people won't like you?

☐ ☐ Do you wish you had more friends?

THE LIFE SKILLS QUIZ

YES/NO **17 DEVELOPING INTIMACY**

☐ ☐ Do you have a hard time understanding what intimacy really means?

☐ ☐ When you start to get close to someone, do you get scared and want to pull away?

☐ ☐ When you see a couple displaying physical affection, do you feel uneasy?

☐ ☐ Even when you are with someone, do you feel alone?

☐ ☐ Do you have difficulty talking about yourself?

18 EXPRESSING SEXUALITY APPROPRIATELY

☐ ☐ Is the mere thought of having sex scary for you?

☐ ☐ Do you feel that being celibate is preferable to risking involvement?

☐ ☐ During sex, do you start out enjoying yourself, but end up feeling afraid, guilty, ambivalent or sad?

☐ ☐ Does a satisfying sex life seem out of your reach?

☐ ☐ Do you sometimes have sex when you really just want affection?

19 MANAGING MONEY

☐ ☐ Do you neglect to count your change?

☐ ☐ Do you rarely, if ever, balance your bank account?

☐ ☐ Do you have trouble paying your bills or taxes on time?

☐ ☐ Do you lack confidence that you can earn the money you need?

☐ ☐ Are you overextended on your credit cards without a plan to pay them off?

20 SETTING GOALS

☐ ☐ Do you have the habit of leaving projects half done?

☐ ☐ Does making plans for a trip or buying a car or getting a new job overwhelm you?

THE LIFE SKILLS QUIZ

YES/NO   Do you make endless lists, and then never actually do what
☐   ☐   is on them?

☐   ☐   Does the idea of setting life goals make you nervous or
        upset?

☐   ☐   Do you 'wing' your way through most situations?

YOUR LIFE SKILLS GOALS

You may feel overloaded, especially if most of your answers were
'yes'. But remember, the skills you are missing can be learned. These
questions will help you to identify specifically what is missing, so you
can begin to acquire the Life Skills you need to create a happier life.

Now that you have assessed your Life Skills, list the particular ones
you want to work on. Those with five 'yes' answers should get
priority. Write them down under Life Skills 1, 2 and so on, then list the
Life Skills with four 'yeses', then three, then two, and one.

Life Skill 1_____

Life Skill 2_____

Life Skill 3_____

Life Skill 4_____

Life Skill 5_____

Life Skill 6_____

Life Skill 7_____

Life Skill 8_____

Life Skill 9_____

Life Skill 10_____

Life Skill 11_____

Life Skill 12_____

Life Skill 13_____

Life Skill 14_____

Life Skill 15_____

THE LIFE SKILLS QUIZ

Life Skill 16_____

Life Skill 17_____

Life Skill 18_____

Life Skill 19_____

Life Skill 20_____

Put your answers to the Life Skills Quiz along with your goals in a convenient place so you can refer to them when you need to.

Now, let me suggest several ways to organize your Life Skills studies. First read Part 1, then use whichever of the following plans suits your needs.

PLAN 1
Turn to the Life Skill with the least number of 'yeses'. Work your way up the list, saving the Life Skills that need the most work for last.

PLAN 2
Read the book straight through, stopping to do the Life Skills exercises that relate only to your goals list.

PLAN 3
Read the skill chapters that interest you.

I recommend Plan 2 if you have more than four skills on your list with three or more 'yeses' each. I have organized the chapters to build on one another. One Life Skill leads into the next one, and so on; just as in your life, particular skills go hand in hand.

THE LIFE SKILLS QUIZ

CHAPTER 3

How to Use This Book

By their very nature most books allow us to sit comfortably and react passively rather than motivating us to become involved. This book is different; it will empower you to take action because it is structured so that you can participate. I invite you to use it as a tool in your life. As you answer the questions and do the exercises, you will find that you have shifted from a passive stance to an active one.

But as you read, be aware that you could fall into a trap where you feel, 'Everything is wrong with me.I need endless fixing and it is hopeless'. In other words, 'I found out more things are wrong with me than I thought'. That kind of thinking will only cause you to feel more hopeless. What I suggest is another, more empowering approach – a rope you can use to pull yourself out of that despair. Always remember:

1) You are fine.

2) You can assess what is missing.

3) There are a specific number of skills missing, not an endless list.

4) You can learn those missing skills.

These four points are the backbone of the Life Skills work. They put the power to change your life in your hands. Here are some additional suggestions for reading this book and using it to assist in your healing:

Read Actively, Do the Exercises
Read this book actively, engaging yourself fully in the material and stories. Use them to look into your own life. Do the exercises, write your answers in the space provided, and discuss your progress with friends.

Allow Yourself to Have Your Feelings

If you have been abused, you may be upset at times without really knowing why. You may cry or get angry. Give yourself permission to experience your feelings without judging yourself. When you need to, set the book down and take time out just to feel your emotions.

Go Slowly

I suggest you stop reading if and when you feel overwhelmed. Close the book; digest and reflect on the material and your responses to it.

Get the Support You Need

Call a close friend and discuss what you are thinking and feeling. At some point you may decide you need professional help in addition to the Life Skills program.

Remember, You Survived

You have survived more trauma than many people will confront in a lifetime. Even though you may feel vulnerable and hurt, you are stronger than you think. This is not to minimize what has happened to you, but to address the strength that helped you survive. Use it now to motivate yourself and to build self-confidence.

Be Willing to Get in Touch with Your Own Inner Resources

Consider the possibility that you have inner resources which you can develop and use to heal yourself. As you make progress, you may have dreams or insights which will facilitate your healing process.

Be open to the possibility of a higher power – nature, God, the Universe. As you release your pain and grow you may sense something greater than you – an inspiring sunset, a comforting dream, a loving smile. When you connect with that force, you are never alone again and you can draw on it for comfort and assistance.

Allow the Good Things

Adult survivors are frequently haunted by a vague feeling that disaster is just around the corner. As soon as things start going well, abused people often feel very uncomfortable, anxious, or even threatened. Know that those feelings are part of your transition and that they reflect your fears, not reality. Slowly, but surely, you can learn to accept good things in your life.

Notice Your Reactions

When you read about other people's abuse in this book, you may

have one of several reactions:
1) You may experience a general feeling of anger, not clearly directed at anything or anyone.

2) You may become angry at specific statements you read here.

3) You may think, 'Such things could never happen!' or 'What does this have to do with me?'

You may be using your anger or denial to cover up painful feelings and memories. If you were not so angry, you would have no protection against your pain. If you were not denying, you would have to acknowledge what *really* happened to you. If you have a strong reaction, try to examine your feelings and see if perhaps you are responding to something else.

Eliminate Stress From Your Life
While people are healing, they often need to simplify their lives. If you feel overloaded, consider allowing yourself more non-scheduled time. You may wish to set aside a specific, uninterrupted time to read and work in this book.

Be Gentle with Yourself
Many people are overly critical and even harsh with themselves. You may not even know what being gentle with yourself really means. While reading, be sure to do some of the following while reading:
1) Tell yourself you are doing a good job.

2) Tell yourself you are OK.

3) Ask a friend to repeat item one and two, or to say something that conveys love and support.

4) Take a five minute 'vacation' sometime during each day.

CHAPTER 4

Distinguishing and Defining Abuse

Now that I have outlined how you can best use this book, let me give you some background information. By the end of this chapter, you will not only learn what abuse is, you will also see that it is shockingly common. You will learn how to distinguish abusive from non-abusive behavior.

The law considers a wide range of behaviors abusive. But you had a private and very personal experience not bound by any legal definition. You may have been physically beaten or emotionally abused from the time you were born until the day you left home. Or in your family, the abuse may have started with a crisis: Dad lost his job, Mom died, the house burned down. Then your mother or father made you their 'whipping boy', venting his or her frustration. Perhaps you were never physically hit, but suffered emotional trauma and damage to your self-esteem because your parents neglected you. Or you may have lived through one devastating event: a rape, traumatic surgery, a beating, or public humiliation. That one event may have been burned into your memory and continues to cause you difficulties.

Whatever your experience, to begin healing you must be able to distinguish abusive from non-abusive behavior. Let us look at ways to distinguish abuse and then some definitions.

DISTINGUISHING ABUSE

If you cannot distinguish abusive from non-abusive actions, then no list or definition will be helpful to you because you will not be able to recognize abuse when you see it. Distinctions enable us to tell one thing from another. When you know your own house from your neighbor's, you can find your way home. When you can tell green from red, life is more colorful. But if you cannot distinguish green from red and you are coming to a traffic light, that can be dangerous, even life-threatening. Some distinctions are that vital.

The following example dramatically illustrates an entire country's lack of distinctions. Several years ago world leaders approached India and asked her government what help she needed to deal with her hunger problem. India said: 'We don't have a hunger problem. We no longer have famines with thousands of people dying; we have no hunger problem.' World leaders replied, 'But you have millions who die of malnutrition and babies who die before their first birthday.' India had never considered that hunger meant not just famine, but chronic persistent hunger.

The ability to recognize 'abuse' is as critical to survival as the ability to recognize 'chronic persistent hunger'. We need to know what is abuse and what is not. Clearly, in extreme cases, the difference can be life-threatening. And when people fail to recognize abuse in milder forms, they permit abusive situations. Adult survivors – not knowing how to determine if they are being abused – often allow strangers, family, and co-workers to abuse them. Although friends may see the situation clearly, the person has a 'blind spot'.

Applying the Distinction
Meet Craig, who learned to distinguish abuse.

Craig T.
Craig, a grey-suited stockbroker with *The Wall Street Journal* under arm, came to my office one day and told me about his childhood. He recounted how first his father and then his step-father had beaten him time after time. His mother had to take him to the doctor for cuts and a head injury inflicted by the step-dad. He said, 'I thought I had done something wrong to deserve those beatings. I could never figure out what! Since then I have worked for several bosses who were much like my father. One boss viciously dressed me down at a staff meeting. I didn't stick up for myself; I just worked harder.'

I asked this successful, but unhappy and fearful man, 'Have you ever considered that you were an abused child?'

'No!' His eyes were wide and incredulous. 'I thought I was just being punished – nothing more than that. I had nothing to compare it to.'

Craig had no idea that his treatment as a child is actually defined as abuse. The notion that he had been abused was startling, but freeing. By making the distinction of 'abuse', he was then able to set the stage for his Life Skills training. Instead of feeling vaguely unhappy, he could identify why and where he hurt. Recognizing that he was abused enabled Craig to see that his father had done something wrong, not him. He could finally begin to stop his 'there-must-be-something-wrong-with-me' thinking which had carried over into his adult relationships and work life. He still needed to learn some of the Life Skills outlined in this book such as Not Letting People Use You, Expressing Anger Safely and Not Overhelping. However, he could now recognize abusive people and situations and take action. This realization gave him power. It freed him from his life-long habit of letting people abuse him over and over again.

During the week between sessions, Craig began to see that most of his relationships were abusive in one way or another. Abuse had become 'normal' to him, because he had no positive behavior with which to compare it. But he came in to our next session with new and important insights: 'I guess I always expected abuse. I assumed I would be treated disrespectfully and I was. I never felt safe because I was always waiting for something bad to happen. That put me constantly on guard waiting to be hit emotionally and physically.'

That inner flinch had put Craig under tremendous stress. I see this stress frequently, this always-on-the-alert stance in adult survivors. They feel tired, haggard, and burned out. But after making the abuse distinction, Craig no longer needed to be on guard.

You can learn to recognize what is causing you to be wary. Once you realize those feelings stem from the past, you can relax your inner vigilance. As Craig explained his new awareness: 'It's as if I have new eyes to see life more clearly. My last therapist said I was masochistic, going after the same destructive type of woman again and again. She told me to stop. Well, I'm not stupid! But I just couldn't see what she so obviously saw. Now I can see the abuse. I recognize when a person is and is not abusing me. And I can visualize the possibility of life without it. Before, life was all the same – abusive in one way or another.'

DEFINING ABUSE

Now that you are beginning to sense that there is a distinction between abusive and non-abusive behavior, these next definitions of abuse can help you evaluate your past. Ultimately you are the only one who can determine whether or not you have experienced abuse. You may remember what happened to you as a child, but you may never have considered it actual abuse. If that is the case, the following definitions may help you view what occurred in a new perspective. As a child, to realize that you were abused may have been too overwhelming; you denied to cope and survive. But now, as an adult, you may be ready to acknowledge the truth. Or you might be fully aware of your past abuse in which case these categories could shed new light on old issues.

Parents' Anonymous, an organization which works with parents who abuse their children, defines four forms of abuse. Physical, verbal, emotional, and sexual. Considered the leading self-help organization in the abuse field, Parents' Anonymous has chapters in every state with several thousand participants in groups throughout the country.

No one form of abuse is inherently more harmful than another. The important points: to recognize the abuse and to understand its impact on your life.

Physical Abuse
Physically injuring a child by hitting, striking, slapping, shaking, and even spanking is child abuse. Some adults batter children using coat hangers, cooking pans, belts, or other objects. People who abuse often cannot tell the difference between fair punishment and excessive, abusive treatment. Venting anger excessively or through unexplained punishment also constitutes abuse.

Earl G.
'My father hit me so hard I had a handprint on my thigh. I had to wear short little pants to first grade. I was mortified that I had five red welts shaped like his fingerprints that all my friends could see. After years of beatings, I turned off my feelings. I still don't feel very much.'

Karen H.
'Dad was out of control. He threw his full coffee cup at Mom. It gashed her cheek and crashed to the floor. Then he started throwing plates and dishes at me. Broken dishes were all over the room. Food splattered on the walls. Mom and I huddled in the corner. Loud noises still freak me.'

Tony D.
'Mom had been drinking. She told me to wipe that look off my face. Then she started punching and slapping. Now I'm quick to anger; I'll take a swing at someone very easily. No one is ever going to treat me like that.'

Frank M.
'My sister and I always got a beating before Christmas. Mom would say, "I know I forgot to whip you for something. Santa doesn't bring presents to bad boys and girls". I began drinking heavily at 18; I beat my first wife.'

Verbal Abuse
Verbal abuse means verbally stripping the child of self-esteem through name-calling, using terms like bad, ugly, dumb, or

clumsy. Tone of voice, word selection, screaming, shaming, and profanity can also be considered verbal abuse. Such abuse can cause deeper and longer lasting scars than physical abuse. Many of my clients tell me they have internalized negative messages once yelled at them by their abusers. Ten, twenty, and thirty years later, they still believe those harsh words.

Tim M.
'I can still hear Mom screaming, "I hate the sight of your face. You look exactly like your father, and he never amounted to anything. Neither will you". As I grew up, I looked more and more like my real father; I constantly reminded her of him. I have never been successful at anything. I have this dreadful fear that Mom is right.'

Joyce K.
'When I was five years old, Mom began calling me "a piece of shit". She screamed, "You're a dirty, bad child; your sister is the good one". I guess I believed her. As an adult, I have let men do anything they wanted to me sexually. I've also allowed my bosses to overwork and demean me.'

Jim F.
'I found myself calling my son every nasty mean name my father used to call me. I felt just like I was eight years old again, when he used to walk in after work. I was shocked! That's when I knew I needed help.'

Susanne A.
'My parents never raised their voices. But they put me down and referred to me as the "dummy". My older brothers took that as permission to tease me at school, and of course, everyone else joined in. All my accomplishments and successes have been like I'm trying to make up for something.'

Emotional Abuse
All the other forms contain emotional abuse, the most common kind. It occurs whenever an adult deprives a child of love, a sense of belonging, of unconditional acceptance and security. The emotionally abusive parent provides a negative rather than a positive emotional environment for the child. And often those who were emotionally abused, without being physically or sexually abused, may not recognize the effects until years later. Because these wounds leave invisible scars, they are far more insidious and difficult to see. The survivor of emotional abuse is often unable to distinguish abusive from normal behavior.

Patti O.
'I worked all summer to earn money for a car. Dad promised me I

could buy one if I worked to pay for it. At the end of the summer, he suddenly announced, "I've decided you cannot have the car. I'm using the money for something else". It just wasn't fair! That was not the first time he had broken a promise. I was crushed and livid inside. I hated him! I still do. As an adult, I'm quick to anger – particularly at injustice. And I don't trust things are what they seem. I always think there's a catch.'

Rose L.
'Mom was home all day, but usually asleep or passed out drunk. Every morning I made myself a peanut and jelly sandwich for breakfast. I could barely get my hands around the giant-size jars. One day the jar slipped, and it crashed leaving a terrible mess. When I came home from school, it was still there. I don't rely on anyone for anything. I do it all myself.'

Henrietta D.
'Mom usually got out of bed around 11 a.m. She never cooked breakfast. Dad had already left for work by the time I got up. I'd fix myself cornflakes and milk and walk to school. Mom spent two hours dressing and putting on her make-up. She thought the world owed her a living. We never talked or hugged. In the evening they'd call me to get them each another beer. That's all I was good for. What did I do so wrong? Now I don't think I deserve love or anything. When something good does happen, I think it will be taken away.'

Rebecca C.
'From the time I was five until Mom was hospitalized, she used to lock herself in the bathroom for hours. I'd sit on the hall carpet outside the door crying and clutching my Raggedy-Ann doll. She was never there for me. I don't think she even liked children very much. I learned to rely on myself. Now I have trouble believing my own husband will be there for me.'

Sexual Abuse
Sexual abuse means sexual exploitation of a child for the abuser's gratification. It involves far more than just intercourse. It can include sexual fondling, pornography, or any sexual misuse. Such abuse most frequently occurs between male adults and female children, but reports of sexual abuse between children and adults are increasing, including females abusing males, males abusing males and females abusing females. Sexual abusers were usually abused themselves as children. Some have difficulty distinguishing between affection for and exploitation of a child. This distorts the child's concept of family roles and adult male/female relationships.

Pamela C.
'We used to swim at a neighbor's pool during the summer. One time the father took me into the bathroom and showed me pictures of people having sex. He sat on the toilet and let his robe fall open. I could see his genitals. I ran home.'

Sara Beth E.
'Dad would come into my room while I was asleep and start rubbing my back. I'd wake up frightened. He'd comfort me by fondling my breasts. Then he began to touch me all over. I hated it but I longed for the touching and holding. I never was held or rocked. I hated myself. When I became a teenager, I used drugs to numb out during sex. Even though I ached for the affection, I hated myself after. I had a lot of nightmares. Finally, after one man was very rough with me, I just stopped letting anyone touch me.

Katie F.
'My brother used to come into the bathroom and rape me in the tub. He'd hold his cigarette close to my skin and threaten to burn me if I told anyone. This went on for years. Finally, he hit a kid on a bike with his car. Then people realized he had a problem. Now when men give me attention, I get really scared. I'm terrified of a relationship.'

Stella G.
'When I began Overeaters Anonymous, I had about 20 extra pounds around my hips. As I lost the weight I got frightened of being attractive. When I began therapy, I remembered my cousin fingering my genitals when I was three or four. I was so disgusted and upset! I began to understand why I had difficulty having orgasms and why sometimes sex made me sick to my stomach.'[1]

Silent Abuse
In addition to the Parents' Anonymous definitions, I include a category called 'silent abuse'. The silent abuser stands by and watches or has knowledge of the abuse which is taking place. During therapy, many clients report they were abused by one parent but that the other knew about it and did nothing.

The realization that someone you love and trust would allow such harm to come to you can be devastating. Your silent abuser's non-involvement may have added to your feelings that no one would protect you. Feeling safe may still be an issue for you today. You may have recognized your anger toward the silent abuser long ago, or you may just be realizing the impact of the silent abuse for the first time. In either case, you are entitled to your feelings. Your outrage and hurt at the passive parent is an appropriate and essential part of your healing process.

Most of the previous examples involved a silent abuser as well as an active one. So do the following:

Jean D.
'Dad slept in my bed from the time I was eight until I left home. Mom must have known he wasn't with her. He confused me. I out and out hated her.'

Henry X.
'When my big brother beat me up, Mom would stand in the doorway and just watch. I got very depressed and tried to kill myself many times. If this was living, I didn't want any part of it.'

Gigi C.
'Dad molested me while I was doing my homework at the dining table. Mom was only a few feet away in the kitchen. What the hell was she doing anyway!'

Johnny P.
'Dad just checked out. He left early and came home after we were all in bed. I don't think he ever knew half of what went on. How could he have been so blind! We were so little!'

A NATIONAL PERSPECTIVE

To put all types of abuse into a national perspective, the National Committee for the Prevention of Child Abuse states that 2.25 million cases of child abuse were reported in 1987.[2] Although little research has been done on the lasting effects of abuse, studies do show that the child's age, the length of the trauma, the child's relationship to the abuser, and the person's resilience determine the degree of trauma and effect on the individual.[3]

Most child abusers were themselves abused. However, a Yale study estimates that only 30 percent of adult survivors actually become abusers.[4] This dispells the myth that all victims of abuse will perpetuate the cycle.

Finally, remember that all abuse has an emotional impact. Dr James Garbarino, leading authority on child abuse research and author of *The Psychologically Battered Child*,[5] simply states that all abuse is psychological. And most people who were abused do have some difficulties and lack certain Life Skills.

YOU DETERMINE IF YOU WERE ABUSED

I include the five definitions of abuse here so you can have some consistent guidelines to assess your own experience. In therapy, I am concerned with legal definitions when someone is currently being abused or when a client wishes to press charges. I review legal and Parents' Anonymous definitions with clients so they can judge for themselves if they were abused at any time in the past. But whether or not your experience fits into a precise definition, if you feel you were abused, that is what is important. Therapeutically, only you can evaluate your past. As a part of the healing process, you need to acknowledge what really happened and how the abuse is affecting you now. Some people know they were abused and know they are having current problems. If you feel uncertain or confused, do not worry. Many people never considered that they were abused or that childhood trauma could be compounding their present difficulties. When you do so, you are taking the first step toward recovery.

SOME ADDITIONAL GUIDELINES

If you are still uncertain about what is abuse and what is not, I have listed some specific abusive situations:

- A student brings home a 95 percent on his report card. Instead of praising him, his father asks, 'Where is the other five percent?'

- A neighbor exposes himself to a group of little girls.

- After a student flunks a spelling test, the teacher orders her to stand in front of the class, then tells her how stupid she is.

- A parent locks her son in his room and tells him she is leaving him there indefinitely.

- A parent refuses to speak to her child for two days.

- A man asks two eight-year-old girls to look at nude pictures with him.

- For several months a mother leaves her three small children unsupervised from after school until dinner time.

- A father tells his son he will stop loving him if he does not behave.

While you were reading the above descriptions, you may have remembered for the first time an incident when you were physically or sexually abused. Or you may have realized that a particular incident actually was abuse or that a memory fragment or recurring nightmare is not a fantasy, but indeed something that really happened to you. You may have discovered that your 'normal' homelife was in fact very emotionally abusive. All of these insights are healthy because they indicate that you are letting go of denial and acknowledging what actually occurred. You may be feeling powerful emotions for the first time. That too is a good sign because you are getting beyond the numbness and beginning to come alive.

CHAPTER 5

What You Can Expect When You Read This Book and What to Bring to Your Healing

WHAT YOU CAN EXPECT

Life Skills is designed to assist you in healing your abuse and learning Life Skills. This process can be emotionally turbulent and may cause painful and forgotten memories to resurface. So you can better understand the process, I want to describe some common experiences clients have had during the Life Skills program. You may go through all of them, or only a few. Just remember that when you are willing to ride out these emotions and changes, you can begin to free yourself from the pain of your past and learn new skills for the future.

Remembering
Forgetting is the easiest and most common way children have of buffering themselves against abuse. It serves to insulate a child from overwhelming pain and trauma. But as an adult you are now strong enough to deal with those memories. And holding them inside takes tremendous energy.

If you cannot remember significant parts of your childhood, memories may come flooding back as you read this book. Your recalling the past may return in ways which can be both upsetting and disorienting. Here are the basic ones:

Being Triggered
When a person is triggered, he automatically reacts to a situation the way he did to a similar past event. The person usually does not realize the connection at first because he does not remember the past trauma.

34

Mary Kaye E.
'My boyfriend and I were sitting on the couch watching television. Suddenly he raised his hand to swat a bug, and I jumped up and ran out of the room. Later, as I stood in the hall shaking, I remembered my father threatening to hit us by raising his hand. I was as terrified as an adult as I had been as a child.'

This young woman over-reacted to an event in the present because it reminded her of something similar in the past. Hers was not an intellectual response, but an automatic reaction. Anger, loud noises, yelling, or fast movements, as well as isolated incidents which mimic the past, can trigger an adult survivor's memory. But as people begin to release old feelings and memories, they are triggered less and less often.

Reading this book will trigger you in some way or another. That triggering – although painful and awkward – is essential because it puts you in touch with painful memories that need healing. When you allow them to surface, you can examine and release them. Then you have the room to learn new Life Skills.

Nightmares
You may not remember specific scenes but you may have recurring nightmares similar to these women.

Melanie J.
'I have this dream over and over again of a man standing at the foot of my bed. I wake up screaming.'

Roberta B.
'Every once in a while I wake up screaming. I don't remember the dream, but I'm terrified and dripping with sweat. I feel like I've been running to get away from someone.

Those nightmares stop as you examine memories and release the pain associated with them.

Flashbacks
You may have flashbacks. A smell, a sound, a gesture, or a situation can set off a flashback like Judith Ann's or Stan's.

Judith Ann C.
'I had just started therapy. I couldn't remember my father coming into my bed, but my older sister told me he'd molested her and me. One afternoon I was standing at the sink washing the dishes, and all at once I saw and felt the whole thing – even his hairy hands reaching under the covers and my little body trying to crawl away from him. I felt sick to my stomach.'

Stan G.
'I was at a party last week and a drunk friend passed out on me. His horrible beer breath made me almost throw up. Then I remembered my drunk father stumbling home after too much beer. I guess that's why I hate being around it.'

Just Pure Feeling
Sometimes people are overwhelmed with pure feelings. The emotions do not seem connected to any incident. This may happen to you while you are reading this book as it did with these two people.

Dwayne E.
'I find myself feeling like an enraged little boy, but I don't see any images.'

Katelin U.
'In the middle of the day at my desk, I'll just start to cry when nothing has happened to make me feel sad. But the sadness feels like its coming from the past. I have to explain to my office mates that I'm all right. After about ten minutes it goes away.'

As your recovery progresses, these forms of remembering will occur less frequently.

Reactions to Remembering
When memories resurface, they bring with them substantial emotional baggage. As you begin to piece together various traumatic events, you can expect these memories to effect your present life. Some people think, 'Well, my childhood wasn't that bad'. Or you may feel profound grief as you remember your childhood. While you may sometimes experience a direct response to a particular memory, such as anger provoked when you recall one certain event, you will also – as I have mentioned – have reactions which may seem unconnected or even irrational, such as a flood of tears with no apparent reason. For a while, this can be like riding an emotional roller coaster. In time you will come to recognize that these responses stem from your ever-increasing memory and acknowledgement of past abuse. Here are three normal responses clients report as they begin to heal themselves:

Minimizing the Memories
I frequently hear people say, 'Oh, it wasn't really that bad'. As an adult looking back you may think that, yet from a child's perspective your experiences may have been terrifying.

Annette J.
'I always remembered that I spilled black ink on my mother's new

rug when I was four. I know she yelled at me, as an adult I never thought much about it. But when I recalled the incident in therapy, my body shook and I broke down and sobbed. Her shouting had terrified me.'

Frequently, people think they are imagining past abuse. But if you are having nightmares, flashbacks, and you are being triggered, you probably were abused. Know that your mind is trying to remember. Be patient with yourself. Your mind is bringing back the memories as quickly as it can comfortably process them, so do not pressure yourself to remember.

Riding the Emotional Roller Coaster
This 60-year-old survivor describes her version of what I call the emotional roller coaster.

Thelma S.
'Ever since I started remembering how I was abused, I've been on an emotional roller coaster. I'm calm one minute and then I burst into tears. Or I might be at work and a trivial conversation will make me angry. At night I feel so sad for myself. I get out my tattered Teddy bear and hug him as I go to sleep. My mother took him away from me when I was four because she said I was "too grown-up". I guess I need to go back and comfort the child who never had a chance to be a little girl.'

If you are feeling intense emotions while reading this book, emotions which seem to come out of the blue, you know exactly what I am talking about. If you have suffered past abuse, you probably will experience both rage and sadness at times. You may also be unexplainably depressed. The intense feelings do not go on forever; they fade after they have run their course. If you think you need to stop reading, it is all right to put the book down until you get a second wind.

Grieving
At some point while learning Life Skills, a deep sense of grief strikes many adult survivors. This may occur all at once or in spurts. If this happens to you, know that you are mourning your lost childhood. This is a common and important part of healing among adult survivors as this man recalled.

Donald C.
'When I remember, I can't help but feel the pain. I never had fun as a child, I never thought about my own needs. I feel such sorrow for myself. If I were fathering myself, I'd never treat me that way. I sometimes just have to allow the waves of sadness.'

You may experience waves of grief while you are working on a particular Life Skill. If so, just allow the feelings; releasing this grief over time makes room for healing.

Personal Relationships
While working on the Life Skills, your growth may shake up your relationships, family, and friends. You are changing in many ways; so are your ways of relating. Share your feelings with the people close to you so they can support you and understand what you are experiencing. But realize too that some friendships may drift away. Destructive friends and relationships may not change and become healthy just because you do. Eliminating them makes room for more positive people to come into your life. When you let go of a destructive pattern, you create an opening for something new and positive.

A Shift in How You View Yourself
Some clients who have worked their way through *Life Skills* tell me they have had a shift in how they viewed themselves and their abuse. I mention this so you can be open to it and facilitate it happening. One woman described it: 'Before I read your book I felt like I was different...that I would always feel abused. Now I'm starting to feels healed. I don't feel marked for life anymore. I'm a new me.'

Survivors who have read this book can begin to peek out from under the dark cloud that has been hanging over them. When you sense that happening as a result of your work, give yourself a pat on the back and a little smile. Maybe your inner war is over.

WHAT TO BRING TO YOUR HEALING
In order for this book to be most effective in helping you heal and learn Life Skills, you need to bring four important inner qualities to your reading.

1) A willingness to break your silence and to let go of your denial about the past

2) A willingness to stop perceiving yourself as a victim

3) A willingness to heal yourself, even if you are not sure how

4) A commitment to recovery.

Discovering Those Inner Qualities
To help you see how all four qualities interact, meet Karen.

Karen K.
Karen, who was 34 when I first met her, came into my California office looking more like a high school student than a woman well

into her thirties. Wearing sweat pants and sweater with black hair falling to her shoulders, she looked everywhere but at me. As she wrang her fingers, she told me: 'I weigh 95 lbs and I'm 5'8". I don't eat much. My stomach hurts all the time'.

Then she told me of countless times her mother had terrorized the whole family. She'd also beaten Karen in front of her siblings a number of times. She confessed: 'I've been denying it happened. I have never told anyone. I have to now; it's eating me alive!'

As horrible as all this was, that is not what I remember most about Karen. I remember what she did when I said to her: 'You know, you survived your abuse. You are not a victim, you are a survivor. You must be very strong! You could bring that same strength and survival to your therapy. If you took on your healing with that same vengeance, we could get our work done more quickly.'

I was throwing down the gauntlet, as I had done with many other clients. But this time I saw no outward signs of strength in Karen. I knew I was taking a gamble. Then suddenly she sat up straight on the sofa and her eyes became fiery and focused. This frail looking girl grew powerful before my eyes. She proclaimed: 'My mother has taken up too much of my life. I have to get on with it. If it's possible, I want to have a regular, normal life. Let's get to work.'

As our work together unfolded, Karen told me more about herself. At times she was afraid to go to the store alone; she had no friends. She'd taught herself Spanish, but was terrified to speak it for fear of making a mistake. Although she held a responsible job and belonged to a union, she always felt she might be fired and be left without funds. She allowed co-workers to take advantage of her and never spoke up for herself. Whenever she expressed her hatred for her mother in therapy, her body would contort and then relax. Sometimes she would leave our session feeling a little shaky. Before our work began, her body had never known such relaxation.

No matter how rough the going, Karen always brought her strength and will 'to make it' with her to every session. During two years of therapy, she gradually released the pain and anger of her past. She stopped losing weight; she began to look healthy, even pretty. She was no longer terrified of life; she discovered she did not need to protect and isolate herself. In the Life Skills group, she reached out to new friends and found a roommate. She has begun to live a normal and productive life.

Karen realized early on that she had to recognize the abuse in her life and break her silence. Taking charge of her recovery enabled her to let go of her victim posture. She trusted that she would heal. And she applied the same tenacity and commitment to therapy that helped her survive her childhood to therapy.

Calling Forth Your Will

Now you may be thinking: 'Well, people like Karen are special. They have something I do not have. They are courageous or tough or genetically more resilient.'

Everyone of us has that will to survive and the ability to commit to healing, no matter how deeply buried it might be. If you feel you lack Karen's strength, remember – you have the will to survive. Like Karen you can apply that same determination to your recovery. You will discover an inner power you never knew you had. We all have what it takes to change our lives, to heal ourselves. But most people do not realize that such healing is possible, or how to begin the healing process.

Break the Silence and Denial

To begin your healing, look underneath your denial and recognize the abuse. You may already know you were abused and remember it all too clearly, but you may believe what happened to you was not all that bad. That is one form of denial. Another, stronger kind is not remembering at all. As mentioned earlier, you will start to recall your past while you are reading this book. Your abuser may also have told you never to tell anyone, and that old taboo may still have a grip on you. But you need to break the silence, so old feelings can be released. Look at what happened honestly and talk about it.

Let Go of a Victim Attitude

Having been a victim of abuse is different from having a 'victim attitude'. A client demonstrated this attitude when he told me his boss was 'out to get him' again. I suggested that maybe the problem was that he saw himself as a victim and behaved accordingly. He started to argue, but I asked him just to look at what I'd said. He came back the next week announcing: 'I was definitely being a victim. My boss is one of those people who always has to have a scapegoat. It's not personal – that's the way he is. But I don't have to be the one. I told him to stop yelling at me. He stopped.'

Shifting from a victim stance can be a simple, but profound and life-altering. When you have a victim attitude, you behave as if you were helpless, relinquishing control to others. When you declare that you survived, your attitude shifts to, 'I'm in charge of my life; I decide what happens'. Rather than let life happen to you, you now have a say in how you interact with the world. You take back control and responsibility.

Be Willing to Heal

Consider the possibility that you can heal the past and change your life. If at first you do not know it or understand exactly how it can happen, do not worry. Just be willing to allow the positive changes to take place.

Commit to Your Recovery

Finally, you need to commit yourself to your recovery. You can bring what I call a 'rageful commitment' to your work. That does not mean being violent or loud. A strong commitment comes from within. Right now you may be a bit skeptical. That's all right. Most people have difficulty committing to something they cannot see. As you meet the survivors in this book who have healed, learned new skills, and changed their lives, you will begin to see what is possible in your own life. And when you sense what is possible, you can totally commit to your work.

CHAPTER 6

Four Abilities Which Empower the Life Skills Work

This is not a mental calisthenics book or an academic textbook. Four special abilities used along with the Life Skills make it much more than that. Just the skills alone can produce some changes. But to make a profound difference and to end abuse in your life you need four additional abilities. Applying these abilities while you are learning Life Skills will enable you to master the skills and turn them into powerful tools. Instead of just memorizing my list of things to do, you will be able to create the Life Skills for yourself. These four abilities are:

1) Taking a stand

2) Intervening in your internal abuse

3) Establishing and respecting boundaries

4) Recognizing and appreciating Survival Strategies.

Familiarize yourself with these abilities now; they will play a crucial role later in learning a specific skill. Each of the skills chapters gives you an opportunity to recognize and appreciate your Survival Strategies.

TAKING A STAND
You have the power to stop the abuse in your life now. That power is called taking a stand, and it is one of the most important things you will ever do. When you take a stand, you make a positive statement about yourself and the way life will be from now on. Rather than stating your intentions negatively, use strong affirmations:

NOT: I will not be violent toward myself or anyone else.
BUT: I will be violence-free.

NOT: I will not hurt myself or others.
BUT: I will be gentle and safe.

NOT: I will not let people use or abuse me.
BUT: I will live an abuse-free life.

Repeat your statement out loud to another person, someone who is committed to your success. Or write it on an index card and tape it on your mirror. That way, when you lose sight of your stand, your committed friend or written reminder can put you back on track.

Once you have made a declaration about your stand, you have created a new context for your life, what I call a new 'bowl'. Your stand fortifies each Life Skill, so it can make a powerful difference. Without your stand creating a new foundation, your old patterns would quickly undermine the Life Skills. This undermining process occurs when a woman goes through the motions of dieting, knowing deep down she will always be fat. By believing she doesn't deserve to be thin she diffuses her will and begins overeating immediately after she has lost weight. When she takes the stand: I deserve to be a thin person, she empowers her diet to work. When you take your stand, you can use the Life Skills to create healthy and lasting patterns.

When you take a stand, you interrupt a pattern, and that enables you to make a dramatic and immediate change in your life. This can empower you to shift your destructive actions into constructive behavior. I have listened to hundreds of clients take the stand that they will lead an abuse-free life, and they have radically altered not only *their* lives, but the lives of their families as well.

In Chapter 4, Craig stated his stand: *I will lead a safe and peaceful life.* Making his declaration, he felt anger at what he had allowed in the past, and resolved that he would never allow abuse in the future. He also felt relief that the abuse was behind him. For the first time he felt in charge of his life. He describes the change. 'Sometimes I have little chats with myself. "Now I'm the boss in my life; I don't have to settle for leftovers." An inner strength is gathering inside me. I'm not interested in holding on to my anger. That would just feed the abuse cycle and keep it going.'

Let me quickly separate taking a stand from holding on to old angers and hurts. A stand does not mean: *I'm going to get even.* Understandably, you may feel that way. If so, be sure to read Expressing Anger Safely.

You need to be committed, to have a strong desire behind your stand, but you do not necessarily need to understand how you will fulfill it. Not abusing yourself or others or not allowing others to abuse you may look impossible right now. In fact, you may have nothing concrete on which to base your stand. However, making a committed statement about your intention allows you to design a more positive future.

From time to time you may slip, but that does not negate your stand. When you were learning to ride a bike, you probably fell many times but that did not alter your stand to ride a bike. Taking a stand includes your past but creates the possibility for something new.

Another example of a stand: *I will be gentle with my children and keep them safe.* If that is your stand, try telling yourself, 'Just for today, I will be gentle with my kids'. Your stand gives you direction; 'just for today' gives you daily instruction. A stand assumes that you do not have to continue repeating past mistakes, but have the power to conduct yourself differently.

How a Stand Has An Impact on Daily Life
So that you can see how this works in other peoples' lives, let me introduce you to Charlotte and Michael.

Charlotte K.
Charlotte, a single mother, told me the following story when she came to her first appointment: 'One day last month I was sitting in a lecture when I suddenly flashed back to my father hitting me in the car. Then I flashed to another time in the bedroom, then a time when I was a teenager. Tears were running down my face. My older sister told me our father was rough on us, but I had no memory of it. I married a man who has beaten me. I have been hospitalized twice with injuries. Now I have a new boyfriend.'

I noticed a large bruise on her forearm. I had to ask her, 'Is he hitting you?'

'Yes!' She quickly added, 'And, no one is ever going to hit me again. He is out.'

Charlotte ended the relationship. Now that she could remember her childhood, the three relationships fell into a definite pattern. And seeing the pattern, she could recognize the abuse. Abusing is never normal, even though it had become customary in Charlotte's life. When she stepped out of her old pattern and took a stand, she was able to create positive action. Taking her stand, she implemented an important skill, Eliminating Destructive Relationships.

Michael G.

Michael, a postal worker, came to see me after only two weeks of marriage. Painfully, he told me: 'We had a wonderful honeymoon. We are so much in love. Then we started fighting. I just lost my cool and hit her; I broke the front door. I even threw our cat down the stairs. We're both afraid. We want children, but not until I know I can express myself without violence.'

Later, after working together, he said: 'I'm angry that I was abused, but that does not give me the right to take it out on my new wife. She doesn't deserve it. But I have to empty out this old stuff and learn how to control myself. I will not hit my wife. My stand is: *I am non-violent.*'

This man needed therapy to help him release his old anger and heal his past. But he realized that the past did not entitle him to unleash his anger on his wife. His stand was clear; and he learned the Life Skill: Expressing Anger Safely.

Putting Your Stand Into Action

You can begin to see that taking a stand is an important tool which helps people implement certain Life Skills. However, you might be having a hard time seeing how your stand can effect another person's behavior. Be assured that it can. Taking a stand to live abuse-free empowers you to take action. When a person crosses your boundary or invades your space or body in any way, you have a right to stop him or her. Here are some examples of how you can stop someone before things get out of hand:

'You don't need to do that.'

'Stop!'

'It isn't necessary to talk to me that way.'

'Back off.'

'Tell me what I did, but do not insult me.'

'Don't interact with me like that.'

In some instances, these statements will be enough to stop people in their tracks, to make them aware that they are out-of-bounds. But when someone has a well-entrenched pattern of abusing you, your words may not be enough to reverse a life-long pattern. In that case, you have to repeat your statements until they are heard. Or you may need to accompany your words with actions such as leaving the room or refusing further conversation until the abuse has stopped. If you are in danger of physical abuse, you may have to bring in outside help. But remember, when you change your behavior, eventually the other person will too – or he will leave.

To summarize, if you once accommodated abuse by not recognizing it, you can now start to distinguish abusive situations. Then you can take a stand to live abuse-free. You will be on the look-out for abusive people and situations. You will have shifted from being 'done to', to doing something for yourself; from merely living life to creating life. Your actions do make an impact. And taking a stand makes a powerful statement both to you and to the world, that you are in charge and only you will decide how your life will be.

You may not be ready to take a stand today. That is fine. As we get into the individual Life Skills, I will review this material, and you will have other opportunities to take a stand when the time is right for you to do so.

INTERVENING IN YOUR INTERNAL ABUSE

By internal abuse I am talking about the harsh judgments many adult survivors make about themselves which perpetuate abusive patterns. Many survivors mentally beat themselves up.
For example:

I'm bad.

I deserve it.

It was my fault.

I'm damaged.

I'm worthless.

I'm a piece of shit.

People who have internalized their abuse can have a difficult time seeing its effects because they have woven negative judgments into the very fabric of who they are. These harsh statements become part of their identify.

One Life Skills participant explained, 'I would never let anyone talk to me the way I talk to myself'.

Perpetuating the Abuse

Those judgments not only invite abuse, but keep people from moving forward in their lives. Such survivors think they deserve ill-treatment from others and that they do not deserve success and happiness. The internal abuse costs them peace of mind, self-confidence, and just plain happiness. To stop this on-going negative process, I help clients separate what actually occurred from judgments they made about themselves. We not only work on releasing past abuse, but on letting go of those destructive judgments, i.e. the internal abuse. That does not minimize the abuse itself; what happened caused pain and trauma. However, during healing and Life Skills work, you need to examine the judgments you have made about yourself.

When people feel they deserve abuse, their self-esteem is obviously low. And a person with low self-esteem is a sitting duck for subtle jabs such as friends habitually breaking dates at the last minute. Your friend continues to do that because he or she knows you will not stand up for yourself. This pattern not only permits abuse, but perpetuates it. Stopping internal abuse is an integral part of learning Life Skills. To illustrate how abusive thinking can keep abuse locked in place, meet Hillary.

Hillary Q.
Hillary came to see me while I was still practicing in California. An unusually thin woman with circles under her eyes, she told me her parents used to lock her in a small dark closet. She was also beaten for no reason. As a result, she decided she must be 'bad' to deserve such extreme punishments. She felt ashamed. In her adult life, she tolerated several abusive bosses as well as sadistic sexual experiences. She had never been in love or in a nurturing supportive relationship with a man. Her fingers mechanically picking apart her Kleenex, she announced, 'I'm damaged goods'.

I told her: 'You can heal yourself. Maybe you are not permanently damaged. Hurtful things happened to you and I know you feel damaged now. But perhaps during our work together you will realize that while those events occurred, they are over now and you can decide not to be affected by them any more.'

She disagreed, convinced that she was damaged beyond repair. But she agreed to work in therapy. After a year of therapy and Life Skills work, Hillary – her face glowing, hands folded calmly in her lap – reported: 'Because I felt I deserved abuse, I let people do whatever they wanted to me. I was a doormat. I've worked hard to release years and years of hurt and anger. I finally took a stand with my boss. I no longer put up with any crap. At some point in therapy, I realized I was not 'damaged goods' – that was the most freeing thing of all. And I have fallen in love with a kind, loving, wonderful man. We're getting married early next year.'

When Hillary shifted her view from *I deserve abuse* to *I deserve a good life*, she took a stand to live an abuse-free life. That enabled her to let good things and supportive people come into her world. She dropped friends who were taking advantage of her and started friendships with those who were nurturing and kind. Her new friends reinforced her growing positive feelings about herself.

They did not treat her as if she were 'damaged goods', but like the whole woman she was becoming. All that input helped her let go of her *I'm damaged and not repairable* judgment, and she was able to bring that whole person to her Life Skills work and to her life. After a year, she stopped blaming herself and letting people use her, two very important Life Skills.

Shifting Your Abusive Thinking

Now you too may be thinking just what Hillary thought when she began therapy. 'But I secretly do think *I am bad, I do deserve it, I am damaged*'. If you believe that you deserve to be punished you will unconsciously seek out people who will punish you. If you believe that you are not worth much, you will negate positive experiences. As long as you hold on to these judgments, no amount of therapy or Life Skills work will make much difference. Your abusive thoughts are the 'bowl' or foundation which shapes your life. If your bowl is called *I'm bad* and you fill it up with Life Skills, you are still available for abuse because your negative thinking easily undermines the skills. For example, if you buy a pretty dress and think you are too ugly to wear it, it will just hang in the closet. The dress will not make you beautiful. You must change your thinking so that you feel beautiful in whatever you wear. You bring your beauty, your context, to the dress. You must recognize the abusive thoughts which mold your life before you can change them. In other words, you must identify how you have shaped your 'bowl'. The Self-blame Chapter digs into this negative programming more deeply. For now, know you can release those judgments.[1]

ESTABLISHING AND RESPECTING BOUNDARIES

Taking a stand means setting boundaries – loud and clear. But you need other 'boundary skills' as well. Psychologically, setting your boundary means declaring where you will stop. When you state your limit, you say what you will and won't do and what you will and won't allow. Boundary means line, limit or border. Rockelle Lerner describes boundaries:

> When our boundaries are in tact, we know that we have
> separate feelings, thoughts and realities. Our boundaries
> allow us to know who we are in relation to others around us.
> We need our boundaries to get close to others, since otherwise
> we would be overwhelmed . . . When we have healthy
> boundaries, we . . . know when we are being abused.[2]

Developing boundaries is essential to eliminating abuse. As survivors establish their boundaries, they can distinguish abuse and put an end to it.

Non-Abusive Families

In non-abusive families, parents respect boundaries; in abusive families, boundaries are often violated. Within normal, healthy boundaries, children learn to express their needs, and how to have them met. Healthy parents respect their children's feelings and thoughts. They recognize the child's need to say no and assert himself, i.e., to set his own boundaries. They set limits when needed, but never do so by withholding love. In fact, a loving parent sets boundaries to care for and to train the child. For instance, a mother explains to her three-year-old: 'I understand you're angry but you cannot play with the scissors. They are sharp; you may play with the plastic bowls'.

This mother understands her child's desire to play with scissors and the frustration of being stopped, but she sets limits which keep the child safe. Setting boundaries is the mother's expression of love. At the same time the mother validates the child's feelings and wants. Children as well as adults are entitled to their own thoughts and emotions. Both children and adults are entitled to feeling safe, not being invaded or abused.

Abusive Families

In an abusive family, the adult invades the child's boundaries and meets his or her own needs at the child's expense. The parent oversteps limits, emotionally or physically, stripping the child of the safety he deserves. For example:

- An abusive parent beats his three-year-old for playing with the scissors.

- A father fondles his daughter sexually.

- A mother drives her children to over-accomplish so she can feel good about herself.

- A parent reads a teenager's diary.

- A compulsive father orders the kids to scrub the already-clean floor six times in a week.

- A parent tells the son, 'Wipe that angry look off your face; be happy!'

These parents disregarded their children's feelings, thoughts, and bodies. In the last instance, the parent not only discounted the child's feelings, but told him what to feel. All of these parents invaded their children's emotional or physical boundaries. These adults did not create a safe environment in which the child could discover his own feelings, perceptions and needs. When adults continually interfere with this formative process, the child does not develop a clear sense of self or appropriate boundaries, and thus cannot separate and become his own person. Such children do not know where they begin and their parents end; in short, they become codependent.

Taking Back Control of Your Life

Whatever the abuse – a neglectful mother or violent father – survivors who did not learn boundaries often experience a limited and vague sense of themselves as adults. They grow up with an unclear understanding of how to relate; in other words they are unclear about boundaries. They do not:

● Trust their own feelings and perceptions.

● Know they are able to have their needs met.

● Feel in charge of their lives.

Beverly H.

Beverly, 28, was an aspiring actress whose long brown hair half-covered her eyes. Although I had been told she showed talent on stage, she appeared awkward and unsure of herself socially. As she explained to a Life Skills class: 'Growing up I just wanted to fit in. I was raised on a farm in Iowa. I had six brothers and sisters. Whenever I wanted to read or draw, my father hit me for wasting time. If I dressed like the kids at school, my mother would call me "cheap". One time I got my hair cut short with some girlfriends, and Mom slapped me and gave me extra chores. And when I'd practice scenes from plays in my room, she would burst in on me. Then I was the butt of jokes at the dinner table. I never had any real privacy or encouragement. My family just couldn't let me express myself the way I wanted; I was too different. But I never thought my experiences were out of the ordinary. It's just the way my life has always been.'

Beverly never had a safe environment in which to express her feelings, opinions, and wants. As a result, she did not know who she was. Beverly's parents imposed their boundaries rather than allowing her to establish her own. The Life Skills class offered Beverly a safe and supportive environment to define what she wanted, felt, and thought, something she had never been able to do as a child. As she began to express her needs, she realized others were interested in helping her meet them. And as she shared her thoughts and feelings, she found them encouraged and validated. After three months – eyes shining and hair combed back – she summed up her progress: 'I'm beginning to know who I am – where I begin and end. I'm not a blank space. I feel like it's okay to be me, even if I'm a little off-beat. I'm a woman; I can fill myself with my own thoughts and ideas and wants. I am getting a sense of who I am and I'm creating my own life.'

Boundaries and Life Skills

If this section describes you, you may feel a bit concerned. However, you can teach yourself to set and respect boundaries, particularly in the chapters about Being Used, Overhelping, Sexuality and Intimacy. Defining boundaries and taking control of your life takes time, but the Life Skills work accelerates and strengthens that process. It not only assists you in taking control of your life, but gives you tools so you can live it competently.

RECOGNIZING AND APPRECIATING SURVIVAL STRATEGIES

As children, survivors consciously or unconsciously design their own Survival Strategies as a way of staying physically or emotionally alive. Here are a few Survival Strategies my clients have told me about:

'I lied so I would not get yelled at.'

'I stuffed my anger so the fighting would stop and I'd be safe.'

'I did what anybody wanted just to keep the peace.'

'I let myself be used because it looked less dangerous than confronting people.'

Almost every behavior listed in the Life Skills Quiz also describes a Survival Strategy – a method of operating that once protected you in your family. Lying, supressing anger, overhelping, pleasing, being invisible, putting yourself last, denying and letting yourself be used are all Survival Strategies. Turn back to that section for a moment and look over the questions to which you answered Yes. See if those questions also describe any of your Survival Strategies.

Outgrowing the Old Strategies

You may still think you need protection, approval or other benefits of Survival Strategies. But the Survival Strategy that you needed as a child may not be useful now. In fact, it is very likely limiting. For example:

● An adult survivor refuses to experience his pain because he still feels he needs to protect himself from his feelings. This limits him not only from releasing past pain, but from learning how to express emotions in a positive and productive way. Consequently he doesn't have close friends and has never been in love.

● A woman avoids conflict because she still fears punishment.

This prevents her from expressing anger appropriately. Instead she has recurring headaches. She pushes issues under the rug so nothing ever gets resolved.

- A man feels he must help everyone or life will fall apart as it did when he was little. His need to overhelp keeps him from learning to support people so they can solve their own problems. This keeps him from dealing with his own issues. He feels burdened and resentful that no one is there for him.

Natalie K.

Natalie, 33, in sales, offers another example of how Survival Strategies which were useful in childhood can become a burden in adulthood. One day at work she suddenly exploded at a customer. Her manager referred her to me. She began: 'My anger got me through my childhood. I'd grit my teeth and tell myself, "They aren't going to get to me!" But now that anger is about to cost me my job. But if I can't use my temper, how will I protect myself?'

Natalie recognized exactly how her anger had served her, but was afraid to let it go. I suggested that she would always have her anger, but that she could learn additional ways of relating. That way, instead of totally giving up a behavior which made her feel safe, she could simply learn additional skills to give her a wider range of choices.

Making Room for New Learning

When you see yourself using one of your Survival Strategies:

1) Appreciate how the strategy helped you survive.

2) Be aware of your emotions, especially fear, anxiety, and anger.

3) Understand how the strategy limits you.

4) Decide to set the strategy aside at least temporarily.

5) Be open to learning something new.

When you do set a strategy aside, you are able to learn a new skill. That way you are not giving up your old strategy but acquiring a new skill. In several Life Skills chapters I refer to the concepts just discussed, so you will have many opportunities to practice them.

Many adult survivors' lives have been so filled with abuse they cannot even imagine their lives without it. Taking a stand gives people a powerful tool to say, 'No, this abuse will stop!' Putting an end to internal abuse lets people realize they were not permanently damaged. When people set boundaries, they limit overt abuse and prevent people from taking advantage of them in any way. Recognizing Survival Strategies enables people to see how their early strategies served them but also how those same strategies are limiting them now.

These tools will help you stop abuse patterns and learn new Life Skills. I will refer to them throughout the book. Here are some assignments to help you apply these tools to your life.

QUESTIONS AND ASSIGNMENTS

1a) Do you need to take a stand on your being abused?

Yes _____No _____

b) What is your stand? Write it down in the space provided.

Examples:
   I will be safe and gentle with people.

   I will live an abuse-free life.

   I will demand to be treated well.

_____

_____

2a) Have you been abusive to someone else?

Yes _____No _____

b) Do you need to take a stand about that?

Yes _____No _____

c) What is your stand? State it in the space below.

Examples:
   I will be gentle and respectful to the people around me.

   I will treat my loved ones well.

   I will be non-violent.

_____

_____

3) Have you already taken a stand on abuse?

Yes _____No _____

If so, take a moment to remember the event which sparked it. Although in the past taking a stand may have arisen from a crisis, you don't need to create a crisis to take a stand now.

Examples:

When I was 14 I grew four inches in one summer. That's when my mother hit me for the last time. I yelled at her to stop and she did. I'd had it, and I was big enough to do something about it. I guess that's when I took a stand. She never hit me again, and no one else has either.

I came home drunk one night and heard my daughter crying. She looked so afraid of me. That was it. Something clicked. I stopped drinking.

My business partner said he didn't want to work with me any more because I caused so many fights. I finally saw what my temper was costing me. I was determined to stop exploding. That's when I took my stand.

4) What harsh judgments have you made about yourself as a result of your abuse? List them here.

Examples:

I deserved it.

I'm bad.

I'm a mistake.

I'm worthless.

I don't count.

_____

_____

_____

5) How did your parents or the adults who raised you emotionally or physically invade your boundaries? Write an example or two of your own below.

Examples:

My brother 'accidently' hit me or spilled hot water on me. Then he'd say, "Oops, I'm sorry". But these kind of accidents happened almost daily.

My mother used to read my diary even though I asked her not to, and even after I had hidden it so she wouldn't find it.

I had an uncle who used to brush up against my breasts and behind. Even though he never actually molested me, he always found ways of touching me where he shouldn't have.

_____

_____

6) What are the Survival Strategies you used as a child?

Examples:

Lying — Did you feel you had to skirt the truth in order to avoid a beating or harsh punishment?

Denying — Did you often make excuses for your parents' behavior such as 'He's just not feeling well', or 'She's just in a bad mood?'

Not feeling — Did you learn not to cry when you got hit or punished, because feeling the pain would be too overwhelming?

Being hysterical — Did you resort to tantrums, crying or stamping your feet as a way of controlling the abuse?

Exploding — Was anger your method of keeping people at a distance or denying your sorrow?

Overhelping — Were you overly solicitous as a way of keeping the peace?

Being perfect — Did you try to be perfect, thinking that would keep 'all hell from breaking loose?'

Being used — Did you let people use you rather than risk confrontations?

As you read further you may discover more. If you used a strategy not mentioned here, write it down.

_____

_____

_____

7) What Survival Strategies do you still use as an adult? List them here.

_____

_____

_____

8) What benefit does each Strategy give you? Safety, approval, avoiding conflict?

_____

_____

PART II

Learning
New Life Skills

SECTION ONE

Building a Firm Foundation

The first three Life Skills – Building Trust, Not Dissociating, and Expressing Emotions – give you a firm foundation for the other skills. When a person has these skills or is at least starting to trust, feel and be present in the body, he or she is better equipped to learn all the others.

Trusting, Not Dissociating and Expressing Emotions, are fundamental skills because they are used to develop and define a healthy, expressive, interactive sense of self. Once these skills are utilized, you begin to trust your own feelings, perceptions, and decisions. Bringing these capabilities to the Life Skills lessons, you are not just learning mechanically and then passively turning control over to others; you are actively directing your life while applying the new skills on a daily basis.

There is a direct relationship between trusting your body, trusting yourself, trusting your feelings, and trusting others. When you are present and trust your body, you can rely on yourself and your feelings. When you trust yourself, you can trust others in a healthy and balanced way.

CHAPTER 1

Building Trust

GOALS

- To give you practice trusting yourself

- To teach you some criteria for trusting

- To help you identify Survival Strategies related to trust

This chapter encourages you to trust yourself, rather than believing others know more than you do. It gives you criteria for trusting others, so you can make good decisions about whom to trust and not trust, instead of taking chances. It helps you identify Survival Strategies concerning trust.

WHAT SURVIVORS MISSED

People who have been abused have trouble trusting because their trust has been violated. A person they once trusted to care for them abused them instead. That person – whether a family member or close friend – violated a special relationship, stepping over critical boundaries. The person who was abused grows up guarded and suspicious. Some do not even trust their own feelings and perceptions. Others have shied away from friends, family and relationships to avoid replaying old patterns. But by isolating themselves, they have denied themselves the nurturing and love that comes from positive human contact. Without being able to trust, they cannot get the support every human being needs.

Kay G.

Kay told how she learned not to trust people: 'In my family people disappointed me time and time again. Once, after my father divorced my mother, I sat for two hours waiting for him to pick me up. He never came. So I decided the only person to rely on was me. I don't trust anyone except myself.'

Once violated, trust can take a long time to re-establish.

OLD PATTERNS
Overly Trusting, Yet Distrusting
A typical survivor trusts too much in some situations and is overly cautious in others. Such people simply do not know whom to trust and not trust because they lack proper criteria.

Laura S.
'I never open my front door for anyone. My friends had to get back in their car, drive to a pay phone and call me, before I'd open the door. On the other hand, I recently went to Las Vegas with some people I had just met. They were big gamblers, I'm not. I thought they knew more than I did, so I let them bet my last $200. Of course, I lost. I do that kind of thing a lot.'

Debbie K.
'I'm extremely suspicious of people in business. Most people call me shrewd; some people are even a little afraid of me. But with men, I become a whimp. I defer to them totally.'

Robin J.
'I trusted my husband no matter where he went when he travelled; I was stunned when he left me for another woman. Yet I demand a detailed account of my responsible teenage daughter when she goes out. Even though she's never given me any reason to distrust her, I'm always suspicious of her.'

Trusting Too Much
Another type of survivor trusts too much. This person often thinks that other people know more than he does, even when they are wrong or obviously incompetent. In essence, they trust others more than themselves.

Juan G.
'When I was a kid, I knew something was weird about our family – Dad and Mom hit each other and us too. But we never talked about it. It was a secret that we all knew about but never discussed – like the Emperor with No Clothes. Now I have a hard time trusting my perceptions. I had a bad feeling about a business deal, but I was so sure my partner knew more than I did that I relied on his judgments. Later, I found out I was right, but of course it was too late.'

Sylvia C.
'I let my husband be in charge of everything. I don't trust my judgment or perceptions at all. When I was growing up, my mom always put down my feelings and ideas. She said they were silly. I guess I believed her.'

Bea F.
'As a child, I never had any friends. I figured there must be something wrong with me because I got punished all the time. I got sent to bed at 4.30 in the afternoon; I never knew why. Now I trust people immediately so they'll like me. I have lent money to people I hardly know without asking for anything in writing. In relationships with men, I'll do what ever they say without stopping to think if it's appropriate.'

Always Suspicious

This last type of survivor trusts no one, suspects everyone. This person has been burned and disappointed so many times that he or she has decided not to trust at all.

Ronnie E.
'My mother was always in and out of hospital; she was crazy. One night a cop found her vacuuming the street "Because it was snowing", she said. It was July. My father ignored it all and worked later and later . . . and finally left. The only person who bailed me out of trouble was me. Now I don't trust a soul.'

Sally A.
'My father left us for another woman. My husband of 10 years left me for my neighbour. My last boyfriend had another woman waiting in the wings. Needless to say, I don't trust men very much.'

Jamie S.
'My parents were both alcoholics and unpredictable. After 15 years, I know my law partner is honest and reliable. And my wife is wonderful – always there for me. But I can't quite bring myself to trust them. I keep waiting for them to pull something.'

WHAT YOU CAN DO
Going Beyond the Survival Strategy

Whether adult survivors mistrust or overtrust, their behavior probably originated as a Survival Strategy. Some survived by mistrusting everyone, thus keeping danger at a distance. Others trusted everyone to avoid confrontation or to placate. Being docile, passive, and pleasing kept them alive. These strategies may have served a purpose in the past, but now they are likely to handicap you.

Some of you need to risk more. One gentleman realized how scared he was of a woman he was attracted to. The woman met all the trust criteria in the assignments section so he finally risked asking her out. Others need to learn to be more cautious and exercise good judgment. Another man reined himself in from his usual impulse decision-making and did not sign a business deal until he consulted his partners. The exercises at the end of the chapter will help you begin to practice trust skills. In that way you will have a variety of responses and guidelines for using them so you can learn to make the best and most rewarding choices.

Developing and Earning Trust
People whose trust has been abused often lack good criteria for trusting. Many adult surivors decide to trust or not trust instantly. Some regard trust as a black-or-white issue – they trust totally or not at all. They do not realize that people should earn trust by demonstrating trustworthiness over a period of time. One Life Skills participant described herself:

Evelyn R.
'Everyone became my best friend instantly. I had no rational basis for trusting. I was too scared that I'd be alone because I was lonely most of my childhood. Now that I'm not desperate for friends, I value myself more and have learned to take my time and let trust develop slowly. People don't just become my good friends auto-matically. I'm still friendly and outgoing, but I have categories called strangers, acquaintances, buddies and really intimate friends. Now I trust the people in each group differently.'

Let me reiterate two notions that can help you make better decisions about trusting:

1) Trust develops over time.

2) People must earn your trust.

These ideas imply that trusting happens by degrees and is not a black-or-white matter at all.

SUMMARY
Abused people can have problems with:

● Trusting too much

● Not trusting anyone at all

● Naively trusting in some situations and not giving their trust when it is deserved

● Using over-trusting and/or mistrusting as Survival Strategies

People can learn:

● Trust is built gradually and must be earned

● Ways of evaluating when and whom to trust or not trust

QUESTIONS AND ASSIGNMENTS

1) Do you trust people too quickly? Do you accept rides from strangers or confide intimate details about yourself on first meetings? If so, briefly describe one incident when that happened.

_____

_____

_____

2a) Are there times when it is hard for you to trust? When someone is nice to you, do you suspect him of having ulterior motives? If so, briefly describe one incident when you sensed it was appropriate to trust someone, but you could not.

_____

_____

_____

3) Do you over-trust in some situations and distrust without cause in others? If this is your pattern, describe it briefly.

Examples:
   After one date I fall head-over-heels in romantic relationships; but in business I'm suspicious of everyone.

_____

_____

_____

4a) Have you used excessive trust or distrust as a Survival Strategy?

Yes _____No _____

b) If you answered yes, write down how this strategy has served and protected you.

Examples:
   I trust everyone so people will like me.

   I don't trust men because I don't want to get burned again.

_____

_____

c) Write down how this strategy limits you now.

Examples:

I don't have any truly close relationships in my life.

I'm easily duped.

_____

_____

5) Regarding people close to you, can you distinguish those you can trust from those you cannot? Are you able to trust one friend who has always been supportive and kept your secrets, but not another who has frequently lied and betrayed your confidences?

Yes _____No _____

6) I have listed below some trust criteria. As you practice building trust, you may want to add some of your own.
a) Does this person treat you with kindness and respect? By this I mean, does he or she respect your ideas, wishes, needs, and your right to say no? Does this person say things like:

I want to hear what you have to say.

I think your idea is a good one.

I want you to have what you need.

Let's work out a compromise.

I don't like your choice, but I respect your right to make it.

I don't like that you turned me down, but I understand.

b) Is the person genuinely concerned about you? By this I mean, does he or she:

Listen without interrupting?

Show an interest in your life?

Allow you to be angry, sad, happy, and not try to change or suppress you?

Let you express your opinion even when it differs from his?

c) Does this person generally keep appointments? When this person is late, does he or she apologize?

d) Does this person keep your secrets?

e) Does this person reveal secrets someone else told him in confidence?

f) When this person says he will do something, does he follow through? By this I mean, when a friend says he will be there on Saturday, he shows up.

Write down a friend's name _____

Regarding this friend, review the trust criteria just listed. Does your friend meet these criteria?

Yes _____No _____

7a) Check the actions which let you know you should question a friend's trust. Your friend:

_____Is habitually late

_____Talks behind your back

_____Forgets to call you

_____Doesn't show up for a date and doesn't call

_____Dates your boyfriend

_____Borrows money and doesn't repay it

_____Fails to give you an important phone message

b) Add other actions in the space below which would cause you to question a friend's trust.

_____

_____

_____

c) If your friend or family member repeatedly does things on this list, then he or she has a pattern of untrustworthy behavior. Write down what you would like to say to him or her. Communicate honestly and responsibly.

Examples:

Please try to be on time.

Next time you are going to be late please call.

I'm not going to lend you any money until you pay me back what you owe me. And I'd like to know when you'll pay me back.

_____

8) If a person gives you a double message you should be cautious of trusting him or her. A double message means saying one thing and doing another. Often one message is spoken while the other is nonverbal.

Examples:

I love you/I hate you.
A mother tells her son she loves him while she is slapping him for no reason.

Come close but stay away.
A lover who is warm and passionate at night, but disturbingly cool and withdrawn the next morning.

I like you but you threaten me.
A new friend calls every day, makes plans and then suddenly breaks them, stops calling and has second thoughts about seeing you.

I love you (while physically moving away).
A husband tells his wife he loves her, but works more hours than necessary and clearly prefers the company of his male friends over her.

We all experience ambivalence at times. When people can communicate ambivalent messages responsibly, then they may be worthy of trust. For example, he or she might admit:

I love being with you, but sometimes I feel very threatened.

I want you close, but sometimes when you are close I get scared and I push you away.

Left unspoken, such messages are confusing and suspect. But when they are honestly confronted and discussed, they open a path for building both trust and closeness.

a) Recall an incident when a person gave you a double message. Write it down in a few lines.

_____

_____

b) Now write down what that person could have said to communicate both messages clearly and honestly and still demonstrate trustworthiness.

_____

_____

9a) Write down your decisions about trust. After each decision, write down when you made it and under what circumstances. In some cases, you may have had one dramatic incident which you can pinpoint immediately. In other instances, you may need to reflect on a series of events which led to your decision.

Examples:

You can't trust men – When I was 12, my father said he was going on a business trip – and he never came back.

I can't count on anyone but me – I remember getting up every morning and fixing breakfast for my brothers and me while my parents slept it off.

I trust others more than myself – My parents were always telling me they knew what was best for me and they constantly reminded me of my mistakes.

I trust everyone – My older brothers would never let me play with them, so I'd do anything to get them to like me; I became a little 'yes man'.

_____

_____

_____

_____

_____

b) Consider the possibility that the decisions you made as a child may be limiting you. By replacing each with a more flexible and freeing decision, you open up your life to new possibilities.

Examples:

NOT: Men can't be trusted.
BUT: You can trust some men but not others.

NOT: I can't count on anyone but myself.
BUT: I can count on some people, besides myself.

NOT: Everyone knows more than I do.
BUT: I can trust myself.

Write down your new decisions.

_____

_____

_____

_____

10) Choose someone whom you think you could learn to trust:
someone who has shown continued love and support and has earned
your respect. Write down the qualities you think make him or her
trustworthy.

Examples:

My friend is almost always on time, and calls if he's going to be late.

He does what he says he'll do.

When I tell her something in a confidence she keeps it to herself.

He never says bad things about other people.

_____

_____

_____

_____

11) Choose a person in your life with whom you want to build trust.
Ask him or her to do a small favor.

Examples:

Return a phone call.

Be on time to a meeting.

Return a book on a certain day.

Pick up an item at the market for you.

FURTHER READING

HUNT, Irene.
   The Lottery Rose (New York: Charles Scribner's Sons, 1976).

PATTERSON, Katherine.
   The Great Gilly Hopkins (New York: Avon Camelot Books, 1978)

CHAPTER 2

Not Dissociating

GOALS
- To help you identify dissociating characteristics

- To teach you simple methods for re-entering and reawakening the body

- To help you begin to be more in your body

This chapter defines dissociating as the state a person is in when he goes numb or 'leaves the body'. Let me explain what I mean by that. Dissociating, or not being in the body, describes a particular phenomenon with specific characteristics. The dissociated person feels very little emotionally or physically, is distant or removed, appears wooden or dead, and speaks in a monotone or flat voice.

WHAT SURVIVORS MISSED
Everyone distances himself from time to time; people daydream o mentally 'space out' for a moment or two. This is natural. But can that same person be fully present, conscious and aware when needed? For the traumatized person, the answer is often no. This person has stopped feeling as a way of blocking out physical or emotional pain. However, the problem is much more severe than simply not feeling emotions, which I discuss in the next chapter; dissociating can mean blocking out literally all sensations.

The survivor who has dissociated does not feel at home in his body, something which most people take for granted. This experience leads such individuals to feel at war with their bodies or even with life itself. They sometimes report that the most basic acts of living – getting up in the morning, going outside, speaking to another person – feel threatening.

OLD PATTERNS

In my work with survivors I have seen two types of dissociating. In the first instance, the person leaves his body to avoid a specific situation and then decides that being in his own body is permanently dangerous. Other cases involve people who generally numb themselves and experience life minimally.

It's Dangerous to Be In the Body

Some survivors decided at a certain point that being in their bodies was dangerous. They may actually remember a specific experience of being out of the body. Yet their recollections are distinctly different from the near-death experiences Ray Moody reported in *Life After Life*. [1] Moody discovered that the people he interviewed often found their out-of-body time to be profound, life-altering, and even spiritual. Many decided to come back and live their lives more fully. The experiences were positive, even empowering. Not so for the adult survivor who left the body or dissociated as a Survival Strategy to avoid or deny or cope with pain.

Several clients have told me they consciously separated themselves from their bodies to escape pain or danger. Many had decided *Life is dangerous* or *My body is dangerous* or *It's dangerous to be alive*. Years later, they were still operating out of these decisions. A new client who had been brutally and repeatedly raped coped with her unbearable situation by 'removing' herself from the scene.

Helen D.
'I sat on the mail box and watched them rape me over and over. They raped me five times.'

Her face was wooden, it looked thick and stiff. Her voice sounded flat. She told me she had felt little emotion since her ordeal. She liked her work at a crisis center, because the highly-charged emotional situations never got to her as they did the other counselors.

Phil H.
'From a safe spot on the bookcase, I watched my father beat me. I counted my head bouncing on the window sill 13 times.'

This man was very sensitive and emotional, but he had decided early on: *My body gets me in trouble*.

Clarissa C.
A woman professor told me her mother was psychotic. She was put in abusive foster homes starting at four years old. She decided not to feel the pain. And now, years later, the man she is living

with hits her regularly. She showed me bruises on her face and arms. I was not as alarmed by the bruises as I was by the fact that she was not concerned. Her 'whistles and bells' as I call them, those inner signals alerting us to danger were out-of-order. Of course, this made her a prime candidate not only for abuse but also for remaining in abusive situations, with little motivation to get out.

Numbing: Not Feeling At All

I discovered another group of clients who simply numbed themselves so they did not have to feel the pain. Sometimes the deadening started during one abusive incident and sometimes it occurred over time. And this group of survivors had no specific memory of leaving their bodies.

Tracy N.

'I just numbed myself. I told myself I wasn't going to show any feelings. I wouldn't let him see he was getting to me. It was the only thing left I could control.'

This woman did not feel much at all. She described herself as subdued. Such people can experience emotional 'numbness' some or all the time; this means they have little emotional color in their lives. Sometimes they appear wooden, stiff, frozen, or unfeeling.

Robyn T.

'When I stuff myself with food, I can feel my stomach. When I don't, I have no sense of my body and I get scared. When I am eating I feel connected to my physical self.'

Heather C.

An anorexic woman told me: 'I don't feel any physical pain. The doctor said I should have pains and other symptoms, but I don't feel anything.'

When a person numbs all sensations, the body's normal response to danger gets short-circuited. Clearly, this can be disasterous because the survivor lacks the normal ability to sense fear or pain. This distancing can also lead to depression and ultimately to mental instability. Over many years dissociating undermines the survivor's mental health as well as his physical well-being.

WHAT YOU CAN DO

If this section describes you, you may have trouble with speaking, listening, reading, motor tasks, or memory. For instance, one woman came into a Life Skills class looking detached and vacant. She described her childhood beatings as if she were giving the weather report. Although she said she was listening in class, she looked like she was daydreaming. She often asked that comments be repeated twice or three times.

To assist her I had to find a process directly involving the body, more than just verbal therapy. I chose Sensing, a work developed by Charlotte Selver. It focuses conscious attention on breathing, gravity, and gentle movement to restore body awareness and aliveness.

After my client did the tapping sequence, which is based on Sensing work and other exercises at the end of this chapter, she not only looked more 'present' but she was more alert and did not need things repeated. When people re-awaken and re-enter their bodies, they can experience their emotions more fully and can begin to trust those feelings and perceptions. They are also more competent at interacting with others and conducting everyday tasks.

Needless to say, not being in the body can effect every area of your life. So retraining yourself to be present may help sharpen all of your learning skills, especially the more cognitive Life Skills in later chapters. Many people have found that when they healed their dissociation, other problems began to resolve themselves.

ADDITIONAL CASES
To see the results of re-entering the body, meet Terri and Louise.

Terri L.
During a session, Terri, 27, remembered an automobile accident. She reported: 'I realized I had never felt safe in my body since the accident. My body was the enemy because it got me hurt. I have not been fully in my body since then – I was only six years old.'

Terri displayed several characteristics of dissociation:

1) She sometimes felt like she was seeing life through a sheet of glass.

2) Her face often looked frozen and lacked animation.

3) She did not feel deeply; she was never dramatically angry, happy or sad.

Terri continued: 'I used to think I was just quiet and dull. During therapy I re-decided I could now count on my body and be safe. I 'entered' it as though I were filling a lamp with light. I remember slapping myself all over, playfully singing I light up my life. Now I find I have a wide range of feelings; my face is more relaxed and open; I don't feel as separated.'

Louise F.

Louise, whose parents invalidated her feelings as a child, told me: 'I remember our family taking a trip to the Grand Canyon when I was a little girl. I had so thoroughly trained myself not to feel, that when I stood overlooking the edge, I felt nothing. The view so inspired the woman standing next to me that she cried. I felt nothing; I was numb. After 30 years and much personal work, I went back to the Grand Canyon this summer.'

Louise also had been tapping herself as described at the end of this chapter twice daily for two months. She continued: 'This time everything was vivid and alive; the wind on my skin, the sun on my face, the bright colors . . . and I was so moved I cried. Even when things are unpleasant now I can stay with it and not go away. I'm alive again.'

How can you know whether or not you have split off from yourself? Although we have no specific criteria for dissociating, professionals do recognize certain signs. Here are some ideas to consider:

SUMMARY

- People who have been physically or emotionally abused can and often do dissociate

- Dissociating can take the form of numbing, denying feelings and memories, or being out of the body

- Any of these conditions can serve as a Survival Strategy to avoid physical and emotional pain

- Survivors may actually look wooden or frozen

- They may not feel much emotionally

- They may have trouble sensing danger

- Prolonged dissociation can led to mental instability

- Sensing and other gentle body work coupled with therapy can assist you in re-integrating

QUESTIONS AND ASSIGNMENTS

1) Do you feel numb some or most of the time?

Examples:

I really don't feel much.

I feel like I'm wrapped in cotton.

I don't have much of a reaction to things.

Yes _____ No _____

b) If yes, describe your experience in a couple of lines.

_____

_____

_____

2a) Do you remember a time when you left your body or split off?

Examples:

When I had my ski accident, I left my body while they set my leg.

I turned off when Mom screamed. I just started listening to her attacks as if they were happening to a character in a movie.

Yes _____ No _____

b) If yes, describe that time briefly.

_____

3a) Do you feel distant or separated from your feelings and what is going on around you, as if you were separate from life itself?

Examples:

When our son was so sick, my wife was worried, upset. She got mad at me for not caring. I care; I just felt cut off from my feelings.

I told my boss I was angry, but I didn't feel it. Mostly I fake my feelings.

Yes _____ No _____

b) If yes, write down what your experience is like.

_____

_____

_____

4a) When you should sense danger, do you feel nothing?

Examples:

After the fire our fellow tenants were furious with the landlord for not having smoke alarms. I felt nothing.

A guy tried to stab me with a knife. I just took the knife out of his hand. Danger? I didn't feel any.

Yes _____ No _____

b) If yes, write down a time when you should have felt danger, but sensed little or nothing.

_____

_____

_____

5a) Do you feel like your body is the enemy?

Examples:

I can't count on my body. My body gets sick or has something wrong with it all the time.

I wish I didn't have to have a body. It just gets in the way.

My body is always getting hurt or into trouble. I'd like a new one.

Yes _____ No _____

b) If yes, describe briefly how you feel about your body.

_____

_____

_____

6a) With your eyes closed, stand easily with your feet slightly apart. Take a deep breath, and without forcing, allow the exhalation to complete itself. Do this two or three times. Now allow your breathing to remain in your awareness as you begin to shake your arms vigorously. Now lift one leg and shake it, holding onto a chair or wall for balance. Then, lift the other leg and shake it. With your eyes still closed, stand restfully and notice what you feel.

Examples:

I feel a tingling.

I feel warmer.

I feel more awake.

My arms feel heavy.

I'm more aware of my legs and feet now.

b) Identify your sensations, not judgments or concepts, as specifically as possible.

Example:
NOT: I feel better.
BUT: I'm more aware of my legs.

NOT: I feel sensations.
BUT: I feel tingling in my lower limbs.

7a) With one arm hanging gently at your side, tap that arm all over with the flat part of your other hand a few times. Then let the tapped arm hang and compare the different sensations in the two arms.

Example:
I can feel the tapped arm more than my other one.

It feels more 'there,' bigger, more alive.

It feels heavier.

My shoulder dropped.

b) Write down what you experienced.

8a) Now you are going to tap yourself with gentle slaps all over your body. Start at your head and with your fingertips tap your head and face. Now move over the rest of your body using the palm of your hand. Tap fairly vigorously, but kindly. Be sure to tap your arms and under your arms. Spend extra time reaching to tap your back, buttocks and legs. People don't have as much awareness in these areas.

After a few minutes, and before you tire, stop and let yourself feel the sensations.

If you feel a little nervous, just do what seems comfortable and tolerable.

b) Write your reactions below.

Example:

I can feel my feet and legs.

I feel bigger and more in touch with the ground.

I am breathing more deeply. I am not holding myself so tightly.

I felt something let go in my back.

I felt anxious, now I feel calm. For the first time I can feel the lower half of my body.

_____

_____

_____

c) If you need to wake up in your body, I suggest you give yourself this simple tapping exercise two or three minutes in the morning, again in the evening as well as any time you notice you feel cut off from your body. [2]

9a) Sitting or lying down, close your eyes and relax comfortably. Take a few deep breaths and let them out, gently, without forcing them. Now imagine you are a hollow lamp and that you are going to fill that lamp with liquid light. Begin pouring your energy or liquid in at the top of your head. See the light illuminating your head, shining out of your eyes, down your neck, into your arms and fingertips. Now see it going down into your chest, filling your vital organs and abdomen and back. Now see the light flooding down both legs, knees, into your feet and toes. Take a deep breath and breathe light all through your body.

Say out loud *I am safe and alive in my body* three times.
Open your eyes.
(You can read this into a tape recorder and play the instructions for yourself.)

b) Write your experience in the blanks below.

_____

10a) When you feel yourself spacing out next time, focus on what you are sensing. Ask yourself these questions:

● What colors do you see?

● What do you smell or taste?

● What pressure or temperature do you feel?

● What are people saying?

● What noises are you hearing?

Focusing on the blue sky, feeling the soft grass under your feet, or hearing the traffic will bring you back into your body.

b) Fill in this sentence:

After I spaced out, to bring myself back again I focused on:

FURTHER READING
BROOKS, Charles V.W.
   Sensory Awareness: The Rediscovery of Expression (New York: Viking Press, 1974).

KEANE, Betty Winkler.
   Sensing: Letting Yourself Live (New York: Harper & Row, 1979).

For information in Sensory Awareness classes in various areas of this country and Europe, contact;
   Sensory Awareness Foundation
   273 Star Route
   Muir Beach, California 94965.

CHAPTER 3

Expressing Emotions Appropriately

GOALS
- To help you identify your feelings

- To help you validate and permit yourself to experience emotions

- To help express your feelings appropriately

Feelings are part of being human. Expressing them appropriately and regularly promotes both mental and physical health. Yet many people have difficulty expressing them. Failure to feel emotions is a characteristic of dissociating; however, some people who are not dissociated do not express emotions.

This chapter addresses the latter group. It will not only give you permission to feel, but will also provide methods of identifying your emotions. Then it will discuss how to express those emotions appropriately.

WHAT SURVIVORS MISSED
Our culture has trained men not to show sadness and vulnerability. Women, on the other hand, have been taught not to act out their anger. In addition to these cultural restrictions, a child from an abusive or alcoholic home may have cut off all emotions as the only way to stop hurting. Having blocked his emotions as a child, he may grow up unable to feel and experience life fully. Another child may have learned to exaggerate feelings or cry hysterically in an attempt to try and control an abusive situation. This person may grow up dominating and controlling, not knowing how to solve problems by mutually working things out. These tactics may have been effective as Survival Strategies, but they now severely limit the survivor's development.

OLD PATTERNS
Benefits of Feeling
When I invited one client to try and revive her emotions, she replied: 'But why would I want to feel all that pain? What good would it do me?'

When people allow themselves to experience their feelings, they can achieve an emotional release. For instance, a widow needs to cry and feel her loss. In doing so, she can heal her grief more quickly. Holding on to powerful emotions for years can cause physical stress and even disease.

Experiencing emotional pain can also be useful in other ways. Pain lets us know something is wrong, whether physical or mental. Systematically suppressing pain can be dangerous. Feeling pain, anger, love – indeed, all emotions – comprises part of our inner guidance system. One client related that he had suffered stomach aches for years. When he finally began to express his anger and sadness about his childhood, his symptoms went away.

When freely expressed, emotions not only provide information but add rich color to our lives. A non-feeling person sees a glorious sunset without being moved, or witnesses the birth of his child and misses the thrill. The experience of being moved or thrilled, i.e. feeling our emotions, helps guide our personal reactions and enrich our lives. Not feeling is never to taste the essence of life.

Feeling Too Much or Too Little
Some abusive parents invalidate their children's emotions by telling them they are not experiencing what they are in fact feeling. This negative training creates problems years later when, as adults, they have turned off their emotions. Others are overwhelmed by their emotions and are afraid of being controlled by so much feeling. Another type I call the 'drama queen' is a person who gets energized from crises and over-emotionalizing.

WHAT YOU CAN DO
Coming Alive
If you have trouble connecting with your emotions, begin by giving yourself permission to let go, at least a little bit. Then notice what you are feeling several times a day. Allow your emotions to surface naturally. As you begin to feel more comfortable, you will not be so overwhelmed. If you have difficulty defining your feelings, read the exercise at the end of the chapter.

Begin to notice that when you do express yourself, you are still safe. Choose friends and associates who validate your feelings.

With practice, you will soon start to become more sensitive and emotionally free.

Becoming Less Dramatic

If you tend to over-emotionalize, then you need different Life Skills. But first you must recognize your addiction to drama. The 'drama queen' loves crises and actually gets high on them. Men can be 'drama kings', but it is more common among women. These people consciously or unconsciously create continual crises. These scenes feed their need for excitement, but never give them genuine satisfaction. The 'drama queen' or 'drama king' can operate as rescuers saving friends and family from disasters, or as victims who continually create personal crises hoping someone will save them. Dr Joy Davidson in *The Agony of It All* [1] describes the drive for drama and excitement in great detail with many helpful suggestions for recovery. She distinguishes between normal, healthy excitement and drama fraught with pain and suffering.

To begin breaking this pattern, you need to take a hard look at the pay-offs you receive from being dramatic and over-emotional. They may include being able to control people and situations receiving attention, or simply the rush of excitement. The drama queen often needs to feel special, even like a heroine. However, this behavior prevents you from authentically working out conflicts so you get what you really need. Many people report that, though their lives are exciting, something is missing. That something might be closeness, satisfaction, a sense of meaning, genuine thanks for a job well done. When you learn to solve problems without melodrama, you can get what you genuinely need.

For instance, a client came in telling me she needed to discontinue therapy. She began sobbing and appeared very upset. I suggested we talk about different solutions so she could have what she needed. She wanted to continue therapy but she could no longer afford to come weekly. When she realized she could just ask for what she wanted without the drama, we then scheduled her sessions to accommodate her budget.

ADDITIONAL CASES

To illustrate how three survivors learned to express their emotions more appropriately, let me introduce you to Cynthia, Kathy, and Frances:

Cynthia R.

As I mentioned, some abused individuals learned to survive by training themselves not to feel. Unfortunately, that decision usually blocks out all emotions, both good and bad. To avoid pain while she was being beaten, Cynthia, 27, had trained herself early-on to feel nothing. She was now studying to be an actress, and for a time had abused drugs and alcohol. She explained: 'When I stopped drinking and taking drugs, I started having anxiety attacks because I was no longer chemically numbed out. I'd get so frightened of what I was feeling in acting class that I'd get sweaty, feel faint, and want to run. I used to black out when I was drinking; then I blacked out emotionally.'

By the time Cynthia started therapy, she had been in AA for five years. I asked if she would experiment and allow in just a tiny amount of feeling, and then notice her responses. I suggested she listen to sad music and pay close attention to her feelings. I had her keep a record of her feelings over a week. During the next few months Cynthia realized that she actually felt quite a lot. At first she was afraid, but each time she allowed in some feelings and saw she was still all right, she felt she had room to open up a little more.

She came into one session saying: 'I'm all over the place. I'm angry at my boss, frustrated with my boyfriend. And I hate the cab driver.'

Cynthia was becoming alive and feeling emotions she had never experienced before. Each week she was able to allow in more feeling. After eight months, Cynthia was very much in touch with her emotions. She reported: 'I'm alive now with all kinds of feelings. Last week I experienced real excitement – I mean like I was actually thrilled when an old friend called. And when my mom's cat died, I cried. I truly felt sad for her. My anger still scares me, because it's so heavy-duty, but the more I let it out, the more I'm starting to get used to it.'

Kathy T.
Because Kathy felt dead inside, she thrived on emotional excitement. Only when she felt intensely did she sense she was alive. She described herself as out-of-control emotionally: 'I never trusted my feelings at all, probably because my parents invalidated what I knew I felt. When I was sad, they'd say 'You're not sad!' Dad would actually write me a check if I'd smile. They trained me to ignore and suppress all my negative feelings. At home I walked around with a fixed smile on my face. At school I sought excitement – rock bands, drinking, staying out all night – anything dramatic just so I'd know I was alive. I had no sense of balance. In high school I drove myself to be busy all the time. I got

good grades and joined every club. I never felt anything negative. I binged on excitement.'

At home Kathy's mom was usually drugged on Valium. If her children got sick, she would tell them to go to bed and 'let me know when you're better'. If they cried or expressed pain, they were punished. Her dad, an alcoholic, often hit Kathy and her brothers. After Kathy performed the lead in the school play, she came home ecstatic. Afterwards her father beat her so badly she was hospitalized.

'Because my parents trained me not to feel, I grew more and more depressed. By the time I was in my early twenties I was suicidal.

'Ten years and a lot of therapy later, I can finally acknowledge the 'bad' feelings. I was so afraid I'd go out-of-control if I let them up, but I see now that suppressing made me even more afraid. Now that I'm really facing my emotions, they have no power over me. I discovered I can stop the frenzied activity. I'm even starting to trust my intuition.

'Recently, I was infatuated with a man. I knew he was crazy and had problems, but I chose to ignore them because I felt such a strong attraction. One night he exploded. then I remembered my first impression. I knew I had to let go of him. Even though I don't always listen to my instincts, I can say I'm learning to trust myself and my feelings. I have people around me now who have similar values. I can trust them to honor my feelings and not overpower me.'

Frances K.
Frances, 28, a word-processor, rescued her friends and created her own share of personal dramas. When she rushed into my office for our first session, she was out of breath.

'Can I use your bathroom? I have to clean up. I just saw an accident and stopped to help the driver.'

That seemed very compassionate, but as Frances told me her story, I discovered she fed on non-stop emergencies. I asked Frances about her early life.

'It was always chaotic – all my seven brothers and sisters screaming and yelling. As the oldest, I went from helping one with a scraped knee to breaking up two sisters fighting, to a teacher's conference for my brother who'd gotten into trouble at school. My mother had divorced my father and she worked full time. I was the family heroine. I loved that role; I guess I still do. I know I gravitate toward people who have lots of problems. It's what I'm used to.'

I asked her, 'Do you see how you play a role in keeping it all going?'

'Of course! But where else would I get my juice from? I'm like a junkie who needs a fix. I have a dear friend in the hospital; I visit her every day. She really needs me. My mother's dying of cancer, so I always have to be on-call for her. Last week the boiler exploded in our building and the tenants were out on the street. I stayed up all night talking to people.'

I asked, 'How long has this been going on?'

She responded, 'All my life!'

I could certainly sympathize with Frances' personal pain and capacity for caring. But her non-stop drama had become an addition which, like a drug, enabled her to avoid dealing with her own issues. She complained that no one was there for her; no one listened to her. And she was beginning to get resentful.

I suggested she take five minutes each day to reflect and sit quietly. I asked her: 'What would happen if you had some peace and quiet? Consider the possibility that you could feel alive even in calm moments.'

'Oh, that would be wonderful, but I don't think I could stand it for very long.'

She started with five minutes. She came in to the next session and reported: 'Five minutes seemed like forever at first. I wanted to jump up and do something. On the fourth day I began to cry . . . I didn't know why. But now I think it's because I live everyone else's life, but not my own.'

We began working on her releasing her feelings and focussing on what she wanted in life.

While reading this section you may have recognized parts of yourself in several of the cases. The stories may have made you feel uneasy and evoked long-buried memories and feelings. If you have anaesthetized yourself, those emotions can help you feel more alive again. They can provide information about your life and help you heal yourself. The questions and assignments will assist you further.

SUMMARY
- Feeling and expressing emotions is natural

- Expressing them promotes good mental and physical health

- Abused people may have turned their feelings off as a means of coping

- Other survivors may be 'addicted' to excitement.

QUESTIONS AND ASSIGNMENTS

1) What beliefs do you have about expressing or not expressing your feelings? Write them down.

Examples:

Expressing feelings is dangerous.

I'll be out of control if I'm too emotional.

Feelings aren't important.

If I feel too much I'll be like my hysterical mother.

If I express my feelings I'll be too exposed.

Feelings are indulgent and a waste of time.

_____

_____

_____

_____

2) Do you give yourself permission to feel whatever you are feeling? If not, begin to make room for your emotional reactions. Write down how certain activities might help you express your feelings.

Examples:

I could let myself cry at the end of a movie, just sit there for a few minutes and let myself sob.

Once a day I could sit quietly and ask myself: What am I feeling?

If I feel excited, I could go ahead and act it out: jump up and down, laugh or scream or yell.

_____

_____

_____

b) The next time you have the opportunity, express your feelings. Then write down what happened.

Examples:

I went to the movies by myself so I wouldn't feel embarrassed. Afterwards, I just sat there and cried my eyes out.

I was so mad at the guy who cut me off, that I screamed. The car windows were rolled up and he didn't hear me, but I felt good.

I just felt kind of sad all day; no specific reason. But I noticed it, and didn't run away.

_____

_____

3a) For one week pay close attention to your feelings. Use this word list to help you identify your emotions.

Examples:

sad	dejected	unhappy
dull	flat	glum
low	discouraged	fearful
timid	shy	restless
anxious	hesitant	scared
shaky	gay	friendly
content	serene	joyous
glad	pleased	cheery
bright	restful	hopeful
enraged	offended	fuming
bitter	excited	bold
certain	calm	misgiving
loving	nurtured	despair
lively	satisfied	suspicious

b) Each evening review your day and select a particular incident which provoked emotion. Then list one or two words which best describe what you felt. You may find that you experienced more than one emotion at once.

Examples:

At work my manager criticized me unfairly. I felt: angry, offended, hurt.

When I was standing in the check-out line, the woman next to me complimented my hair cut. I felt: pleased, self-conscious.

Monday

_____

_____

Tuesday

_____

_____

Wednesday

_____

_____

Thursday

_____

_____

Friday

_____

_____

Saturday

_____

_____

Sunday

_____

_____

4a) List the feelings that are easiest for you to express.

_____

_____

b) List the feelings which are most difficult for you to feel.

_____

_____

5) Answer the following questions:

Yes _____No _____Do your friends tell you that you indulge in your emotions?

Yes _____No _____Do you frequently find yourself telling people, even strangers, about your misfortunes?

Yes _____No _____Do you talk about other people's tragedies and conflicts over and over again?

Yes _____No _____Does a constant stream of dramatic events seem to prevent you from achieving your goals?

Yes _____No _____Do you find it exciting to assist friends who are going through a crisis?

Yes _____No _____Are you easily bored and need continual emotional excitement?

Yes _____No _____Do you cry or get angry easily?
If you answered Yes to two or more questions, you probably over-dramatize your emotions.

6a) Do you over-dramatize everyday incidents?

Yes _____No _____

Examples:
When the lady in front of me dropped her groceries, I screamed for help. Five people came running. She was fine; my heart was pounding with excitement.

While I was at the mall, a car in front of me took my parking place. I jumped out and threatened to punch the driver. I loved the thrill of it.

My friend went to the doctor's for a cold. She wasn't that sick, but I took off work early, went shopping for her and brought her dinner. I loved being the hero.

When I broke up with my boyfriend I carried on for weeks — crying, suffering. I knew deep inside it was over, but I wouldn't admit it. I was angry and wanted his attention.

b) If yes, write down an example.

_____

_____

c) What was your payoff from being overly dramatic? Circle the ones on the list and add others that you discover.

Attention

Excitement

A rush

A challenge

Feeling needed

Feeling special

Feeling like a hero

Relief from boredom

_____

_____

_____

d) What did you really need that you did not get from that interaction? Closeness, satisfaction, being genuinely productive, a sense of meaning, thanks, recognition?

Examples:

I wanted the woman to say thank you, but I know I embarrassed her.

I wanted the man to apologize for taking my parking place.

I wanted to feel satisfied that I'd helped; but I just felt empty when the excitement was over.

I wanted my boyfriend to say he was sorry. I'm sorry too. Then maybe we could say goodbye like two adults.

_____

_____

_____

e) Next time you see yourself being overly dramatic, ask yourself, What do I genuinely need that I'm not getting?

FURTHER READING
CAMERON-BANDLER, Leslie and LEBEAU, Michael.
  The Emotional Hostage: Rescuing Your Emotional Life (San Rafael, Cal.: FuturePace, 1986).

DAVIDSON, Dr Joy.
  The Agony of It All (Los Angeles: J.P. Tarcher, 1988).

PADUS, Emrika.
  The Complete Guide to Your Emotions and Your Health (Emmaus, Pa.: Rodale Press, 1986).

VISCOTT, Dr David.
  The Language of Feelings (New York: Pocket Books, 1976).

SECTION TWO

Taking Care of You

'Having fun? What fun! Taking care of me? I've been so busy just staying alive, I can't imagine having fun or doing something nice for myself!'

When I mentioned self-nurturing, having fun and attending to personal needs at the first Life Skills class, this was typical of the reaction I received. People felt a little threatened, as if I were speaking another language they did not understand. This might very well be your reaction as you read this. Life Skills participants have reported feeling anxious, afraid, angry, and sad. Whatever your feelings, they are natural given that your growing up may have been void of fun and nurturing of any kind. Now, as an adult, you may draw a blank when asked to think about fun, needs, or taking care of yourself.

However, just as people from rural communities can learn to drive in heavy traffic, or people from the city can learn to milk cows, you can learn these skills. But having fun, expressing needs, and nurturing affect the emotional quality of your life no matter where you live or what you do.

Learning to take care of you will be easier if you:

1) Let go of the need to suffer.

2) Give yourself permission to take care of you.

CHAPTER 4

Having Fun

GOALS
- To help you let go of the need to suffer

- To discover what is fun for you

- To discover a sense of play and fun in everything you do

- To create a healthy, self-generating relationship to fun

Fun means enjoying yourself, being amused, playing. By having fun I mean not just going to the movies, taking a vacation, or going to an amusement park, but creating a sense of fun with whatever you choose to do. That sense of play can bring joy to all aspects of life. This chapter talks about both kinds of fun. You will have an opportunity to discover what is fun for you and begin to discover a healthy sense of play.

WHAT SURVIVORS MISSED
Fun May Feel Foreign
For adults from alcoholic or abusive homes, play may be totally foreign. They never saw Mom and Dad laughing together; the family did not play recreational games, take vacations that were enjoyable, or just have fun at the dinner table. On the contrary, attempts at fun may have ended in terrible fights. Playing games meant getting hurt or being made fun of.

Children from abusive homes often had to grow up too fast. They were given or took on the burdens of raising younger sisters and brothers. Or they took on parenting their own parents. Sadness and hurt filled that child's life instead of fun and laughter. As a result of over-responsibility, adult survivors often feel unable to have fun and feel intimidated by 'fun-loving people'. They may not even recognize that fun is missing from their lives.

OLD PATTERNS
Letting Go of the Need to Suffer
Many adult survivors have a deep commitment to suffering and struggle even though the actual abuse may have stopped years ago. I recently talked to a woman in a Life Skills course who earns over $100,000 a year. She had just returned from a Caribbean vacation with her husband and children; they live in a professionally decorated home.

Rita S.
At 40, Rita has many of the luxuries people desire. But, even with her tan, she looked haggard. When we began talking about fun, she said: 'I never have fun. I really do not enjoy myself.'

As we explored this further, we discovered her attachment to suffering no matter how good life gets. She said: 'I think I should suffer. It feels familiar. It's Christian. I always feel something disastrous is going to happen and take my money, my family, and my life-style all away.'

No matter how much money she had or how many recreational activities she did, they did not satisfy or nurture her. I suggested she consider fun a quality she could bring to any activity, work or play. I also asked her to consider that the 'war was over', meaning she no longer needed to live in fear of her violent father. Perhaps she could let go of the fear and suffering that kept her from enjoying the present.

I realize you may not earn over $100,000 or have just returned from an expensive vacation, but I invite you to look at your own suffering. Beliefs shape our lives. They form the box in which we live. If the box only has room for suffering, that is what we will create.

Reading this section, I hope you are beginning to see that if you believe you have to suffer, you will. Even when people have money, security, or material things, they cannot enjoy them if they feel they *have* to struggle. Even though you may be upset discovering your commitment to struggle, you can also rejoice in that discovery. By that, I mean, you have recognized a basic filter that colors your entire life. If you can stop looking through that filter, you can see that life is not comprised of endless suffering.

This thinking requires that you be willing to take responsibility here and not be a victim. You may be tempted to be angry with me or feel hopeless. But I invite you to ask yourself: What am I committed to – suffering or taking care of myself? Just be willing to consider setting the suffering aside and be open to the idea: there is life without suffering.

WHAT YOU CAN DO
Give Yourself Permission
When you let go of suffering, you have space for something new. You have room to give yourself permission to have fun.

Mitch D.
Mitch, 30, tells about his difficulty doing this: 'At my house we got yelled at for eating food after school, for playing games when we weren't supposed to, for day-dreaming, for dawdling. Now you want me to sit idle and do nothing! Having fun feels like I'm breaking Dad's rules even though I hate those rules.'

As the Life Skills class progressed, Mitch realized he no longer lived in his father's house, and under his father's rules. Mitch could make his own rules. During one class he stood up and announced: 'To hell with my father's rules. I'm entitled to have fun when I want it. I'm entitled to have needs whatever they are. I'm giving myself permission to take care of me.'

You may need a little time as Mitch did. But only you can give yourself permission. I strongly suggest that you begin to let go of struggle and give yourself permission to take care of you.

Set Aside Time For Fun
People also need to set aside time for fun. With too much scheduled work and regulated activity, people often forget the simple joys of relaxing and having just plain fun. Abused or not, adults can think fun is frivolous and just for kids. They can feel pressure to act mature. People who value productivity can think fun is a waste of time. However, rediscovering fun improves health, attitude, stamina, and relationships. Playing can reduce stress and promote closeness with family and friends. People who have relaxed and enjoyed themselves can be more productive when they return to their jobs.

John A.
At 32, John was a young manager who worked later and longer hours as he became more successful. He found less time for bike riding and baseball and other hobbies – they had been his weekend passions. He began to believe they were frivolous and unimportant. During the Life Skills workshop, John decided to play ball with his young son before dinner. His son beamed with laughter. John told the class: 'I feel closer to my son than I have in months. I seem to let go of the day's stress; I'm not as crabby with my wife, and I am sleeping better. Twenty minutes of playing ball is such a simple thing, but I am going to keep it in my routine. I may even start back to my model-making. I'll bet my son will enjoy that too.'

John made a conscious effort to set aside time for fun. He gave himself permission to enjoy his passions and his son. He rediscovered his enjoyment of hobbies and sports. And he found they enhanced his family relationships.

Be Willing to Try Things

A friend told me that as a child she had fallen off her bike so many times she was terrified to ride again. Last week, this 30-year old woman bought a bike. She started riding around the block on the sidewalk. She did that for two weeks. Then she rode in the park only on week days when there was little traffic. Now she rides several miles a week.

This woman was willing to try again. She began slowly so she could overcome her fear. Now she rides to exercise and enjoy herself. You may have to take risks as well.

Laura S.

'My father molested me when I was five years old. My mother walked in on us and beat me, screaming that I was bad. I believed her. I became an alcoholic; I married one. I let people abuse me. Fun was the last thing on my mind.

'During the Life Skills course I met a wonderful man who had a similar background. Neither of us played much or knew what was fun. So we began exploring all kinds of activities. We went on picnics, climbed mountains, swam in lakes — lots of outdoors stuff. Although we did not think we were athletic, we so enjoyed nature and vigorous exercise. We even bought a 30-inch plastic alligator for the beach — just for fun. We call him Wally — The first frivolous purchase I ever made. I never learned to ride a bike. Vince took me to the park one day; and, at age 40, I rode a bike for the first time. I'm having a great time.'

Laura and her boyfriend are packing in all the fun they missed out on as children. They have given themselves permission to be silly, try new things, and just have fun. They now set aside time each weekend for recreation.

Bring a Sense of Fun to your Life

Some people seem to have fun with whatever they do by looking at life humorously and being willing to laugh. I keep kazoos on hand. My father recites limericks. Another friend has a funny comment about everything. You can try simple, silly things that bring fun to your life.

Lynne K.

Lynne, 37, now a successful therapist and gay, told a Life Skills class: 'In the fourth grade, a girl named Sherry and her friends kicked me and made fun of me at recess. I must have decided that recess and games were dangerous, because the next year I never went out for recess. Instead I went next door to Mr Mason's room and helped him. No one ever asked me why I did not go out. I just avoided the whole scene.

'As an adult I hated parties and groups having fun. I felt like I was the only one not having any fun. And it must have been written all over my face. I'd go to the movies or to a friend's for dinner, but groups – forget it.'

Her Life Skills class planned a small party to see if they could have some fun as a group. They had fun planning the party. Almost everyone in the class did not like parties. At our next class Lynne said: 'It was great! It helped that I knew everyone. Everyone brought a silly toy to play with. I could talk about how uncomfortable I was. We laughed over jacks, bubbles, pickup sticks, and slinkies. The next step will be to go to a friend's party where I know some of the people. But I'm going to try it. I realize I'm not that pathetic fourth grader anymore.'

Based on her fourth-grade experience, Lynne had decided to avoid groups. But she saw that she might be missing out on enjoying people. So she took a risk and broke her pattern. Lynne brought a sense of fun to the party and it was successful.

These people planned activities with friends, made time to do things they enjoyed, and brought a sense of play into their lives. The exercises at the end of this chapter will help you do the same.

SUMMARY

- Abused people never have learned to play

- Other survivors have had abusive experiences while trying to have fun

- Such people may avoid anything that sounds like the past so they won't get hurt again

- Having fun may feel foreign at first

- To have fun you need to let go of the need to suffer

- To enjoy yourself start by giving yourself permission to have fun

- Then set aside time for play

- Be willing to try new things

QUESTIONS AND ASSIGNMENTS

1) What childhood memories do you have about fun? Birthdays, beach trips, vacations, camp, little league, water fights, singing? They may be positive or negative. Write them down. Emotions may surface as you do this. Allow them.

Examples:

I fell off my bike and have not ridden since.

The kids teased me so much I will not play team sports.

I loved summers. We took vacations to the beach. We took tennis lessons and swam in the neighbors' pool.

I was always good at games, but my playmates excluded me, so I lost out when I had fun.

I loved going to camp. I was away from my family. I had more fun in those weeks than the rest of the year. That's where I learned to ride horses, swim and hike.

_____

_____

_____

_____

2a) What are your beliefs about playing and having fun? Write them down.

Examples:

Now that I am grown up I do not think about fun.

I do not have time for fun.

Fun is for kids.

Fun is frivolous.

Fun is for when you can afford it.

Fun is a waste of time.

Successful people don't have fun.

Fun looks dangerous.

If you have fun you get hurt.

I can have fun after ALL my work is done.

_____

_____

_____

b) Are these beliefs ones you still want to have? List some new beliefs that allow you to have more fun.

Examples:

I can play and get my work done.

I can have fun and not get hurt.

Grownups need to play too.

_____

_____

_____

3) When you are doing a recreational activity do you have a hard time letting yourself enjoy it?

Yes_____No_____

4) Do you usually feel guilty when you are having fun?

Yes_____No_____

5) Do you find yourself suffering or struggling when others are having a good time?

Yes_____No_____

6a) If the answer to #4 or #5 is yes, I suggest examining your rules about suffering. Here are some rules. Circle the ones that apply to you.

I have to suffer like my parents.

I can't be the only happy one in my family.

I'll never be happy; so why try?

I can't stand it to be too easy.

Suffering is familiar.

If I'm never happy, I'll never be disappointed.

I suffer to fit into my family.

b) Use the space below to write your own.

_____

_____

_____

7a) Write: *I give myself permission to have fun* on an index card. Put it on your mirror. When you look in the mirror say this affirmation out loud to yourself. This little card can evoke powerful responses. So you can feel comfortable with your own reactions, here are some responses people have reported:

I am angry, but I don't know why.

Why should I have fun or discuss needs? Someone is just going to take it away.

I don't think any of it is possible.

I feel like crying.

I don't deserve it.

Give yourself permission to have your experience. By allowing the feelings to release, you can move through them and create room for new learning.

b) Write your reactions.

_____

_____

8a) List 10 things you like to do. Use this list and then add your own ideas.

Biking	Dancing
Swimming	Building models
Gardening	Flying
Writing	Painting
Driving	Drawing

Baseball	Sewing
Travel	Playing pool
Hiking	Going to the theatre
Meeting friends	Going to museums
Knitting	Discovering new places
Watching TV sports	Going out to eat

1) _____

2) _____

3) _____

4) _____

5) _____

6) _____

7) _____

8) _____

9) _____

10) _____

b) You may have difficulty coming up with ten items. Whatever number of activities you have is fine. Some people find simple things fun; some enjoy sports. Some find fun in anything. What did you learn about yourself?

Examples:

All my activities are free.

I do all my activities alone.

I haven't done something fun in years.

I need another person to do my activities.

I don't even take time to read, my favorite thing to do.

I'm afraid to paint or draw again.

I keep myself from the things I love to do.

Most of my ten are so simple.

c) Select one activity from your list and do it.

9) Buy several children's toys or games that cost under $3. Play with them.

Examples:
   Liquid bubbles

   Frisbie

   Pick-up sticks

   The Giant Bubble Thing

   Jacks

   Jump rope

   Wiffle ball

10a) What are some fun things you have always wanted to try? List them. Here are some ideas. Write your own in the blanks below.

   Biking

   Skipping

   Jumping rope

   Telling a joke

   Reading a children's book

   Planning a surprise for a friend

   Running through the waves at the ocean

   Making a sand castle

   Para-sailing

   Going to a concert

   Learning to sail

   Learning to swim

_____

_____

_____

---

b) Check off the ones you really are going to try, even if you are scared. Invite a friend if you need support. In the space below write your plan to try your new activity.

---

11) Rent a comedy video.

Many people want to continue giving themselves a FUN assignment in addition to later assignments. Sometimes it takes time to integrate a life-style change. You may want to give yourself a Fun assignment every week.

FURTHER READING

CASSIDY, John.
   The Klutz Book of Jacks (Palo Alto, Cal.: Klutz Press, 1989).
   The Klutz Yo-Yo Book (Palo Alto, Cal.: Klutz Press 1987).

CASSIDY, John and RIMBEAUX, B.C.
   Juggling for the Complete Klutz (Palo Alto, Cal.: Klutz Press, 1977).

CASSIDY, John and STEIN, David.
   The Unbelievable Bubble Book (Palo Alto, Cal.: Klutz Press, 1987).

CASSIDY, John and STROUD, Michael.
   The Klutz Book of Magic (Palo Alto, Cal.: Klutz Press, 1990).

HSU, Flanders.
   Balloon Hats and Accessories (San Francisco, Cal.: Contemporary Books, 1989).

CHAPTER 5

Asking For What You Need

GOALS
- To discover your beliefs about needs

- To give yourself permission to have needs

- To learn what you need and how to express it

- To create ways to have your needs met

This chapter provides learning that you may have missed while growing up. It helps you to discover your needs and your beliefs about them, and shows you how to meet those needs.

WHAT SURVIVORS MISSED
Meeting Emotional Needs
All living creatures have basic needs – the need for food, water, and shelter. People have emotional needs as well. The need to be loved, wanted, and touched; the need to express, to be heard, to relate; the need to be productive, satisfied, and included, whether a person is working, relaxing at home, or spending time with a loving partner or family, each person has a right to have his or her own needs met.

When parents assist each other in meeting their own needs and their child's needs, that child learns that needs can be met. He or she sees parents expressing their needs and having them met as an expression of their relationship. Mom asks Dad to help her with the dishes. He helps her, but *after* he finishes a phone call. Mom needs to talk to Dad about her day; then Dad has some quiet time. Children from such homes grow up naturally expressing their needs knowing they can be met.

OLD PATTERNS
Needs That Are Forgotten
In an abusive family, parents can easily forget the child's needs. In fact, the children may have parented their own parents, forgetting their own needs. As a result such children did not have an opportunity to develop their own likes and preferences.

If you survived abuse, you probably never or rarely had time to focus on you. Your family lived from crisis to crisis. You may have taken on bringing some order the the chaos, fixing meals, organizing younger sisters and brothers, parenting your parents. You grew up too fast with too much responsibility too soon. You learned: *My needs come last*, or *My needs will never be met*, or *My needs are not important*, or *I don't deserve to have needs*.

You tried to bring control to an uncontrollable situation. Now you may still need to control others rather than taking care of yourself. This is Melody Beattie's definition of codependence from *Codependent No More*.[1]

You may have learned to set aside your needs to keep the peace, to stay safe, or to please. You do not feel entitled to have needs and do not expect to have them met.

WHAT YOU CAN DO
You may be reading this chapter asking yourself: 'What needs? I never thought about my needs'. The very topic may make you feel a little uncomfortable. That is fine. This section gives you the tools to start looking at what you need. I have broken down meeting needs into four steps.

1 Give Yourself Permission to have Needs
Many survivors never thought about their needs. Or they grew up believing that having needs is selfish. Having needs is a natural part of being human. Now mentally say to yourself: *I give myself permission to have needs*.

2 Ask Yourself the Question: What Do I Need?
Now what do you need? I suggest that you write that question on an index card and put it on your mirror or desk so you can look at it frequently. You may not know how to answer it yet. But you will start thinking about it. If you have never considered your needs, using the index card will help you begin to include them in your life.

3 Write Down Your Needs
Your needs will change throughout the day and throughout your life. Sometimes you will need to be with one person, and sometimes with people. Sometimes you will need to be productive and,

at others, relaxed. Sometimes you will need times to be held, and at other times you will need to be alone.

4 Make a Plan to Meet Your Needs and Act on It

In the exercises at the end of this chapter you will have a chance to list your needs. After each one, write down how you plan to fulfill it. Writing down your needs will assist you in integrating them into your life.

As you begin to recognize your needs, you may feel angry and resentful that they have been denied. Allow these feelings to release so you can replace them with new patterns.

ADDITIONAL CASES

Now let me describe some people who did not feel entitled to what they needed and taught themselves how to express and fulfill their needs:

Stephen L.

At 50, Stephen has been married three times and has had a series of jobs. With seven brothers and sisters, Stephen was the baby. His parents never let him forget he was an afterthought. During one fight as a kid, he remembers his mom shouting, 'You were an accident!' He told us: 'I always felt like the 'bad boy'. The nuns beat me with a paddle at school, then I'd be punished with a strap at home for the same thing. I rarely finished dinner without being sent to my room for something. I was always trying to keep my 'nose clean'.'

'By college, I thought girls would not like me for just me, so I decided I'd do whatever the other person wanted to in order to be liked. I became a pleaser.

'Years later, in jobs or relationships I got so frustrated that I wasn't getting anything I'd blow up and walk out. I walked out on two wives. Now I see I set myself up by never expressing my needs. I let my boss schedule me seven days a week – no days off and no lunch or dinner break.

'When my new wife and I bought our house, I liked one, but I said let's buy another one because I thought she liked it. As it turned out, she liked yet another house altogether. We bought a house neither of us liked.

'After I realized I had needs and I was entitled to them, I started scheduling days off and lunch hours. My boss still thinks I'm a good employee! I told my wife to stop dawdling and making us late. She still loves me and she's ready on time. I'm not being nasty, but I'm speaking up. I feel much better about myself and I'm still working on expressing my needs.

'I am also noticing when I am pleasing. A neighbor asked me to help him clean his garage. I noticed my knee-jerk reaction to say, 'Sure. I'll help!' But I did not offer. I tell myself: *I'm o.k. without doing anything extra.* I don't need extra points to build my self-esteem to zero. And – this is a shocker – I'm o.k. even when I say NO! My wife and I are learning to negotiate now that I am speaking up with what I need. I love my job. I am replacing that vague resentment I had most of my life with real happiness and feeling good about myself.'

Stacy K.

At 32 Stacy was a recovering alcoholic and office manager for a law firm. Talking about her abusive family, she said: 'I always gave in to keep the peace. The few times I remember asking for something, we had a terrible fight. We were very poor and did not have much meat. I asked for a steak for dinner one time. My father yelled: 'Shut up, kid!' He could have just said we can't afford it. With such a harsh put-down, of course, I never brought up the topic again. It only took a couple of 'shut up, kid's before I did. It was safer to keep quiet.

'During my first marriage, we did have money for steak and anything we needed. But when I brought up going back to school or my plans for a business, my husband said they were silly. He said I wasn't smart enough. Once again it didn't take much to suppress me. I realize now he needed me to be dependent on him. My working was a threat to him. I eventually left him.

'After the Life Skills course, I began speaking up for myself. And I began to tell the difference between people who needed me to be weak and those who wanted me to grow. Now I realize I only want to be around people who support me. And that means they want me to get my needs met. With my new husband, we discuss what I need and what he needs. Last weekend he wanted to go to the country and I wanted to go shopping, but we wanted to be together. We did both. We negotiate and look at options. We both are willing to work things out. He supports my school idea; he is not afraid of my growing.'

Carol D.

At 35, Carol, a stockbroker and gay, said: 'When I was about seven or eight, my parents had a fight. I went into the kitchen after supper, put on mom's apron, and washed and dried the dishes. Then I went into the bedroom and found them asleep. I covered them up. Standing there I made a decision: *I was a grownup.* That is when I started parenting my parents. I set my needs aside; I thought they needed me to do what they needed. When I was in the fifth grade we needed to move because of my dad's health. I hated leaving my friends, but I never said anything. I said fine.

How could I say NO?!

'I also had a powerful model for putting my needs last . . . my mom. She put up with my dad's moods, terrible temper, and selfishness. More than once I was watching a mystery on TV and, just as it was ending, Dad switched to the football game. I couldn't get my needs met. Mom worked full-time, did the shopping and all the housework. She never considered herself.

'I copied her exactly in my relationships with women. It never occurred to me to include my own needs. I thought: A good lover says YES to everything her lover asks. I ran myself ragged. We split up. In later relationships with women, it took me some time to put out my needs.

'I kept getting stronger at stating my needs. Once a friend asked me to bring my car to pick up some chairs for her. I told her it would be difficult for me. We worked out another way for her to get the chairs. I was surprised that she wanted me to have what I needed. Now I am not surprised.

'I used to over-book myself socially because I couldn't say NO to a friend. Now I can say NO if I need some time to myself. I look for friends and lovers who are open to mutual needs being met.'

SUMMARY

- Many survivors put their needs last and do not know what they need

- They do not think their needs are important or can be met

- As children they may have parented their own parents, neglecting their own needs

- People can learn to express and meet needs by
  1) Giving themselves permission
  2) Asking themselves what do I need?
  3) Listing their needs
  4) Making a plan to get their needs met and doing it

QUESTIONS AND ASSIGNMENTS

1) What was it like in your family regarding needs? Here are some statements about families and needs to help you get started. Circle the ones that apply to you. Use the space below to write down additional insights about needs.

- It was every man for himself.
  All my brothers and sisters scrambled to get what they could. I stopped trying.

- No one considered your needs.
  Mom announced the way it would be, so she got taken care of. She never consulted us.

- No one ever really got their needs met.
  My family was very sad — a lot of lonely people all living together.

- You learned to put your needs last from one parent.
  My mother sacrificed everything for her family. I learned to do the same thing.

———————————————————————————

———————————————————————————

———————————————————————————

2a) Circle the beliefs about needs that describe you. Write additional beliefs in the space below.

- You should always anticipate others' needs. They should know what I want.

- Needing is being selfish.

- Sacrificing for others is good.

- I'll never get what I need so why ask and be disappointed.

- I can do without.

- I can only count on myself, other people are disappointments.

- If I don't think about my needs, I won't feel deprived.

- I come last.

———————————————————————————

———————————————————————————

b) For each negative belief you circled or wrote down, write a more positive belief.

Examples:

I deserve to have my needs and get them met.

You cannot always know what others want and they cannot always know what you need. You have to tell people what you need.

I can get what I need.

I can get what I need and others can too. No one has to lose.

_____

_____

_____

3a) As an adult, do you think you are entitled to your needs?

Examples:

I don't think I have the right to have needs.

I don't deserve to have needs.

It's better not to have any, then I won't be disappointed.

Yes _____ No _____

b) If no, give yourself permission to have needs. Say out loud: *I give myself permission to have needs.* It may feel awkward at first, but you will get used to it.

4) Do you give up your needs when you are with someone else? Many people succumb to another person's needs to avoid conflict or to please.

Yes _____ No _____

Examples:

When I'm with my girlfriend, I usually let her choose the movie. That way we don't disagree.

I always let my friend have her way. I never thought of it as giving up my needs, it's just easier.

If we do what my family wants all the time, I hope they will think I'm a good mother.

5) Write: *What do I need?* on an index card. Tape it to the refrigerator or medicine chest or desk. Ask yourself that question several times a day. You may not be able to answer it at first. Use the list in #1 for ideas. Write your responses daily for a week.

Examples:

'I asked myself the question but I couldn't come up with an answer today.'

'I need to get away and be quiet.'

'I need to relax.'

Monday

_____

_____

Tuesday

_____

_____

Wednesday

_____

_____

Thursday

_____

_____

Friday

_____

_____

Saturday

_____

_____

Sunday

_____

_____

6) Brainstorm with yourself. Make a list of sample needs in all areas.
Add your ideas to the list.

Examples:

I need to be quiet.

I need someone to listen to me.

I need to talk.

I need to be outdoors.

I need to be with people.

I need some space to myself in the house.

I need to read the paper.

I need to spend quality time with my family.

I need to relax.

I need to speak up sooner.

I need supportive friends.

I need to quit my job and make more money.

I need to tell you how angry that made me.

I need to feel wanted.

I need to be independent.

I need to be productive.

I need to be acknowledged.

I need to be included.

I need to excel.

_____

_____

_____

_____

7) Pick one need from #3 and create a plan to fulfill it. Carry out the plan. You play an active role in having needs met. Don't make excuses for ignoring your own needs. Start with a small step that is likely to be a success.

Example:

'I need some time for myself. I will ask my husband to take care of the children each Saturday morning for one hour so I can go for a walk alone.'

'I need to relax more. I bought a relaxation tape. I'll use it before I go to bed.'

8) Many survivors never had time to develop likes and dislikes. This exercise helps you do that. Practice expressing your likes and preferences. Here are some questions to help you:

What kind of food do you like?

_____

What color do you like?

_____

Where do you want to go?

_____

What weather do you prefer?

_____

Where would you like to live?

_____

What is your favorite season?

_____

What famous person would you like to spend an evening with?

_____

What is your favorite movie?

_____

FURTHER READING

RAY, Sondra.
   I Deserve Love (Millbrae, Cal.: Celestial Arts, 1987).

SIMON, Sidney B.
   Values Clarifications: A Handbook of Practical Strategies for Teachers and Students (Dodd, 1985).

CHAPTER 6

Self-Nurturing: Giving To Yourself More Than Just What You Need

GOALS
- To help you discover how you do not nurture yourself

- To learn ways of self-nurturing and practice them

While you have been learning to have fun and to express and meet your needs, you have also been nurturing yourself. In real life, the Life Skills are not separate but interrelated; when you strengthen Fun and Needs, you are automatically taking care of yourself. So you have a good, healthy start.

Self-nurturing means going beyond just meeting your needs; it means discovering healthy, positive ways to take care of you. That does not include self-destructive, compulsive habits – drinking, overeating, over-spending, gambling, taking drugs. This may seem obvious, but many survivors have tried to meet needs and attempted to take care of themselves with drink, food, sex, gambling, or drugs. These may lift your mood temporarily but they are a poor substitute for genuine healing and real emotional nurturing. This chapter teaches you positive ways to give to yourself more than just what you need.

WHAT SURVIVORS MISSED
Functional Families Learn to Self-nurture
When people nurture themselves they feel satisfied and taken care of. When they do not, they can feel resentful and angry. In the following examples, the children learned from parents who nurtured themselves. Having had positive models, Eric and Gloria found that self-nurturing became a natural part of their adult lives.

Eric F.
'When I was growing up, Dad took his time when he came home from work. He read the paper in his chair; Mom kept us away from him until dinner. Then we had time with him, and Mom usually sewed or read. Now that I have a family of my own, my wife and I have a similar routine in the evenings.'

Gloria D.
'When I was a teenager, sometimes I asked to stay home alone when the family went out. I'd listen to music or just hang out. I realize now I was learning to take care of myself. I still find time in my schedule just for me.'

Abusive Families Do Not Teach Self-Nurturing

In abusive families, parents do not take care of each other emotionally let alone nurture themselves as individuals. This provides negative modelling for the children. Such children grow up lacking any self-nurturing examples. Maggie and Jerome describe their experiences.

Maggie F.
'When Mom came home from work, she would start drinking and calling her girlfriends. I fixed dinner. She ate and talked on the phone. Then I did the dishes while she talked some more on the phone. She never asked about my homework or my friends or my report card. I was the mother; she was the teenager. I'm very resentful. I can fix meals and keep my hair combed, but be nice to myself? I don't even understand the sentence.'

Glen S.
'By the time I was six I could do for myself. I learned my parents would not do anything for me, so I had to. I survived. Now I make a nice salary and have a nice place to live, but I find it impossible to spend money on myself or even furnish my apartment. The idea sounds so indulgent!'

WHAT YOU CAN DO

Put Yourself in the Picture

This means including yourself in your daily plan, learning that you count, that nurturing yourself is important. You may feel selfish at first, but you will get used to caring for yourself. You will discover self-nurturing helps to keep you emotionally sound and happy.

Treat Yourself Like an Honored Guest

If you find it difficult to focus directly on you, pretend you are an honored guest. How would you treat such a house guest? You would give them your favorite room, invite them to take a long bath, prepare special food, buy their favorite music, rent a special video.

Build Your List of Ways to Self-nurture

As you read the cases and exercises, develop your repertoire of positive self-nurturing activities. You may spend years collecting favorite ways to nurture yourself, but start now.

Do Something Self-nurturing Each Day

Schedule time to yourself or do something nurturing every day. Even if it is just a few minutes, write it on your calendar.

ADDITIONAL CASES

Here are two people who did start nurturing themselves:

Dennis K.

Dennis, 26, had five brothers and sisters and an alcoholic father. The oldest, he never had time for himself.

'My father left when I was 12, so I was in charge while Mom worked. I did chores and organized lunches and homework. As a teenager, once in a while, I'd go out with friends.

'Now I have my first job and an apartment. I don't have all that responsibility, but I live like I do. I have a schedule for everything. My chore list is always longer than I have time for. In the Life Skills class, I decided to take time for me. At first it made me very edgy. But now I schedule a day when I do just what I want. I still feel like I'm squandering time, but I'm having a ball. I'm a lot happier.'

Ruth Ann S.

At 40, Ruth Ann is a lawyer. She took work home evenings and weekends. Her husband also worked long hours.

'My husband and I smiled at each other over our stacks of papers. We rarely went out for fun. We both were just trying to get through piles of work.

'Growing up, I threw myself into my studies at school. That was the way I stayed away from the endless arguments and fights. In the Life Skills class, I realized I love my husband and his company. I don't need to hide from anything. We don't have much time, but we've started planning outings. We even book evenings when we don't bring home work. One of us will fix dinner for the other as a surprise. I found that nurturing myself meant spending quality time with my husband.

'Also I have a card on my desk that says, 'Are you being nice to yourself today?' And another one that says, 'Does this have to be done right now?' I see that I can nurture myself. Now I can be creative and find new ways.'

SUMMARY

- Adults who were abused were often too busy surviving to learn to nurture themselves

- They can learn to nurture themselves

- They can start by putting themselves in the picture, being more gentle with themselves, building a list of self-nurturing activities, and doing one daily

QUESTIONS AND ASSIGNMENTS

1) How could you be good to yourself? How could you be gentle with yourself? How could you take better care of yourself? Write down your own ideas.

Examples:

Don't get up until you want to one morning.

Let yourself know you are doing your best.

Treat yourself to a massage.

Walk slowly enjoying the day.

Drive the long way home and enjoy the scenery.

Listen to your favorite music.

Tell yourself you did the best you could today.

Buy yourself a stuffed animal to cuddle.

Take a bubble bath.

Read a book for pure enjoyment.

Give yourself a pat on the back for working so hard on yourself.

Plan a day when you do just what you want to.

_____

_____

_____

2) Do at least one nurturing activity a day even if it is one minute long.

3) Make a list of self-nurturing ideas. Keep adding to it. Gather ideas from friends.

4) Be gentle with yourself this week. Treat yourself like you would treat your best friend or an honored guest. Write down your reactions.

Examples:

This made me very uncomfortable. The only way I could think of being good to myself was to picture being my own best friend. I gave myself a foot massage.

I'm a dorm floor counselor on duty 24 hours a day. I put up a sign on my door that said closed for 15 minutes.

I took a bath instead of a two-minute shower.

4) Put an index card that says: How can I be good to me today? on your mirror.

FURTHER READING

JOHNSON, Dr Spencer.
One Minute for Yourself (New York: William Morrow Inc., 1985).

SECTION THREE

Ending the Abuse

The last two sections dealt with developing a healthy and positive relationship with yourself. This section helps you develop and strengthen the Life Skills that you need to end self-abuse and abusive relationships with others. The first chapter in this section explains how to recognize and overcome blind spots. This is key to ending abusive relationships. The next describes how to express anger safely. In Not Letting People Use You, you have an opportunity to practice setting limits. The Ending Self-Blame and Self-Sabotage chapters explore how to stop self-abusive habits.

CHAPTER 7

Overcoming Blind Spots

GOALS

- To discuss how blind spots can develop

- To begin to recognize blind spots

- To give people tools to overcome blind spots

This chapter is the heart of the Life Skills program. If people cannot recognize abuse, they have a blind spot and they tend to put up with the abusive behavior, which perpetuates the abuse cycle. This chapter explains what blind spots are, how to begin to recognize them, and what to do to overcome them.

WHAT SURVIVORS MISSED

Not Seeing the Obvious

The vast majority of my adult survivor clients have some areas where they cannot see the obvious. They are not stupid; quite the contrary, they are intelligent, educated, hold responsible jobs. However, in one or two specific areas, they have a blind spot. A man cannot see that his wife is abusive to their children. A woman cannot see she is marrying another alcoholic. With both of these people, a natural cognitive ability – their ability to see and recognize a pattern – has failed them totally. The 'blindness' can be in not seeing their own negative or positive qualities, not seeing a particular relationship pattern, or not seeing qualities in other people. Here is an illustration:

Rachael S.
'My friend had to point out to me that I have had three abusive boyfriends before I saw the pattern.

Janice D.
'My boss tells me I'm angry, and that's what gets me in trouble with clients. They don't want to work with me. I just don't see it.'

Why People Have Blind Spots

Survivors who have a blind spot did not learn to see people and circumstances as they really are. Some abused people inherited their parents' blind spots. A woman marries an abusive husband just as her mother did. Others unconsciously decided not to recognize the obvious because this strategy protected them. If a child does not see that his parents are truly cruel to him, he does not have to feel the pain. The blind spot protects him and serves as a Survival Strategy.

Some adult survivors have no positive frame of reference. They consider abuse normal because they had nothing to compare it to. For instance, they thought all families fought because they never saw a family that got along.

Frequently, clients come into therapy suspecting they have a blind spot becuse they have repeated their pattern so many times. Barbara tells about her lack of a positive frame of reference and her blind spot.

Barbara H.
When this 26-year-old college graduate came into my office, she began: 'My friends all told me that Ray, whom I lived with for two years, was no good – that he had other girlfriends. I didn't believe them. One evening, a friend came over to tell me he was engaged to another woman. I just didn't want to see it. She drove me over to the other woman's house so I could see Ray's car in the driveway and Ray sitting at the kitchen table. It took my actually seeing him there before I could finally get what was going on.'

Barbara could not see that while Ray lived with her, he was also engaged to another woman. In fact, he had fathered a child by this other woman while he lived with Barbara.

The reader is probably thinking: 'How could she be so blind? She's not dumb; how did she miss that?' Or, 'How could he hide his other life so well?' Ray would tell Barbara he was going on a business trip for three days, but really he was staying with another woman. When Ray and Barbara went out for an evening, he sometimes made as many as 15 phone calls from 15 different pay phones. He'd send Barbara to her mother's for a week as a present.

Barbara related, 'I never suspected he was buying time to be with her.'

Friends of a co-alcoholic – person who lives with an alcoholic – react similarly when that person marries the third alcoholic. 'Can't she or he see what is happening?' Well, no, they cannot.

Barbara's father, who was mentally ill while she was growing up, created an inconsistent reality. When she was sad, her father told her she was happy. He sat in the living room holding a shot gun to protect the family from unseen enemies. When her father started watering the kitchen floor to see if the grass would grow in the kitchen, Barbara did not realize her father was mentally ill, she just turned off the faucet. She did not think anything was peculiar. She perceived, as normal, events that most people would call abnormal. Barbara didn't question his behavior or Ray's. At the same time, her father invalidated her perceptions, so she grew up distrusting her own sense of reality. Events or people that were not quite right looked normal to Barbara.

Because Barbara's case is so extreme, the reader may have difficulty identifying with it. The examples in the Old Patterns section will help you recognize your own.

OLD PATTERNS
Why and how people develop blind spots warrants more thorough study. However, through my investigations, I have discovered five reasons for blind spots.

1 Naiveté
By naive, I do not mean stupid; I mean a person who does not know a certain behavior exists. When that person does encounter the behavior, he or she cannot see it. Here is an example of naiveté that prevents a person from seeing:

Nora B.
'My husband told me my best friend was coming on to him at a party. I couldn't believe that my friend would do that. I continued to trust her. Months later I saw her make advances toward another man. I was stunned.'

Nora could not conceive of her best friend playing around. Nora's limited view kept her from seeing her friend's behavior accurately. But when it happened again, Nora began to see. Often, people begin to see the pattern because two incidents occur close together.

2 Denial
This person denies events. A survivor might say: 'My parents were not alcoholics. They just drank a lot.' To keep the denial in place, this person has to blind him- or herself to seeing the family alcoholism. Cherie's case illustrates this denial:

Cherie S.
'I idealized my mother for years. She was a good mother; I was a bad daughter. And she always reminded me of that. Only recently,

I started remembering she was cruel and mean. Now I am also seeing that I let friends be mean and nasty. I not only do not see it, but I don't say anything.'

With the help of her therapist, Cherie began to break up her denial. She took a more honest look at her mother. When that happened, she could recognize her friends' cruelty. Children often idealize abusive parents because dealing with the truth would be shattering. But that denial causes its own problems.

3 Not Feeling Emotions

Consistently blocking emotions creates a barrier to seeing accurately. For instance, if a person does not allow himself to feel his own anger, this can prevent him from recognizing anger in himself and in others. Only when this person begins to feel anger can he recognize it in himself and others. For example:

Marion N.
'I never felt my anger until I was in my twenties. I was a nice girl. I didn't realize I was enraged at my parents. And I did not see when other people were angry. When my husband would put me down, I couldn't see it. My mother would make jokes at my father's expense, but I did not see her viciousness. I could not assess accurately people or situations involving anger. When I did begin to feel my anger, I started seeing it in others.'

Marion has started unravelling a childhood pattern that will allow her to see anger in herself as well as others. This scenario can be applied to other emotions as well: sadness, guilt, fear. When the survivor begins to feel the emotion inside, he can begin to see it in others.

4 Lack of Healthy Distinctions

Here people lack the ability to distinguish abuse, cruelty, or abnormal behavior, as I described in Chapter 4 of Part I. Remember, Barbara did not realize anything was wrong with her father who tried to water the kitchen floor expecting grass to grow. Then, as an adult, she did not think anything was peculiar when her boyfriend made 15 phone calls during their date. In other cases, children grow up thinking love and abuse must occur together. These children often become adults who expect abuse from people they love.

Jennifer V.
'I thought I'd done something wrong, but when I started therapy, my counselor suggested that my dad sounded very disturbed. My dad would beat me while he told me how much he loved me. This was the first time I realized maybe something was wrong with

him. But I still think people who love me are going to hurt me.'

With other survivors who do not have a healthy sense of distinction, their parents never took time to understand them. So, as adults, these people expect to be misunderstood. Such people do not demand to be understood or to be treated well.

5 Double Messages

'Go away, but come close' and 'Talk to me, but be quiet' are double messages. They create confusion and an uncertain world-view. What is really going on becomes blurred.

Sam D.
'Dad yelled and punished us unfairly, but Mom and Dad never talked about it. In fact, Mom promoted 'Nice people don't yell', and at the same time 'Dad is a great guy'. I grew up very confused. I think people are terrific, even if they are cruel and mean. It's fuzzy for me. I guess I don't want to see their abusive nature.'

Children from such homes can be confused about the truth. These survivors need to pay close attention to the difference between what people say and what they do.

WHAT YOU CAN DO
How to Overcome Blind Spots

I asked people who had overcome blind spots to describe how they learned to see accurately. After examining the stages they went through, I have outlined five steps. You may not need to go through all five, but they can help you map out your own road to clear seeing.

1 Recognize that you have a blind spot

This is the beginning of seeing, to realize you are blind in one area. You may recognize a blind spot after reading these examples.

2 Be willing to look honestly at the past

This requires the courage to confront the often painful truth about people or situations.

3 Feel unexpressed emotions

Allow yourself to feel the unexpressed anger, hurt and sorrow regarding the person or situation. You may find those feelings come up spontaneously while reading this section.

4 Learn new distinctions

This means teaching yourself to recognize abuse. You can learn to tell the difference between abuse and non-abuse, healthy and unhealthy, cruel and kind behavior. You may have a person in your life who can help you with this.

So you can learn these four steps, here are some people who recognized their blind spot and trained themselves to see more accurately.

ADDITIONAL CASES
Hal A.
A 47-year-old businessman, Hal, who was badly abused as a child, had trouble seeing abusive situations as an adult. In fact, people duped and lied to him. During his years of recovery, he was selected for jury duty. He described how the judge helped him overcome his blind spot.

'The judge instructed the jury on how to detect lying in the witnesses. 'Look for body language, sincerity, facial expression, and your own gut reaction', he said. During the deliberations, I tested his guidelines using my fellow jurors as sounding boards. More important to me, I had specific ways to assess people and situations in my life. I began to use them rigorously with good success.'

Hal recognized he had a blind spot: he could not tell when people were lying. Although painful, he looked honestly at many incidents when people had snookered him. The judge actually taught him new distinctions when he gave the jury instructions. Hal borrowed the judge's more masterful seeing and applied the judge's instructions to his life. He began watching body language, looking for sincerity and facial expression, and trusting his gut reaction.

Josie R.
At 38, Josie had a Masters in Public Administration. She reported how she learned to see: 'I just had to have a man . . . Any man. I wasn't concerned about the quality; I married George because I wanted a man. He didn't want us socializing with other couples. He did not like my spending time with my friends. I wasn't allowed in the kitchen because he had his special way of organizing everything and I messed it up. When I succeeded professionally, he was verbally abusive. He withheld his affection, was mean and manipulative.

'I was naive; I believed everyone was good. In my experience, people are kind to each other. He was very jealous. I couldn't imagine my own husband being so mean; I dismissed it because he still loved me. I concluded, 'He loves me, so I must be wrong'.

'I never felt my anger. Anger was scary to me. Not until I began to feel my anger did I see what was really going on.

'At a marriage counselling session, the therapist was angry at my husband's over-controlling and taking advantage of me. When

I saw her anger, I began to feel entitled to mine. That gave me the permission I needed. When our neighbor's car broke down, the husband just naturally picked her up . . . no problem. When my car stalled, my husband complained. I saw how difficult he was; I'd given up my point of view on everything. He didn't work; he really didn't want children as I did.

'I read *Women Who Love Too Much* and I attended a support group. I began feeling my rage. I borrowed their point of view; that helped me shift mine.'

Josie began counselling knowing she was unhappy, but not knowing she had a blind spot. The counselor helped her to realize that she had not let herself look at certain aspects of her husband. Then she allowed herself to feel her rage. Through counselling and reading she learned new distinctions. She borrowed the support group's seeing so she could expand her own perceptions.

Brenda S.

Brenda, 24, with two small children, was on public assistance. Her father slapped and punched Brenda and her sisters and brothers. One time, he pulled Brenda out of bed, waking her from a sound sleep, and threw cold water on her.

'Daddy would promise not to beat us. I wanted to believe him so bad. I had to believe in the fantasy *I'll always be there for you, I love you, I'll never hit you again.* But he'd drink and he'd disappoint us again and again.'

Brenda relied on the promises to create a false sense of security. The words became her security, rather than the actions. Because she trained herself not to recognize the truth, everything she said became distorted.

'After my boyfriend hit one of my kids so hard he left a bad bruise, I told him he could not come into the house if he had been drinking. I took a stand with him and then finally I broke free from him.

'My next boyfriend did not have a drinking problem, so I thought, this is good. But one night he slugged me so hard I fell and broke two teeth. I did not see his abuse until I looked in the mirror at the hole where my teeth were. Just because he didn't drink, I thought he wasn't like my father. But he was just another version of him. Now I can see it.

'I'm going for my high school equivalency test. They tell me I'm smart, but I have trouble seeing that. But maybe if those tests say I'm smart, I'm not seeing something good about myself.'

Brenda realized she had a blind spot only after her boyfriend knocked out her teeth. That jolted her into recognizing his abuse. She was willing to see that he was just like her abusive father. In doing this, she was able to distinguish abuse. She did not need to borrow someone else's seeing, she could see the truth for herself.

SUMMARY

- A blind spot can be an inability to see personal qualities, or relationship patterns, or situations.

- People develop blind spots because of naiveté, denial, unexpressed feelings, lack of healthy distinctions, or receiving double messages.

- To overcome blind spots, people need to:
  1) Recognize they have one
  2) Be willing to look honestly at the past
  3) Express unexpressed feelings
  4) Learn the needed distinctions
  5) Borrow a more senior person's seeing.

QUESTIONS AND ASSIGNMENTS

1) Do you have trouble seeing the good qualities about yourself?

Yes ——No ——

2a) Below are a list of qualities. Assess yourself objectively. Circle the ones that apply to you:

Kind	Clean
Thoughtful	Good dresser
Neat	Pleasant
Helpful	Cooks well
On time	Early riser
A good friend	Makes the bed every morning
Eager to please	Loyal
Hard working	Responsible
Considerate	Healthy
A good listener	Easy to please
Able to hold down a job	Adaptable
Careful driver	Thorough

b) Ask a friend to add to your list about yourself. Write the new qualities below.

_____

_____

_____

c) Put a star by the ones you cannot see in yourself.

3a) Do you start out thinking a new friend is wonderful, only to find out he or she lies, breaks promises or cannot be trusted?

Yes _____No _____

b) Describe a time when you did this.

Examples:
   My office mate was nice to me my first day of work. I immediately thought she was great. Then she stopped paying attention to me and broke lunch dates. What happened? Another co-worker said she does that with everyone so you'll do her favors.

_____

_____

_____

4a) Do you see someone's negative behavior pattern only when a friend points it out to you?

Yes _____No _____

b) If yes, write down a short example.

Example:
   My husband left me standing at a bus stop in subzero weather. He went home without me. Once he lost me while we were shopping. I searched the store for two hours. Years after we divorced, a friend said, 'He certainly rejected you'. I didn't see it until then.

_____

_____

_____

5a) Do you have a hard time knowing when you are feeling a certain emotion? For example, anger, sadness, fear.

Yes _____ No _____

b) If so, what is it?

Example:
   I do not feel sad when I know I should be.

_____

c) Do you have a hard time recognizing that emotion in others?

Yes _____ No _____

Example:
   As a result, when my friends are down or sad, I don't really want to acknowledge their feelings. I think it scares me.

6a) Did the adult who raised you say one thing and do another? In other words, did you get double message as a child?

Yes _____ No _____

b) What were they?

Example:
   My mother loved and hated me.

   My father was loved and respected in the community, but he beat us and made life miserable for my mother.

_____

_____

_____

c) How do these double messages affect your seeing as a adult? You may not be able to answer this question now. You may have an insight later on while reading the book. If so, turn back to this page and write in the answer.

Examples:
   I can't recognize love without it being connected to hate, abuse and turmoil. In fact, when I see abuse, I think there must be love.

   My parents never gave clear messages. In business, I can't tell when a client is trying to put one over on me.

_____

_____

_____

7) Do you have a repeating pattern that you suspect may be a blind spot? Describe what happens.

Examples:

I keep dating the same kind of men who say they want a relationship, but leave me.

People say my mother is cruel to me, but I can't see it yet.

I do something to turn people off, but I don't know what it is.

_____

_____

_____

FURTHER READING

FORWARD, Dr Susan and TORRES, Joan.
Men Who Hate Women and the Women Who Love Them (New York: Bantam, 1987).

NORWOOD, Robin.
Women Who Love Too Much (New York: Pocket Books, 1985).

CHAPTER 8

Expressing Anger Safely

GOALS
- To help you begin to release old anger safely

- To assist you in expressing new anger safely

- To recognize your style of expressing anger

- To discover if you cover up your anger with sadness or cover your sadness with anger

- To help you discover if you feel entitled to your anger

- To invite you to take a stand regarding anger

WHAT SURVIVORS MISSED
Many do not feel comfortable with their own anger, let alone someone else's. In addition, for survivors, anger can also mean danger, and not just physical danger. Growing up, people not only were physically hit, but they were beaten up with words, set up, and manipulated. Watching and interacting with parents, other adults, and siblings, children learned destructive ways of expressing anger. So, as adults, some avoid anger at any cost, never expressing their own and certainly not allowing others to express their anger. Other people explode, using their tempers to control and dominate situations and people. Usually, people continue expressing anger as adults in the way they learned to as children.

For children who were abused, expressing or not expressing their anger was a Survival Strategy. Their behavior, whether agressive or passive, became a strategy for staying safe and alive, protecting themselves and others. Clearly such survivors missed learning how to express anger safely. So it remains buried or erupts from time to time causing problems.

Old Anger

This unexpressed rage from the past I call Old Anger. Abused people have an extra dose. They have powerful rage at their abusers that they have not resolved. When survivors do not release that Old Anger, they continue to spray it on to present situations. Old Anger is unresolved, past anger that spills onto a present situation.

You are probably expressing Old Anger if you get angry out of proportion to what happened. If you want to strangle your child because he spilled some milk, you are probably not angry at him but at something unresolved from your past. When you can begin to examine your over-reactions and look at what you are really mad at, you can stop potentially destructive outbursts. These outbursts lead to fights and abuse. This chapter teaches you how to recognize and deal with your Old Anger. Old Anger can be expressed or unexpressed, explosive or implosive. This chapter gives many examples of each.

Meet Simone and Steven, who learned to express their Old Anger constructively.

Simone T.

'My husband, the kids, and I drove 14 hours to my brother's for Thanksgiving. We walked in tired and glad to see him and his family. We were 15 minutes late, but the minute my brother saw me, he blasted me with the most awful tirade. I was floored and hurt. I could not figure out what I'd done or what he was so mad about.'

After a disappointing holiday, Simone called me to express her own frustration and to look at what had happened. I suggested: 'Maybe his anger was Old Anger. Old Anger is unresolved anger that people add on to a current situation. They get triggered and react out of proportion to what is going on. Most of us have unresolved anger that we carry into the present.'

With that notion, she called her brother and found out that he was still mad at her for the times she beat him up as a child. After he had expressed his feelings, he realized that he did not want to hold on to it. They agreed to try another weekend.

Steven P.

Steven also needed to release Old Anger. Steven, 26, received his MBA from an excellent graduate school, and several firms were recruiting him. The placement officer who sent him to me told me, 'There's something keeping him from being hired'.

When Steven came for his session, he sat coiled in the corner of the couch ready to pounce. He began: 'I have a terrible 'chip' on my shoulder. I know it and I think I know why, and it is keeping me from getting hired. I can't get rid of it myself. Can you help me?'

As our work together developed, he told me about his family: 'I defied my father over and over again. He'd say, 'You can't get a job'. And, I went out and got a job. He'd say, 'You can't go to college'. I went to college. He'd say, 'You'll never amount to much'. I graduated from Columbia. I paid for it all; he didn't give me a cent.'

His tone of voice let me know how outraged he was at his father. I said: 'So your anger has served you well. You used it to motivate yourself. You have had to fire yourself up all your life, and you have done a good job'.

I wanted Steven to realize how his anger had protected and motivated him. Then I pointed out that his Survival Strategy was getting in the way. I told him: 'But your anger may cost you getting a job, because people see it immediately. They are afraid of it. I'd like you to consider laying down your 'arms' during job interviews and even on the job. You will always have your anger if you need it.'

Steven had been taking his Old Anger to the interviews. He was really angry at his father. When he began letting go of it, he could walk into job interviews without having his guard up. When a prospective boss asked him how he spent his summers or what part time jobs he had had, he answered questions without looking for a fight. After a lengthy process, he accepted a good job offer.

Identifying Your Old Anger

Here is the question to ask yourself so that you can identify Old Anger: *Am I angry out-of-proportion to what happened?* That usually means you are not just angry at what happened, but you are angry about an old situation. At first, you may be able to see this in others more easily than you see it in yourself. But as you begin to apply this question to your behavior, you will begin to analyze it objectively.

New Anger

You are expressing New Anger when you are angry at something that just happened and you are not over-reacting or being triggered. You are angry at the person who cut in front of you, or the noisy neighbor, or your daughter for leaving the bathroom a mess.

Feeling and expressing this anger is normal, appropriate, and healthy. But how do you state angry feelings honestly without blaming or putting others down? I suggest you memorize this fill-in-the blank sentence from Thomas Gordon's *Parent Effectiveness Training* [1]

I FEEL ANGRY WHEN YOU_____
(describe the behavior),

BECAUSE_____
(describe the impact the behavior has on you).

Here are some examples:

I feel angry when you walk in at two in the morning because it worries me.

I feel angry when you tell me I'm stupid in front of our friends, because I think you do not respect me.

I feel angry when you forget to call me because it leaves me hanging.

Now that I have defined Old and New Anger, let us look at abusive styles of expressing Old Anger so you can identify your patterns.

OLD PATTERNS
Abusive Styles of Expressing Anger
I have noticed seven basic styles of expressing Old Anger. Some people use a style that directs their anger outward while others use a style that directs their anger inward.

1 The explosive person
This person explodes verbally at the people around him or her. These explosions can be abusive and cause family and friends to fear the person.

Nancy K.
'My dad used to yell at us, but we were never allowed to yell. I was boiling inside. I would scold my Raggedy-Ann doll and hit her. Then I'd comfort her. As a mother I exploded, but only with people I had some control over . . . like my children. This insured my authority and control. I had become just like my father. My youngest was afraid of me.'

Nancy felt justified in exploding. As she examined her pattern, she began to see the cost of her outbursts. When explosive people recognize these two elements, 'justified' anger and its cost, they can gain some control over their behavior.

2 The person who turns anger inside
The survivor who holds anger in puts himself under great pressure. Keeping that rage inside can give this person stomach aches

or other physical ailments; it can even lead to overeating or other addictions.

Dora F.
'When I was angry as a teenager, I headed for the refrigerator and ate a half gallon of ice cream. Only in Overeaters Anonymous did I realize I'd been stuffing my anger and overeating for 30 years. It looked safer to eat than express what I was really feeling.'

Dora realized her overeating was directly related to her anger. Other people who keep their anger inside can suffer from jaw spasms, headaches, or hypertension. Such people use tremendous energy to keep a lid on their anger. When people do finally express it naturally, they often feel emotional and physical relief and are far more relaxed.

3 The person who cannot tell when he or she is angry
People who are afraid of their anger often have buried their own rage so deeply they are no longer aware of it. As a result they have no idea when they are angry. Natalie's story illustrates this style.

Natalie M.
'After my father died, my uncle came to live with us. He'd come home from the plant after we were in bed and yank me out of bed by my hair. I felt nothing after a while; I went limp. As an adult I don't feel any anger. But when I drink, I black out sometimes. My friends tell me I go into rages and when I wake up I don't remember anything.'

This woman sublimated her rage to endure extreme circumstances. Not everyone has such a past, but some do not realize when they are angry. They have tight stomachs, sweaty palms, or other symptoms. These survivors can use their symptoms to begin to recognize when they are mad.

4 The vicious person
The vicious survivor expresses anger as mean jabs or sarcastic remarks. He or she blames or judges or condemns others. Such behavior can be abusive and destructive to relationships.

Mollie E.
'My parents did not hit, but they gave each other vicious tongue-lashings. 'You fat bitch! I'd be better off without you!' Mom countered: 'You would not last two minutes without me. You wimp!' Even though I told myself I'd never be like them, I found myself saying horrible things to my children.

Mollie's worst nightmare had come true, she had become just like her parents. And this is how the abused child grows up to be the abuser and passes the pattern on to the next generation. But seeing her own pattern, Mollie has a chance to stop it and change.

5 The resentful person

This person does not express what he is really mad at. Instead he or she turns the anger into resentment that comes out in covert and subtly hostile ways.

Reggy G.

'I found myself resentful of my children even though I love them very much. I was resentful I had to provide for them. They reminded me of myself. I had to heal the little boy in me, so I could love my children without resenting them.'

Fortunately, Reggy saw his resentment and began releasing it. Unfortunately, many others let their children trigger their unresolved feelings. Resenting yet loving their children puts survivor parents in great conflict. One moment they hate their children, the next they adore them. Giving the children these double messages confuses them. It is a subtle but very real emotional abuse. Recognizing the resentment is the key to ending it.

6 The provocateur

This person provokes manipulating, goading, or needling in others. He gets people around him to explode or start a fight, and then pretends he had nothing to do with it.

Ralph K.

'I was and am angry, but underground. My brother had a temper. I'd needle him until he'd lose it and throw his trucks against the bedroom wall. Then Mom spanked him. When I was married, I needled my wife. She took a punch at me, then I felt I had the right to really hit her. When someone else did it first, I felt entitled to my rage . . . That's how I survived! But my wife left me. I had to lose her to stop provoking people.'

Although Ralph consciously provoked his brother and then his wife, other survivors do so unconsciously. By pretending innocence, they do not have to take responsibility for their anger and their actions. These survivors need to understand their own abusive behavior before they can change it.

7 The violent person

This person becomes physically violent when he or she vents anger. Although some violent people can control their rage, others go out of control.

Richie T.

'My parents did not fight, they just seethed. We were all angry and never let it out. As an adult, I jumped over a desk once and almost hit my secretary. I got fired for decking a fellow worker. When I knocked my wife across the kitchen so she was out cold for a few minutes, I got scared. I knew I had a problem.'

The abuser and the abused can most easily identify the violent person. When this person sees the cost, he or she can usually stop the violence. Then the survivor needs to examine the feelings underneath it, meaning: What or whom is he really mad at?'

The people you have just met have discovered their own styles of anger. The questions and assignments I have listed at the end of the chapter will help you determine yours.

Covering Up Anger with Sadness or Covering Up Sadness with Anger

No matter what your style of expressing anger, you may cover up your anger with sadness or cover up sadness with anger. You do one or the other, but not both.

Our culture trains men to express anger freely but the culture inhibits them from expressing their sadness. On the other hand we train women to express vulnerable emotions easily and limit their expression of anger. However, I have found women with tempers, and men who cry easily and cannot get angry.

Some people can use anger to cover up their sadness. Or others turn their anger into tears. As a Survival Strategy, some turn anger to tears since anger looks dangerous. Others do not show their sadness, keeping it hidden underneath their anger. For these people, being sad looks too vulnerable and unsafe. Rhonda and Evelyn describe these two different strategies.

Rhonda B.
Rhonda, 29, an expecting mother, told me: 'I have always had incredible rage, since I was a child. My mother was so frustrating. I screamed and stomped. But when I began therapy, I got in touch with the lonely, sad child underneath. I have been afraid of being a mother because I have been so angry. After working on my anger a year, I can allow myself to feel the sadness and empty out those old feelings. I know I'll be a good mom.'

Evelyn F.
'I cry very easily – at the sentimental TV commercials, at the *Star Spangled Banner*. When my husband and I argued, I just cried. Then I could not talk. He would get mad at me for crying.'

At 50, this bookkeeper was very sensitive and caring and certainly loved her husband. But she converted her anger to tears so fast, she never felt mad. After a month she could feel anger for 30 seconds, then two minutes. After a couple of months she told me: 'Now when we have a disagreement, I can say *I'm angry* and I feel it. I thought I'd hurt somebody with my anger, but my husband loves it, because I'm being honest. I feel like I've grown up.

WHAT YOU CAN DO

Develop Your Own Non-abusive Style of Expressing Anger

In dysfunctional, abusive families, people communicate poorly when they use the Anger Styles I described earlier. They confuse, distract, blame, or punish – anything but take responsibility for feelings and actions. They often do not know how to resolve differences and conflicts, express feelings openly and genuinely, display affection, and promote each other's growth.

Even though you may have learned these destructive styles, you do not have to continue using them. You can develop your own non-abusive style. To be effective and non-abusive, you need to:

1) Be heard.

2) Express your feelings safely.

3) Resolve differences in a mutually supportive way.

4) Not threaten or harm anyone.

As you empty out Old Anger, you may find you do not have to shout and yell as much. You can simply say, 'I'm angry!' As you express your anger, you will find your own healthy and non-threatening style. You may naturally be soft-spoken so merely saying that you are angry will be enough. Or you may need to raise your voice sometimes. If you don't feel and express anger easily, you may need to practice getting mad. If you anger easily, you may need to practice controlling your anger. If you go on 'anger binges,' you may need to discover what these binges do for you and what they cost you. The point is – whatever you say, however you say it – that you can learn to communicate anger safely, effectively, and without harm to yourself or someone else.

Act Even If You Are Afraid

Even after you start practicing your non-abusive style, you may still be afraid of your own anger. And you may quake at other people's anger. Although this terror diminishes as you feel safer with anger, it can paralyze you so that you cannot act when you need to. Here are two examples:

Example 1
   'When my husband yells, I cannot talk; I freeze up.'

Example 2
   'Our neighbors fight a lot, but I don't complain. I don't want them to be mad at me.'

In each example the person is angry, but not necessarily abusive. Let us change the circumstances slightly in these examples so they are clearly abusive:

Example 1
'When my husband yells, he puts me down. The kids cry even though he doesn't touch them. They think they have done something wrong.'

Example 2
'When our neighbors fight, I hear thuds like they are throwing furniture.'

In the first example the children have already internalized their father's abuse, thinking they have done something wrong. They are already suffering from internal abuse. The thuds coming from the neighbors in Example 2 could mean a person is hitting someone or throwing him against the wall.

To stop abuse, you need to act. What actions can you take in the examples? In Example 1, the wife could talk to her husband, go to counselling, call the Childhelp Hotline or Parents Anonymous, talk to a minister. In Example 2, the neighbor could talk to the neighbors or call the police. In the Lisa Steinberg case, neighbors heard sounds next door and thought nothing of it. Later, they and police discovered that a father or mother had beaten a child to death. I would rather call the police and find out that my neighbors were moving furniture, than find out a child had been killed.

If you are in an abusive situation, what actions can you take? You can walk away, call for help, call police, scream, make a complaint, find a new job. You do not have to put up with abuse. You deserve to be treated well.

Letting Go of the Need to Hold on to Your Anger
When I began researching anger as it related to the abused person, I must have read a dozen books about it. However, I suspected that some abused people exhibited a particular relationship with their anger that was not mentioned. During this time a therapist friend told me about a client who was a Viet Nam veteran. My colleague described one session: 'We'd been working for some time to get him in touch with his rage. One day during a session, he got very angry and began throwing my notebook and smashing plants against the walls. After a few minutes, he settled down. I asked him if he was still angry. He said: 'Yes! He would always be angry!'

I asked my therapist friend, 'Why did you let him tear up your office?'

She said, 'Because he needed to express his anger'.

Then I saw the missing anger piece: This veteran – even if he emptied out his rage regularly – would just fill himself up again. The Vet felt entitled to his anger; he had a right to rage. And so do many people who have been raped, beaten, or abused. They – and you may also – feel entitled to their anger. But I ask you to consider that holding on to your anger may start costing you too much. Meet Philip who saw that for himself:

Philip T.
Philip, 30, a cabby and young father, came for a session telling me his wife was going to leave him if he did not control his violence. He had had a fist fight with another cab driver. He decked a neighbor when they argued over the garden hose. As he talked I was a little scared that he might explode in my office. I asked him if he wanted to work on his anger. He said, 'Yes, but I feel I've earned the right to be angry after what my old man did to me!'

We talked about his father's vicious scoldings, non-stop put downs, and whippings. Then he told me about his own daughter: 'I came home yesterday and four and a half year-old Theresa was throwing her dolls against the wall just like I'd thrown her mother. Then she'd gathered up the doll and comforted it, telling her dolly she loved her.'

By now Philip was sobbing.

'That was too much! My own child is repeating just what I taught her. I have to do something.'

Philip was clear that hanging on to his anger because he felt entitled to it was costing him not just his marriage but his daughter. He was binging on his anger. He continued releasing his old anger and the grief underneath it, but his rages and fights stopped. And I was no longer concerned that he might erupt in my office.

Take a Stand
In Chapter 4 of Part I I introduced the ability to take a stand. Remember a stand is a declaration you make about yourself and your circumstances and how you would like it to be. Say it to another person or write it on an index card, to remind you when you forget your stand. Taking a stand gives you the power to create your life. You may fail. However that does not alter the commitment to your stand. When you were a child, your stand *I'm a bike rider* was still there even when you fell off your bike. So you may lose your temper or allow abuse, but you can return to your stand immediately.

Taking a stand regarding your anger will assist you in expressing it safely. And will enable you to set a boundary with people who have abused you.

If You Have Allowed People to Abuse You

Many survivors allow others to erupt. Sheila describes how she took a stand and no longer permitted such anger in her life.

Sheila K.

At 40, after working for a large computer firm, Sheila had started her own business. She was starting to earn good money, travel, and be known in her field. When she first walked into my office, she wore a muted purple suit with a silk blouse and dark purple high heels. Nothing about her appearance indicated her violent past and present. She told me: 'My father got violent occasionally when he drank too much. Once he shoved my mother into the living room wall and knocked her out. Another time I got so mad I shoved him; then he grabbed a tire iron and smashed my hand. He broke all my fingers.

'Three years ago my boyfriend started throwing things and being verbally abusive. I had never seen the similarity between my father and my boyfriend until that night. I didn't see that I accommodated his behavior just like I did with my dad. I certainly did not recognize that they were abusing me.'

Sheila and her boyfriend came to therapy together. They set up rules for expressing anger safely. Sheila took a stand: *I will live an abuse-free life*. The boyfriend took that stand also.

If You Have Been Violent

If you have expressed your anger by physically hurting others, you may need to exercise your ability to take a stand. David tells how he did that.

David Z.

A young waiter, 21 and gay, told me that one night a table of well-dressed, big-eating customers ran up a $350 bill. They left, apologizing that they did not have enough money to leave him a tip. David stormed into the kitchen and began throwing freshly washed glasses against the wall. The shift manager fired him on the spot.

David came into therapy ready to work on his temper, knowing it cost him his job. He began telling me about his father's rages. During his childhood, his dad always stormed through the house angry at one thing or another. His father called David a 'fag' and a 'weirdo'. David swore he would never be like him. He told me, 'I've become just like him!' But losing his job motivated him to discover other more positive ways of expressing anger. 'I'm taking a stand that I will be non-violent.'

In this section I have outlined four concepts designed to help you express your anger safely. First, develop your own non-abusive style of expressing anger. Then, act – even if you are afraid. And let go of your need to hold on to your anger. Finally take a stand to express your anger safely.

SUMMARY

- When people release their Old Anger, they do not overreact and are less likely to abuse others.

- Communicating New Anger cleanly and safely brings people closer together and builds intimate relationships.

- Often survivors have developed abusive ways of expressing anger including exploding, turning anger inside, not recognizing anger, being vicious or resentful, provoking others, and being violent.

- For some, anger covers up sadness, while others turn their anger into tears.

- People can develop their own non-abusive style of expressing anger that includes being heard, expressing feelings safely, resolving differences, and not threatening or harming anyone.

- Survivors need to train themselves to act in abusive situations even when they are afraid.

- They can learn to let go of feeling entitled to their anger.

- Taking a stand to end the violence breaks the abuse cycle. The abuse ends with you.

QUESTIONS AND ASSIGNMENTS

1a) Recall a time when you were angry as a child. Write down the style of expressing or not expressing anger that you used. It may have been exploding, keeping anger inside, not knowing you were angry, being vicious, being resentful, provoking, or being violent.

Examples:

By not expressing my anger I did not escalate fights.

I exploded because then other kids would leave me alone.

I provoked my sister; she got in trouble and not me.

_____

_____

b) When you were last angry at home, what style did you use? You could have used a combination of more than one.

Examples:

I provoked my husband and hit my son.

I took sarcastic jabs at my friend and was resentful.

I didn't realize I was angry at first, but I woke up with my jaws aching.

_____

_____

_____

c) When you were a child, in what way was your anger style a Survival Strategy?

Examples:

It kept me safe.

People were afraid of me.

I put people on the defensive.

_____

_____

_____

d) How does that Survival Strategy limit you now?

Examples:

Nothing ever gets resolved.

When I don't express my anger I get stomach aches and insomnia.

My temper keeps my friends away; they are afraid of me.

_____

_____

_____

2) What are your rules about expressing anger? Write them down in the space below.

Examples:

Anger is dangerous.

Nice girls don't get angry.

Anger is never productive.

If I get angry, I won't be able to stop.

Anger is beneath me.

_____

_____

_____

_____

3) Do you react with anger out of proportion to the situation? If so, Describe a time when you did so.

_____

_____

_____

_____

4a) If you are someone who does not know when you are angry, see if you can identify some bodily reactions you may have. This may help you begin to feel your anger. Circle the reactions that you typically have. Write in ones that are not listed.

tight jaw

clenched fists

stomach ache

sweaty palms

shortness of breath

tight muscles

_____

_____

b) During the week, notice when you are having these bodily reactions.

5a) Does your anger protect you from feeling your grief?

Yes _____No _____

b) If yes, briefly describe a time when it did.

Example:
 After I had to put my dog to sleep, I came home and threw the clean dishes in my dish drainer against the wall. I was so angry!

c) If you need to cry, set aside some private uninterrupted time and allow yourself to cry. Try the bath tub or shower.

_____

_____

_____

_____

6a) Do you cry instead of allowing yourself to feel anger?

Yes_____No _____

b) If yes, write down a time when that happened in a few lines.

Example:
 I was at the bank on a Friday at ten minutes to three. The bank teller told me he had lost my deposit with my paycheck in it. I was so mad, I burst into tears.

_____

_____

_____

_____

c) If you turn your anger to tears, put away the Kleenex. Try safely pounding your fists on the couch or padded chair. Let yourself be angry for 30 seconds. Say what or who you are angry with out loud.

7) Practice using the sentence:

I FEEL ANGRY WHEN YOU _____
(describe their behavior)

BECAUSE_____
(describe their behavior's impact on you).

Remember, do not use judgments, namecalling, or put-downs.

8) Describe a time in your past when you should have acted.

_____

_____

9a) Describe a time when you would assume a person was in danger.

_____

_____

_____

b) What action would you take?

_____

_____

10) Describe a time when you would call the police.

_____

_____

11) Describe a time when you would walk away from a volatile situation.

_____

_____

12a) Do you feel you have a right to be angry because of what your parents or your abuser did to you?

Yes _____No _____

b) If yes, what does holding on to your anger cost you?

Examples:

ulcers	a close relationship
sleep	my job
friends	peace of mind
being liked	happiness

_____

_____

_____

13) Whom in your past are you really angry at? What did they do? Write them a letter that you will not send. As you are writing, allow yourself to get angry and express it in the letter.

Dear _____

_____

_____

_____

_____

_____

_____

_____

_____

_____

14) Close your eyes and visualize the person you are mad at. Tell them out loud what they did and why you are mad. Let yourself feel the anger and other emotions as you do this. Then see your Old Anger filling up a big balloon. Now release the balloon and watch it disappear. (You may have more than one person you need to write to

or visualize. If so, do these exercises for each person.)

15a) Do you need to take a stand about not allowing others to abuse you?

Yes _____ No _____

b) If so, what is your stand? Write it down. Say it out loud to a person who supports your stand or write it on an index card and put it on your mirror.

_____

_____

16a) Are you someone who is or has been violent or abusive?

Yes _____ No _____

b) If so, what is your stand? Write it down. Say it out loud to someone who supports your stand or write it on an index card and put it on your mirror.

_____

17) If you have a history of hurting others with your anger, next time you are angry practice walking around the block and cooling off if you need to.

18) Next time you get really mad, try rolling up your car windows and screaming for 30 seconds.

19) Using a tennis racket, bat, or pillow, beat the bed or couch for 30 seconds.

20) People are more apt to fight when their blood sugar is low. If you feel a slump during the day and find yourself more irritable, try eating fruit, cheese, or a non-sugar snack to keep your blood sugar high.

21) Ask yourself if you are ready to release your anger – even a percentage of it. Now place your left hand under your right ribs covering the liver. Let your thumb rest on your ribs. Wait several minutes until you feel a mild heat under your hand. Now imagine that heat has a color – say red. When you are ready, begin to pull away slowly with your left hand, see that color emptying into your hand. When you have all the heat and red in your left hand, clap your hand loudly on your other hand to break the connection.

FURTHER READING

BACH, George and WYDEN, Peter.
The Intimate Enemy: How to Fight Fair in Love and Marriage (New York: Avon, 1981).

GORDON, Thomas.
Parent Effectiveness Training in Action (New York: Bantam, 1976).

LERNER, Dr Harriet Goldhor.
The Dance of Anger (New York: Harper and Row, 1985).

PADUS, Emrika.
The Complete Guide to Your Emotions and Your Health (Chapter 16) (Emmaus, Penn.: Rodale Press, 1986).

RUBIN, Theodore.
The Angry Book (New York: Collier Books, 1969).

SATIR, Virginia.
Peoplemaking (New York: Science and Behaviour Books, 1972).

CHAPTER 9

Not Letting People Use You

GOALS

- To explain the ways people use each other

- To help you identify if you let people use you

- To teach you how to set limits and boundaries

- To encourage you to speak up for yourself when needed

This chapter defines how people misuse others: manipulating, promising one thing and doing another, and betraying a trust. When children are misused, that sets them up for being used as adults. I outline the cost and payoff of that. Then I describe simple ways you can set boundaries, stand up for yourself, and say NO.

WHAT SURVIVORS MISSED

Parents who do not misuse their children consider their children's needs, look out for their interests, and protect them. When an adult uses a child, he or she betrays him. A father encourages his son to save money for a bike, then the father spends the money on liquor. That father met his own needs at his son's expense. Abused children were often used by a parent or another trusted adult. However the parents used the child, the experience of being used and betrayed devastated the child. That emotional pain can last for years. And, such a child grows up often allowing others to use him or her.

OLD PATTERNS
Ways People Use Others
When little children are used by adults, they are too young to know their parents are doing something wrong. But they certainly feel disappointment, anger, hurt, and confusion. I categorize three ways people use others:

1 Manipulating others
Manipulating means maneuvering another person to your advantage and at their expense, without their permission.

Oliver Z.
Oliver's mother set her son up and manipulated him.
    'Mom asked me to come into the bathroom and wash her back while she was in the tub. She was very suggestive. Then she'd slap me for being a nasty boy.'

2 Promising one thing and doing another or not doing it at all
This is a kind of lying, telling a person one thing and doing something entirely different.

Nora W.
Nora's mother promised her something and never delivered on her promise.
    'My mother dressed me all up and told me we were going out. I was so excited! All she wanted to do was show me off to her lady friends. I was her doll. We didn't go anywhere.'
    In these two cases, the parents used the child to satisfy her own needs, not considering the effects on the child. However, parents who misuse do not necessarily physically punish or publically humiliate their kids.

3 Betraying a trust
In this case, using means violating a trust for your personal gain.

Martha T.
Martha's father betrayed his daughter's trust.
    'I had my father deposit money I earned one summer in my own savings account. I was so proud! When I found the passbook, it read $0. I confronted him. He'd spent the money.'

Being Used as an Adult
Children who have been used often grow up continuing to let other adults use them. Allowing others to do this can lead a person into abusive relationships and situations. The misuse may not be as obvious, but nonetheless it is there. For example:

Margaret G.
'I let my neighbor drop off her kids and stay at my house any time. She does not pay me. She says she'll be by at 9 p.m. and shows up around midnight.'

Andrea E.
'My mother calls me and complains about my father all the time. She talks for an hour and never asks how I am. This has been going on for years.'

If you have difficulty seeing the manipulation in an example, you may have a blind spot. Look into your own life and see if that example illustrates how people use you.

The Payoff of Being Used

People who allow themselves to be used often believe they *have* to allow it. Even though they may fully understand what is going on, they allow it to continue because they think they are getting something from it – a payoff. Usually the payoff is love, acceptance, approval, safety, or protection. Margaret continues to baby-sit for her late friend because she wants her friend's acceptance and is afraid of losing the friendship. Andrea does not confront her mother because it feels safer than having a fight. Because they are getting some love, these people allow themselves to be used.

Such a person can allow a boss, spouse, or friend to use him because he thinks it safer than confronting the situation. Whatever the payoff, people who let others take advantage of them usually do not feel very good about themselves. However, Life Skills students have proven it is possible to break this pattern and learn new skills. And when they do, their self-esteem goes up.

WHAT YOU CAN DO
How to Stop Allowing People to Use You

If you were abused as a child, you could not stop your parents; you were too small. But you can now. To stop allowing people to use you requires three steps:
    1) Recognize that you are allowing people to use you.
    2) Realize that you are getting the payoff – love, approval, protection – at a cost.
    3) Learn to set limits.

1 Recognize that you are allowing people to use you

If you have a problem with people using you, you may say to yourself, 'People use me'. Or, you may say, 'They are doing it to me'. I suggest saying to yourself, 'I allow people to use me'. This lets you know that you have something to do with people using you. It gives you power to do something about it. For example:

Instead of: My friend talks too long.
Try: I allow my friend to talk and talk when I have to go.

Instead of: My boss overworks me.
Try: My boss gave me work at 5 p.m. knowing I had an important appointment. But I did not say a thing.

Instead of: My boyfriend is stepping out on me.
Try: My boyfriend tells me he goes out with other women. It upsets me, but I don't take a stand.

2 Realize you are getting a payoff at a cost

As I mentioned, when you allow someone to use you, you assume you are getting love or approval. But rather than receiving unconditional love or acceptance, you are getting love with strings attached. 'I'll love you if you allow me to use you.' Abused people sometimes believe that the only love they can get is conditional. That is not true. You can give and receive love with no strings attached.

If you think you get protection by allowing yourself to be used, you are allowing yourself to be blackmailed. One woman stayed with her husband who used her emotionally because she thought she needed protection. You needed protection as a child, but you are big enough to take care of yourself and ask for help when you need it.

3 Learn to set limits and draw boundaries

The third step requires you to learn to set limits. When you set your limits, you are stating clearly what you will and will not do. 'I will go to the store, but I'd like you to put away the groceries.' When you set the limits for your child or employee or friend, you say clearly what is expected. When you need to clarify the limits, you find out what is expected of you. When you are drawing boundaries, you say here is the line over which you may not cross. Keeping boundaries vague can set people up for arguments and problems. Many fights start because of such misunderstandings.

While you are establishing limits, you are speaking up; you are asserting yourself. You make a statement that you will not be used. You are not a victim available for misuse, but a person to be treated respectfully. You have taken back your power. If people around you are not used to hearing you speak up, you may have to interrupt or be a little loud: 'Wait a minute. I have something to say. You forgot me.'

When you practice these skills, you become 'abuse resistent'. You are less likely to be used or abused.

I find, when teaching these skills, that people need specific sentences they can use over and over again. I list below different examples for setting limits and boundaries. They may not fit your situation exactly, but you can modify the language for your use. Here are some sample sentences to help you as a friend, parent, lover, and employee.

As a friend – you can incorporate these phrases into your conversation when they are needed:

I don't want to talk about that now.

I only have five minutes.

I want to be your friend, not your girlfriend.

You can borrow my car but please bring it back by 10.

The problem you are talking about is out of my league. You need professional help.

If you are going to drink, I'm not going to be around you.

I'm tired, I can't talk now, but we can talk tomorrow morning.

Please don't call me after 11 p.m.

If you are a parent – be clear and consistent in setting your limits otherwise your children can easily use you. They can break rules that you did not clearly establish.

You are due home by 11 p.m.

You need to finish your chores by Saturday at noon.

When you've finished your homework you can play.

You can express your feelings, but don't talk back, sulk, or hit.

If you are a spouse or lover – boundaries can be undestood, but at times they may need to be stated. They provide ground rules for your relationship.

You can tell me you're attracted to another woman, but don't act on it.

We can yell and argue, but don't hit me.

You can tell me you are angry, but don't put me down.

If you are an employee – ask what your boss expects. He or she does not have the right to abuse you. Working overtime should be agreed upon ahead of time. And you can express yourself:

I'll gladly type that, but I have to leave at 5.30 p.m. today. I'll come in tomorrow.

I want your critique, but please don't yell.

When you tell people beforehand that this is what you expect, then they can choose to do it or not. You are not using people. Conversely, when you find out ahead of time what the job is, you can choose. You informed yourself, so you are less likely to be used.

A Special Skill: Saying No!
Because many people have difficulty saying NO, I discuss it here as a separate skill. Saying NO is a specific way of setting a

boundary or limit. Everyone is entitled to say NO when he or she has a good reason.

When you say NO the first time, it may sound harsh or rude. You may even feel angry because you have allowed people to walk on you in the past. You need to practice. Here are some sample sentences:

No, I can't go with you.

No, I can't give you the money.

No, I'm not available.

You do not need to explain your reasons. You can say no politely without sounding rude. After a while 'no' will become easier and part of your everyday vocabulary.

The Zealot Phase

When people first start setting limits, they can become over-enthusiastic. After years of being a doormat, the person zealously guards against being used. This can create mischief. To illustrate, a friend who had allowed people to use her was practicing these skills vigorously. She met a wonderful man. But when he was 15 minutes later for a lunch date, she broke up with him. 'He's using me!' She broke up with him six more times over his lateness. However, the 'zealot phase' seems necessary to integrate these skills. People can swing from one extreme of being used to the other, 'don't tread on me'.

Eventually the skills become natural and people learn when to stand firm and when to negotiate. Setting boundaries does not necessarily mean that you need to be flexible. You can negotiate rather than give in.

I need this, you need that; let's work it out.

I can't go Monday, but how about Tuesday?

ADDITIONAL CASES

Here are some people who recognized their patterns and trained themselves in new skills. Use these examples to gain insight into your pattern. After the stories, you will find some questions and exercises so you can assess your own patterns and develop new skills.

Fred A.

Fred's 12-year-old sister had raped him when he was six. She used and manipulated him most of his life. He so adored her, he would allow her to do anything. 'One time I let her scratch her initials on my arm. I was 8.'

Fred learned that to get love you have to allow people to use you. He continued relying on this Survival Strategy into his adult years. He lacked the ability to set limits on what he allowed people to do. At 41, Fred had just ended another relationship with a man. Although Fred had had female lovers, he felt safer with men. Yet he allowed his lovers – male or female – to abuse him.

'One woman called me her toy! Another put me down in front of friends. I lent a man money and he never paid me back.'

The more they used him, the nicer he was. When he began therapy, he did not see that he was being used. Fred began expressing his pain and anger. He began to see how he allowed people to use him. He also began to distinguish between people he could and could not trust. As he felt he was entitled to being treated well, he practiced speaking up, saying NO, expressing his needs. He memorized sentences from this chapter, so he knew what to say when he set his limits.

He realized he had been attracting people who used him. He shifted and started seeing a man who was nurturing and kind. He not only liked him, he felt safe with him.

Brian P.

Brian, 28, worked for an insurance company. He told me, 'My brothers beat me up. But worse, they taunted me. Once I wanted to play ball. I begged them for hours. Then they finally said yes. I went outside with the ball and bat and waited. They came and said: 'We aren't going to play. We just wanted to see yur reaction.' '

Brian continued: 'I was crushed! They did this kind of thing over and over again. I wanted their approval and love so badly, I always fell for it.'

Brian had learned to allow himself to be taken advantage of. As an adult, Brian continued to let people use him. He was available to do any chore, run any errand, talk to any friend, day or night. He was beginning to resent his friends. He discovered he really didn't like several people who were just taking from him.

He ended one friendship. He had a productive discussion with his co-worker during which he spoke up for himself. Before he did a friend a favor, he looked to see if he was being used. If he was, he would not do the favor. He set limits on helping his friends. These skills helped Brian break an old pattern, feel better about himself, and find a mutually satisfying way of relating with others.

SUMMARY
- People use others by manipulating, promising one thing and doing another, betraying a trust, taking advantage of them, or

infringing on privacy.

- People allow themselves to be used because they think they are getting acceptance, love, approval, protection, or friendship.

- People who allow themselves to be used can have a hard time speaking up for themselves or saying No.

- When people are able to set limits, they become more abuse-resistant.

QUESTIONS AND ASSIGNMENTS

1) Do you allow people to take advantage of you in order to ensure their love or approval?

Yes _____No _____

2) Do you let people use you, then feel resentful or angry?

Yes _____No _____

3) Do you let people use you because you are afraid to speak up or confront them with a different idea, plan, or opinion?

Yes _____No _____

4) Are you aware only afterwards that you have been used?

Yes _____No _____

5) Do you find yourself thinking: They did it to me?

Yes _____No _____

6) Below is a list of sentences that you can use to set limits. Write your own in the blanks provided.

I would love to continue talking to you, but I have to get to bed.

I am glad to listen to you and I have 5 minutes right now.

I want to know what you are feeling, but I am not willing to listen to you if you are being nasty and putting me down.

No thank you!

_____

_____

7) The following stories illustrate people being used.

Muriel's co-worker, Diana, tells other people how difficult Muriel is to work with. When Diana and Muriel have lunch, Diana tells Muriel how wonderful Muriel is. At lunch Diana asks Muriel to recommend her for a promotion. Muriel clearly understands what Diana is doing to her but recommends her 'friend' anyway.

Dwayne, 18, has a mother who continually opens his letters from his girlfriend. Even though Dwayne is outraged, he says nothing.

Caroline's boss tells her to work the weekend and late each night even though her job description clearly states she can leave at 5:30 p.m. Caroline works the extra hours without questioning her boss and without extra pay.

Phyllis's fiancé promised her an engagement ring. She finds out he spent the money on new stereo equipment for himself. Although she is bitterly disappointed, she says it is all right.

a) How is each person letting him or herself be used? Fill in the blanks with one of the following choices:

- Manipulated
- Promised one thing and doing another
- Betrayed a trust
- Taken advantage of
- Having privacy invaded

Muriel is being _____

Dwayne is being _____

Caroline is being _____

Phyllis is being _____

b) What do you think these people are getting from letting themselves be used? Fill in the blanks with the following choices:

- acceptance
- love
- approval
- protection

● friendship

Muriel thinks she is getting——————————————————
by letting her co-worker use her.

Dwayne thinks he is getting——————————————————
by letting his mother use him.

Caroline thinks she is getting——————————————————
by letting her boss use her.

Phyllis thinks she is getting——————————————————
by letting her fiancé use her.

c) What is an appropriate sentence each person could say to set limits or speak up for him or herself? Write it down.

Muriel could tell her co-worker:

_____

_____

Dwayne could tell his mother:

_____

_____

Caroline could tell her boss:

_____

_____

Phyllis could tell her fiancé:

_____

_____

8a) Briefly describe three times you let yourself be used by family, friends, or at work.

1 _____

_____

2 _____

_____

3 _____

_____

b) How would you stand up for yourself or set your limits now? Write a sentence for each example.

1 _____

2 _____

3 _____

9) We are all entitled to say No when we have a good reason. For some, saying No once a day is an accomplishment. For others, you can practice several times daily. When you need to say No, do so.

10) The next time you find yourself thinking *They did it to me*, try asking yourself: *How did I allow them to use me?*

FURTHER READING

BLAKE, Dr Karen.
   Born to Please: Compliant Women and Controlling Men (New York: St Martin's Press, 1988).

BOWER, Gordon and BOWER, Sharon.
   Asserting Yourself: A Practical Guide for Positive Change (Addison-Wesley, 1976).

GALASSI, Merna D. and GALASSI, John.
   Assert Yourself: How to Be Your Own Person (New York: Human Science Press, 1977).

SCALIA, Toni.
   Bitches and Abdicators (New York: M. Evans and Co., Inc., 1985).

SMITH, Manuel.
   When I Say No I Feel Guilty (New York: Bantam, 1985).

CHAPTER 10

Ending Self-Blame

GOALS
- To understand how you learned to blame yourself

- To teach you to stop thinking you deserve abuse

- To teach you to identify who has the problem

- To learn to use a reality check

WHAT SURVIVORS MISSED
Self-blaming means taking the blame for actions that you did not do or things that were not your fault. Many survivors think everything is their fault.

Certainly, many people blame themselves undeservingly even when they are not from abusive homes. But children from abusive or alcoholic homes are more likely to self-blame because their abusers did not take responsibility for their behavior. Such grownups blamed each other, the kids, anyone but themselves. That set up an atmosphere in which the children assumed the abuse was their fault.

Simon P.
Simon, years later in therapy, still feels: 'I must have done something terribly wrong to get beaten all the time. Other kids were not punished as much as I was. But I could never figure out what I had done.'

Children like Simon often generalize, thinking everything is their fault. As an adult, Simon is now terrified to try new activities because he blames himself when things go wrong. He only tackles jobs he knows he can do well. His work involves learning new tasks. His fears increase pressure and decrease his productivity. Simon's objective is to avoid blame rather than be productive.

To survivors like Simon everything looks like it was and is their fault. They missed learning how parents and children take appropriate responsibility for their actions rather than blaming others.

OLD PATTERNS
Being Blamed When It Wasn't Your Fault
Child abuse is never the child's fault. However, abusive parents may blame the child. Sometimes such parents tell the child outright *It was your fault.*

Nadine J.
Nadine still feels the effects of her parents' blame.

'My dad molested me when I was six. Mom walked in on us. She grabbed me by the shoulders and shook me until I thought my neck would snap and my teeth would break. I can still hear her yelling: 'If we hadn't had you this would not have happened. This is your fault!' We never talked about it again. My father left me alone, but so did my mother. She was cold and distant from then on.'

This mother could not deal with her husband's behavior and turned her rage on a safer target – the child. But, more tragically, Nadine grew up not only blaming herself for that incident, but for anything that went wrong.

Susie R.
'When my real father died, I was four, and I decided I'd find us another father. While I was shopping with my mother in our small town, I started talking to a nice man. I invited him home to dinner. After dating my mother one month, they married. I was elated! I'd found a new dad. But he hit my mother and screamed at us four kids. He was a tyrant. My mother and siblings all began to blame me for finding this man. Only after months of therapy did I realize that my mother, a fully grown adult, was responsible for her decision to marry him – not me.'

Susie's mother did not take responsibility for her actions. She did not clarify for her daughter that *she* made the choice to marry this man. The bad marriage was not the daughter's fault.

The Family Scapegoat
In certain abusive families, the whole family non-verbally selects a scapegoat. The family conspires to blame one person over and over again.

Alice G.
'When my mother found Dad's empty liquor bottles, I got hit.

When she found out he'd spent their money on other women, I got hit. Since I was the oldest, when my sister or brother did not do well in school, I got hit. My sister and brother never got it like I did.'

Alice became the outlet for her mother's anger and frustration. She was punished whenever things went wrong in the family. She assumed it was all her fault. As a young adult, she became very depressed and attempted suicide. She certainly felt pain and hurt and anger over the beatings. But the lasting damage to her sense of self came from concluding: *I am bad*. When she began to express her own rage and grief in therapy, she felt more alive. When she began to see that her mother, not she, had a problem, she realized she was not inherently bad.

Thinking You Deserved It
Thinking you deserve the abuse cements self-blame into place. If you think *I'm wrong*, you will blame yourself as a natural outgrowth of that thinking. Chris and Josie explain how they felt.

Chris S.
'Why would they have punished me so much? I began to believe I was the problem.'

Josie W.
'After my father told me I deserved it over and over, I guess I believed him. I thought it was my fault.'

This self-blame makes these people targets for future abuse. They have signs around their necks, *I deserve to be abused*.

WHAT YOU CAN DO
Re-evaluate the Past
People who have internalized abuse and feel they deserve blame must shift their thinking. They must re-evaluate their abusive pasts. Looking back, they need to see that the abusive adult had a problem, not them. A survivor – however many years later – needs to realize the beating, neglect, or humiliation were not his or her fault.

As you begin to re-evaluate, you may be very angry at your abuser, but also at yourself – for putting up with the abuse. That is healthy. You are seeing it with new eyes and separating yourself from what happened. Then you can put the abuse in the past and remove that *I deserve it* sign. This means acknowledging that the abusive parent did something wrong. Because children are taught to 'Honor thy father and mother', people can feel disloyal to their own parents. One man, who was trying to reconcile dishonoring his abusive parents, asked the family priest about it. The priest said: 'God puts people here, but he does not make their choices. People make their own choices. And your parents made some inappropriate ones.'

It takes courage to look at such abusive situations and tell the truth, because you have to allow that your parents were not wonderful, but cruel. Here are two people who have:

Sonja F.
'I did not do anything so terribly wrong. I was just a regular kid. I see now my father and mother were terribly angry and did not like children very much. I just happened to be theirs. They both had problems.'

Rebecca L.
'Because I was the oldest, Mom got her hands on me first. She got in the habit of hitting me when she was mad about something else. It's taken me months, but I finally see maybe I wasn't really bad.'

Ask: Who Has the Problem?
People who self-blame cannot tell the difference between 'your problem' and 'my problem'. In fact, they have no category called 'your problem'; it is all 'my problem'. I ask Life Skills participants to look at situations and ask themselves *Who has the problem?*

Mentally giving back problems that you have taken on can be freeing. Here are some people who are practicing this in their everyday lives:

Fran S.
'My husband came home grumpy. My knee-jerk reaction was 'What did I do wrong?' I had done nothing. I asked him how I could be helpful, rather than blaming myself.'

Les G.
'When it rained on the day I picked for the picnic, I saw that I had nothing to do with it raining. This was not my problem.'

Linda Z.
'After my boyfriend left me and went off, he spent the night with another woman. I thought, what had I done? Only after a friend got angry at him did I have permission to be outraged.'

Check Things Out
When you find yourself thinking *I must have done something*, check out your assumption. This is called a reality check. If you are not sure, here are some sample questions to ask:

Did I do anything to make you mad?

Is there something I've done?

Have I said something I should not have?

Am I in trouble?

Using a reality check will let you off the hook, and stop your automatic response to self-blame. Checking things out can give you information about how others perceive things.

Ed T.
'I thought we did not get the job because of me. I asked my supervisor, and he said it was economics.'

Lisa J.
'I felt awkward because I thought I had done something wrong. But my friend said I had not done anything.'

You will probably grasp *Who owns the problem?* and a reality check fairly easily. But you may need some time to put them into practice. Be patient and do not blame yourself for slipping from time to time. Remember, you are breaking habits that you had established for years.

ADDITIONAL CASES
Meet Paula, Wanda, and Shirley, who learned not to blame themselves.

Paula P.
At 31, Paula managed the office of a large printing office. Her black hair hung loose to her shoulders; she wore jeans, tennis shoes, and sweaters, and no make-up. When she began therapy, Paula told me about her painful past: 'When I was 8, my little brother was born retarded. My parents were never the same. They were incapable of accepting any responsibility or expressing their own grief and guilt, so I became the scapegoat. When Nicki had a seizure, I got hit. Mom would scream, 'You hate Nicki; you are filth!' I loved Nicki; no one ever explained to me what happened to my baby brother. Mom sometimes locked me out of the house.

'After a while I believed them, and started blaming myself. I had several abusive bosses. I volunteered to make reparation for anything that went wrong. Somehow I got a little dignity by admitting blame.

'One time I worked all day preparing an expensive dinner for a man. After we ate, he left saying he had another date. I assumed there was something wrong with me. I wasn't good enough.

'In the Life Skills, I learned that it's not all my problem. When I began using a reality check, I saw that all problems were not mine.

Recently, my husband was looking for a new job. I confronted him about not making any appointments for interviews. He got mad, but I didn't blame myself. Before, I would have thought it was completely my fault. Now, I can support him. I spent one or two years ending this internal self-blame. It comes up, but I can interrupt those self-blaming thoughts now.'

Paula's new employers and her husband appreciate and respect her. She has peace of mind and less internal stress, because she is not wondering what she did wrong.

Wanda S.

At 21, Wanda was finishing college. Her long, lean body, pulled-back hair, and heavy dancer's bag let me know she was training to be a dancer.

'My mother blamed herself for everything. She usually thought one of her friends was mad at her. When I had trouble with math, she said it was because she wasn't a good mother. When I got involved with a man she didn't like, it was because she wasn't a good mother. I stopped telling her about my life, since she usually turned it into something about her. She doesn't really listen to my problems.

'Of course, I decided I would not be like my mother. I don't grab other people's problems away from them like she does. But I find myself assuming things are my fault. When a professor told our class that one person had pulled down the class average, I knew it was me even though I had an A average. When my roommate says she wants to talk to me, I assume she's upset with me. Last night she just wanted to talk.

'After learning Life Skills, I have been listening to my own thinking. I tell myself: Is this logical? Is it based in fact? The facts are I have an A average; I couldn't be pulling down the class average. The facts are when my roommate gets mad, she tells me right away. By reviewing what's true, I stop my self-blaming. I sleep better at night, and I notice I'm more at ease and happy.'

Shirley D.

At 24, Shirley came to a battered woman's shelter at 2 a.m. with her infant son and two-and-a-half-year-old daughter. Once she was at the shelter, the physical abuse stopped, but Shirley blamed herself. She typifies most battered women. Shirley related: 'My husband works as a day laborer. We've been married five years. As soon as we got married, he told me I had to stop seeing my friends. We moved away from my parents and sisters, so I couldn't see them as often. My father used to hit us, but not until I got to the shelter did I think it was too much.'

Most women who are battered were abused in some way as children. The behavior looks familiar to them and they do not see it as abuse. Although the women are missing many skills, they feel they deserve the abuse. This internalizing of the abuse keeps the pattern in place.

'Johnny started hitting me when we were dating. He was angry and sometimes he'd been drinking. One night he broke my arm, and I went to the emergency room. The night we came to the shelter he was hitting my daughter. I thought he'd kill her. We just had to get out of there.

'Now that I've been here four weeks, I'm beginning to see what abuse is. And that I've blamed myself not just in my marriage but as a kid. I've never known another way. The counselors here have taught me to value myself. I'm starting to feel good about myself; stopped blaming myself. And nobody is going to hit me or my babies again. I've taken a stand that me and my family will be safe. I have a lot more work to do on myself, but it's a start.'

SUMMARY

● Some children assume blame for things that weren't their fault.

● Other children were blamed unnecessarily.

● Others became the family scapegoat.

● To stop self-blaming look at who has the problem.

● Check things out before you assume blame.

QUESTIONS AND ASSIGNMENTS

1a) Growing up, were you blamed for things that were not your fault?

Yes _____ No _____

b) If yes, write down an example.

Examples:

I was blamed for my parents divorce.

My mother blamed me because I looked like my father. she hated him.

I ate something my mother planned to use for a party. She blamed me for ruining her party.

Growing up, the kid who used the last of the milk, or cookies, or peanut butter got in trouble.

_____

_____

_____

_____

2a) Did you assume blame for problems that were really not yours at all?

Yes _____ No _____

b) If so, when? Write down an incident.

Examples:

I assumed my father leaving was my fault.

I felt my mother's unhappiness was my problem.

If my sister was sad or in trouble I felt guilty and responsible.

_____

_____

_____

3a) Did you get punished for things someone else did?

Yes _____ No _____

b) If so, when?

_____

_____

_____

4) Do you usually assume something is your fault?

Yes _____ No _____

5) Write *Who has the problem?* on an index card. Tape it on your refrigerator, medicine chest, or mirror. As situations occur throughout your day, ask yourself that question. People have three responses:

a) I see I assume everything is my problem.

b) I cannot see.

c) I'm beginning to see when something is my problem and when it isn't.

Write what you learned doing this exercise below.

_____

_____

_____

6) Practice using a reality check. Ask others before you assume your perception of the situation is accurate. Write down what happened when you used a reality check.

Examples:

I was terrified my new boss would scapegoat me like my family did. But he says he likes me and my work.

I was all ready to blame myself for a bounced check. I discovered the bank made a mistake.

When my friend didn't call I thought she was punishing me. Later I asked her and she had been caught in traffic.

_____

_____

_____

FURTHER READING

NAMKA, Lynne.
   The Doormat Syndrome (Deerfield, Fla.: Health Communications, Inc., 1989).

CHAPTER 11

Not Sabotaging Yourself

GOALS
- To identify how you sabotage yourself

- To learn ways of intervening in self-sabotage, so you can have what you want in life

People who have been abused can have difficulty having it good, being successful; they often undermine themselves. These people are so used to struggle that they keep creating difficulties rather than enjoying success. They don't know any other way. This chapter helps you identify self-sabotage and gives you ways of breaking that pattern.

WHAT SURVIVORS MISSED
Some survivors missed feeling comfortable with successes as a natural part of growing up. They are more comfortable with struggle and chaos. When things start getting good, these people sometimes get scared and even try to stop their success. Strange as it may seem, the survivor feels safe and familiar with struggle. Coming from a chaotic family, the survivor may cling to struggle as a security. When they begin to enjoy life beyond struggle – to have non-abusive relationships, experience success, and realize goals – they may be frightened. To the survivor fear means danger, so they halt the success; in other words, they sabotage themselves. Here are three illustrations:

Belinda F.
'I got the part. Then I was late for the show. My understudy went on.'

Edna C.
'I meet a great guy. Then I'm rude and nasty to him.'

Earl J.
'I got a good job. The first day I played incompetent. I noticed I purposely played stupid.'

OLD PATTERNS
Why People Sabotage Themselves
When I asked my clients why they undermine themselves, they gave three reasons:

1) To keep control

2) Fear of success

3) To affirm the belief *I don't deserve a good life.*

1 To keep control
Some people feel out of control, on unfamiliar territory, when they start getting successful.

Rhea L.
'When I started selling a lot of houses at work, I felt like the whole thing was running away from me. I had a big deal cooking. I purposely didn't return one phone call, and I lost the deal to another agent. As long as I am bumping along the bottom I feel comfortable. I may just barely pay the rent, but I feel on top of things in a funny way.'

Rhea confessed she felt odd earning so much more money than her parents. She believed if she did she would lose their love, so she undermined her success.

2 Fear of success
Libby B.
Libby had worked hard to release her abusive past and learn new skills. Her management training program was going well, her marriage back on an even keel, her mother settled in a rest home. She came into a session and said: 'I slept in the morning of an important meeting, I picked fights with my husband and my mother. I've been anxious.'

During the session Libby saw she was terrified of success. 'I'd rather have these same old hassles than a peaceful, good life. I can't stand the success.'

Growing up, Libby's father was fired from many jobs. That put the family in financial crisis. Libby's parents fought, usually over money. And Libby and her brothers picked fights with each other. Libby's parents did not set any example by being productive and successful. They created a home environment where fighting was the main event. When Libby finally stopped the fighting in her adult life, she felt disoriented and afraid.

She continued: 'I'm laughing, but I think you are right. I cannot stand this peaceful, settled life I've worked so hard for.'

3 To affirm the belief: I don't deserve it
This actress explains how her belief that she didn't deserve a part kept her from getting it.

Priscilla G.
'I was called back several times to read for this play. Although I was one of fifty women, I was well-qualified. My agent said I was perfect for the part. After several cuts, the director was deciding between two of us. I looked over at the other girl and said to myself: I don't deserve to get this part. I knew it was over. Of course, she got the part.'

As a child, Priscilla's mother had told her: 'I don't know what your drama teacher sees in you! You don't have any talent. Why are you trying out for the lead?' That undermined Priscilla's self-confidence. At the recent audition, she did not need her mother telling her any more, she had internalized Mom's negative programming. She told herself she did not deserve the part.

WHAT YOU CAN DO
Break the Sabotage Cycle
If this sounds like you, you can break the habit of sabotaging yourself. When your life starts going well and you feel it's moving too fast, you may want to stop it. Make a plan that includes these elements:

1) Allow yourself to feel the fear

2) Reprogram your negative thoughts to positive ones

3) Intervene in your sabotage pattern.

You will find exercises to break self-sabotage in the Questions and Assignments. Then you can retrain yourself to succeed.

ADDITIONAL CASES
When you think you will sabotage yourself, plan ahead to intervene before you do. Meet two people who have trained themselves to do just this.

Jason G.
Jason recognized another kind of sabotage in himself. At 33, he self-sabotaged by over-committing.

'I remember my mother planning her day at the breakfast table. She'd have 17 things to do. When I came home from school she'd be flustered and overwhelmed. She had not done anything. I see now that she sabotaged herself by taking on too much.

'I do the same thing. I plan to do the laundry, the shopping, five errands, and pick up my daughter in 30 minutes. In the Life Skills I realized that, if I were getting my work done on time, I'd be successful and that scares me to death. I wouldn't know who I was.

'But I want to find out. So I have started checking my 'To Do' list with my buddy. He tells me if I have too much on it. I know after a couple of times I'll be able to recognize when it's too much. I've been visualizing myself getting things done and enjoying my success. I'm not there yet, but I'm getting there.'

Rita K.
At 35, Rita was passed over for a promotion twice. She began to suspect she was sabotaging herself.

'My parents told me I'd never amount to much. I quit high school. I finally finished and went to college nights. At my civil service job I've had to take several tests. Each time I've had to give myself a pep talk so I could do it. Then when I got into management I got scared. I did not pass an interview.

'In the Life Skills, I realized I just couldn't let myself be successful. I was terrified. For several months, I examined my negative thinking and reprogrammed it with *You can do it. You do deserve it.* I repeated these phrases over and over even though I did not believe them at first. I used the visualization to practice seeing myself passing the interview. I took the test and interview again and I passed. When my manager told me the results, he said, 'We know you can do the job and you deserve it'.'

SUMMARY
- People sabotage themselves to keep control, to avoid fear of success, and to confirm they don't deserve success.

- You can reprogram self-sabotaging habits by feeling your fear and replacing negative thoughts with positive ones. This new awareness will help you to intervene if it starts to occur again.

QUESTIONS AND ASSIGNMENTS
1) If a benefactor gave you $100,000 and made you an overnight success, how would you feel? Uncomfortable, unworthy, like he made a mistake?

_____

_____

2) Does the idea of success or having life easy frighten you?

Yes _____No _____

3a) Do you suspect that you sabotage yourself?

Yes _____No _____

b) If you do any of the following, check the item off.

_____Schedule too much to do so you never feel you accomplish things

_____Show up late to an important function

_____Be nasty to people you want to be nice to

_____Do not return important phone calls that jeopardize work or relationships

_____Oversleep so you are late for an important event

_____Trip or fall

_____Pretend incompetence

_____Overeat when dieting

c) Write down your own habits of self-sabotage.

_____

_____

4) What are your beliefs about deserving a happy, successful life? Write them down.

Examples:

I don't deserve it.

Life is a struggle.

Being successful is dangerous.

If I mess up at least I'm safe.

Success is unfamiliar.

I'm not worth it.

If I'm successful, I'll be alone.

Successful people are unhappy.

Success means I've made it.

Successful people are happy.

Women can't be more successful than men.

I can't be more successful than my father.

_____

_____

_____

b) For each negative belief, write a positive affirmation on an index card. Put it on your mirror.

Examples:

I deserve a good life.

Life is easy and fun.

I can be successful and safe.

I am safe when I am doing my best.

I'm getting more comfortable with success.

I am worthy of success and happiness.

I'm successful, I have friends, and I'm fulfilled.

It's OK to be more successful than my parents.

c) Write your affirmations ten times daily for 21 days.

5) This visualization uses imagery to help you reprogram your mind with the desired scenario. Select an upcoming event – a party, interview, date, or just your day – that you want to go well.

'Sit comfortably where you can have 10 uninterrupted minutes. Close your eyes. Take two or three deep, slow breaths. Just take a moment to relax. Just give yourself the inner command 'now relax'. Picture the event, interview, or meeting you want to work on. See it in color. Notice what you are wearing, what other people are wearing. Notice how you feel in your body. Now play the action forward like a movie, seeing it exactly the way you want it to happen. Pay attention to what is being said. See yourself relaxed, calm, and confident that it will turn out well. Take a deep breath and appreciate yourself. Open your eyes.'

6) When you feel afraid of success, close your eyes. Imagine yourself going down a playground slide. You are afraid, but safe. You squeal with delight and enjoy the ride.

7a) If you sabotaged yourself once, you may do it again. Name a forthcoming event during which you do not want to sabotage yourself.

Example:

Job interview	Audition
First date	Dinner
Sales call	Your diet
First day of a new job	Monthly budget
Presentation of proposal	Vacation

_____

_____

_____

b) Make a plan to intervene so you won't next time. Ask for support if you need it.

Example:

I videotaped my interview and replayed it, so I could see ahead of time that I did just fine.

I called a friend for support rather than be late to an audition.

I tend to mess up on first dates with guys. So I asked a man friend to walk through the evening with me, so I felt more confident.

I make money to pay debts and handle my financial crisis, but I spend it foolishly. So this time, I banked the money for bills immediately. I wrote down everything I spent. And I asked a friend to review what I spend each day.

c) Write your plan in these blanks.

_____

_____

_____

FURTHER READING

JEFFERS, D. Susan.
   Feel the Fear and Do It Anyway (New York: Ballantine Books, 1987).

POLLARD, Dr John K.
   Self-Parenting: The Complete Guide to Your Inner Conversations (Malibu, Cal.: Generic Human Studies Publishing, 1987).

SINETAR, Marsha.
   Do What You Love, The Money Will Follow (New York: Dell Publishing, 1989).
   The Twelve-Steps: A Way Out: A Working Guide for Adult Children of Alcoholics and Other Dysfunctional Families (San Diego: Recovery Publications, 1987).

SECTION FOUR

Breaking the Pleasing Pattern

Some adult survivors learned to please as a Survival Strategy, a way to be safe and loved. Both overhelping and needing to be perfect originate out of a need to please. A pleaser is a person whose actions are motivated by needing to be liked. This person organizes his or her life around pleasing others. The overhelper focuses on others. And the person striving to be perfect focuses on high standards. Both avoid dealing with their own problems by trying to please. When people begin addressing these two patterns, they naturally begin to address their own issues. The focus shifts from outside to inside.

CHAPTER 12

Not Overhelping

GOALS

- To distinguish between helping and overhelping

- To investigate where overhelping originates

- To learn what is a crisis and what is not

- To provide methods to shift from overhelping people to empowering them

WHAT SURVIVORS MISSED

'When you give a man a fish, he can eat for a day. When you teach a man to fish, he can feed himself for a lifetime.'

This old Japanese adage distinguishes between helping that limits people and helping that empowers people. Overhelping limits people. I define overhelping as helping when the assistance is not called for or when the helper wants love or approval. Here are a few situations where the person is overhelping. I describe them first from the overhelper's point of view and then from the helpee's view.

The Overhelper's Point of View

The Overhelper thinks he is helping, when in fact he may be getting in the way or limiting the person. Rather than teaching the other person how to do something for himself, the Overhelper rushes in to do it for him. These examples demonstrate how overhelping creates co-dependent relationships.

Celia S.

'I just wanted to lend a hand when my daughter moved in to her new apartment. So I went to the store and bought all the cleaning supplies I always use and arrived at her house. I don't understand why she was angry.'

Celia's daughter was striking out on her own and wanted to establish her own independence. Celia did not honor this and ask if she could come over. She simply arrived assuming she was being helpful. She might have helped with the cleaning, but she was not helping her daughter become independent. She did not acknowledge that her daughter was now in charge of her own life.

June B.
'My husband told me he wanted to be an artist. He couldn't work because his mind had to be clear to paint. So I went to work, then I got a second job, and now I work three jobs. I'm getting resentful.'

While trying to help her husband, this woman made him codependent on her. They never discussed who would support the family; June assumed she should. She did not ask him to start carrying his fair share of the expenses; she became a martyr.

The Helpee's Point of View
The helpee often feels resentful and controlled. Sometimes over-helpers make the problem worse by assuming they are superior and the helpee is lacking.

Marion K.
'I told my therapist I felt I had handled my issues and wanted to terminate after my year of therapy. She told me I was resisting. She felt I had other problems I wasn't willing to face up to. I think she needed me in her practice. That's her problem.'

This therapist assumed she knew what was best. Rather than discussing it as equals, she labelled her client as if something was wrong with Marion.

Edgar M.
'When I took my assistant on a business trip, he treated me like I was handicapped. He held my arm as we walked, picked up my phone before I could reach it, waited at the door with my coat. All those things are nice, but his attitude was *I needed help*! I finally sent him home.'

Edgar's assistant was suffocating him, not allowing him to make any moves on his own. Rather than asking what Edgar needed, he assumed he knew what was appropriate. In the end Edgar had to push him away and was left without an assistant.

OLD PATTERNS
Where Overhelping Begins
Some children learned to overhelp from an overhelping parent. They mirrored their parent's behavior. These people don't necessarily overhelp all the time. In other cases, a child assumed adult

responsibilities at an early age. This type of overhelper took on too much too soon. For this child or adult, overhelping seems to be a way of life. Let us look at the overhelping lifestyle.

Assuming a Parent Role Too Soon

I found adult survivors who assumed a parent role too soon because a parent died or left the family or was ill. Or the parent was emotionally unable to fulfill his or her role, so a responsible child, often the oldest, took on the job. Judith Wallerstein and Sandra Blakeslee in *Second Chances: Men, Women and Children a Decade After Divorce* call such young people 'overburdened' children.[1] These children attempted to parent when they were ill-equipped to do so. They tried to solve unsolvable problems like get Mommy and Daddy back together or get Daddy to stop drinking. No one told them to, they just were trying to make things better.

Ann E.

A young woman with an alcoholic father reported: 'I comforted my mother when she cried, but I really couldn't do much. She told me how upset she was and that she wanted to leave my father. I tried to think of things that would cheer her up. I also remember lecturing my father for drinking and making Mom unhappy. I felt responsible for both of them. Now I take on friends' problems as a way of loving them.'

This woman was too young as a child to take on such problems. She felt hopeless and frustrated because her help was not effective. However, she learned to overhelp as her way of loving people. As an adult she helps people who do not want to help themselves.

Dick R.

One man, who was an 'overburdened child', was driving his new wife crazy with his helpfulness. He explained: 'My mother died when I was 12. After that Dad would leave me notes telling me what needed doing after school. I cleaned, prepared dinner, and helped my brother and sister with their homework. Now at home, I just jump and do what needs doing. It's all my job as far as I'm concerned. That's the way it's always been.'

The Cost of Overhelping

The overhelper assumes people cannot solve their own problems when indeed they can. He or she steps in with solutions without invitation. That keeps people weak, dependent on the overhelper. It 'gives them a fish'. This codependence captures a central theme of many abusive relationships. The overhelper takes the problem on so the person cannot solve it himself. If the secretary keeps covering for her alcoholic boss, he never has to take responsibility for his drinking. If the father keeps giving his adult daughter money, she never cuts the apron strings and learns independence. Both the helper and helpee need their roles, without them they would not have a job. They depend on each other; the overhelper needs to rescue, the helpee needs rescuing. Each one needs the other for their emotional survival. Overhelping costs helper and helpee alike.

The Cost to the Overhelper
If people are constantly overhelping others, the helpers can feel burdened. They can begin to feel stressed and exhausted. Over time, they may even burn out. And, when the overhelper spends time and energy on others, he or she does not have personal time.

Betsy S.
'I have no fun or time off. I'm on duty all the time. Lately, when I get a late-night call, I want to slam down the receiver. I don't want to listen any more.'

Betsy has not attended to her needs for so long that the resentment is welling up. She has started recovering from over-helping, because she is feeling resentment and anger at giving and getting nothing back. The feelings indicate that the healing has begun. You may begin having such feelings as you read this section and gain insight into your own pattern.

Let me quickly add that I do not mean to imply that people should not care and be kind to one another. On the contrary, I do think people should be compassionate, but we can offer support in a way that helps people be strong rather than weak.

The Cost to the Helpee
By now you probably have started seeing that overhelping breeds dependence. The person being overhelped does not learn Life Skills. I met a 25-year-old woman who did not know how to start a washing machine or make a bed, because her mother always did it. Moving into her own apartment, she was lost.

Brad S.
'I never did learn how to write a sentence because my dad took over doing my homework. I can't learn to write now; I wouldn't know where to begin.'

But more important than specific skills, the helpee does not feel able. People like Brad believe they are unable to solve their own problems.

WHAT YOU CAN DO
Teach People to Fish
After people stop overhelping, they need to learn to empower

others to help themselves. And they can focus on their own lives. But while overhelpers are making the shift, they may feel a loss.

Cheryl B.
One chronic overhelper cried, 'This rescuing has been so much my way of life, my identity, I don't know what to do with my time!'

Well, if you are not fixing or doing for people, what do you do? Give people back their own problems to solve and set limits on your helping. When you do this, you are communicating to them that they can do it, they are able.

1) Ask if your help is wanted.

2) Support people but don't do it for them.

3) Offer advice and answer questions, but don't give the solution.

4) Assist people in figuring out their way rather than manipulating them to do it your way.

These tools help people stand on their own two feet. Let us apply them to a parent, a wife, and a boss who have shifted from overhelping to empowering people to 'fish' for themselves.

Keith J.
'I told my son I'd answer his math questions, but he had to figure it out. I explained the concept, but he had to solve the problem. He was so used to me doing it that he bridled at my asking him to. But I could see he felt more confident. When he passed the test on his own, we both were proud.'

Shelly F.
'Before, I went shopping for my husband's clothes assuming he needed fixing. I never could figure out why he resented my big favor. Now I give him my ideas, but he decides what he wants. Funny thing . . . he looks great and we don't fight. We have more of an equal partnership.'

Wayne E.
'Now my managers come to me for advice, but I let them solve the problems.'

As you begin to:
1) Give back people's problems
2) Set limits
3) Teach people to fish
You may feel a little disoriented, like you are out of a job. You may even feel bored. That is normal. It will pass as you focus more on empowering rather then overhelping.

Put More Focus On You

Overhelpers fill their lives with others' problems so they do not have to deal with their own. If you overhelp, chances are you have not devoted much time to yourself. As you let go of overhelping, you can handle your own issues and have time for yourself. If you are burned out and resentful, you probably need to focus on you. Ask yourself:

● What could you do for yourself?

● What do you need?

ADDITIONAL CASES

Milly R.
At 45, Milly has a large psychotherapy practice. In addition, she writes articles and leads workshops. Her sunny nature shines through even on the phone. Over lunch she told me: 'My parents did not abuse me. As an only child trying to fit in, I was sure no one liked me. In sixth grade, I saw the best way to build the model oil refinery so I took over. The other kids hated me for it. I was smart and quick, but I had low self-esteem. So I needed to be seen for the brilliant plans and ideas. Mostly my ideas were right, but I forced them on the other kids.

'At home, once a year or so, a cousin or uncle stayed with us after surgery or an alcohol rehab program. I learned to enjoy caretaking: helping my mother make protein drinks and mid-morning snacks.

'Caring for people seemed natural, so I became a therapist. But I still felt *I was not good enough.* Even though I did good work, I felt I had to do 13 good deeds and 17 miracles daily, just to be at zero. Needless to say, my successful practice was not satisfying. And I burned out regularly.

'During my marriage I tried to improve and fix my husband. I know he resented it. I thought I knew what was good for him. After battling for 10 years, we are divorced.

'Then, in a workshop, I began examining my own thinking. At some point, I realized I was more than good enough. I ask before I give my opinion or advice. I stopped needing to be the hero in people's lives. I approve of myself so I don't need other people's approval.'

Christine J.
A high school teacher and 30, Christine usually sat in my waiting room grading papers, and came in talking fast and out of breath as if she never had enough time.

'My dad worked and my mother was confined to bed. I came

home from school, cooked, cleaned, shopped, and did homework. At one point, before we put my handicapped sister in a home, I took care of her. I worked starting in eighth grade. That helped buy clothes and extra things.

'I had no idea, when I left home at 23, that I was doing anything wrong or out of the ordinary. I loved being away from home, but I took on my boyfriends like home improvement projects. I did not see them as any different from my family. I drove 90 miles one night because one friend needed to talk. When I married I tried to solve my husband's problems. He could have had professional help a lot sooner if I had not tried to rescue him. At work my principal loved my go-get-em, but one time I conducted a meeting he should have led. I overstepped my boundaries and got my wrists slapped. Of course, I had a group of puppies (friends) who had money, job, and love problems. I ran my family, my classroom, and my marriage like a drill sergeant. Things got done, but I was not letting people do it themselves.

'In the Life Skills, I began to let up my resentment. Who was going to take care of me? What did I need? When was it my turn? And I had these people all dependent on me. I learned to offer my suggestions so they could solve their own messes. Some friends dropped away; my husband is thrilled; some friends made the change over with me. I have more time for me; I sleep better. I know when to quit and when to back off now.'

Kathleen N.

At 28, Kathleen managed regional theatrical productions – long hours, large responsibilities, and undefined tasks.

'No matter how big or how great the job, I tried to do more. As the oldest, I felt responsible for my parents. My step-dad was verbally and emotionally abusive to all of us. Oddly enough, he came to me for advice on how to handle his marriage. That started around nine years old. I became the peacekeeper. I'd explain to one sister why my brother was mad at her. I learned young to stick myself in the middle of someone else's problem.

'I was counselling my friends in elementary school. That way they'd like me. No one ever took care of me. But I didn't reveal anything about me.

'When I grew up, friends called me at 4 a.m., but no one asked how I was. Of course, I never told them or asked them for anything. I believed taking care of me was selfish. I took on production jobs without clarifying the hours or pay. I was giving my boss advice, talking to him at 2 a.m. My bosses asked me questions just like my father did. I felt needed.

'At my last job, my boss and I got into a terrible shouting match! I quit. I was so resentful and underpaid! I had no personal life or peace of mind. I took a stand tht I would not allow myself to be used. My overhelping was abusive to me. I started saying: This problem belongs to you. This is not mine. This is not appropriate.

'Now, at my new job, I negotiated a contract; I demanded certain pay and specific hours. I still thought I'd be punished, but they treat me nicely. Setting boundaries, the whole relationship changed. The boss likes and respects me. Instead of feeling abused, I feel productive, well-used.'

SUMMARY

- Overhelping keeps people weak so they do not learn to solve their own problems.

- Genuine helping empowers them to figure things out on their own.

- Some people learned to overhelp from a parent.

- Others learned to overhelp because they took on a parent role too soon.

- Overhelping can be necessary in an emergency when a person cannot make decisions for himself.

- To empower others, ask if your help is wanted; give suggestions rather than doing it for people.

QUESTIONS AND ASSIGNMENTS

1) Do you help without asking if it is wanted? Write down a time.

Examples:

I cleaned my friend's apartment without his asking me.

I arrived at a party two hours early to help the hostess.

I carry Band-aids, suntan lotion, and handiwipes in my purse and give them out to people when I see they need one.

_____

_____

2a) Did you learn to overhelp from a parent or adult? Which one?

_____

b) When did they overhelp you? How did you feel? Write down an incident.

Examples:

When I was in high school my mother threw out my old clothes without asking me. I was furious!

For my eighth-grade assignment my father made my map of Europe, not me. It stood out like a sore thumb. I was so embarrassed!

_____

_____

3) Do you think people's lives would fall apart if you were not holding them together? Write down the things you do that you believe hold other people together.

Examples:

If I didn't shop for my husband, I think he'd starve and go naked.

If I didn't call my mother every morning and evening, I think she'd die of loneliness.

I have to listen to my friend even when I don't want to, because I think she'd get hysterical if I didn't.

I would have divorced my wife years ago, but I stay married because I think she would go crazy.

_____

_____

_____

4) When you help, what are you looking for? Approval, love, or self-esteem?

Examples:

I helped my friend move, not because I wanted to, but because she'd like me better.

I don't need the money, but I work overtime so my boss will like me.

_____

5) How does overhelping limit the people around you? Write down other ways you see it limiting.

Examples:

My son doesn't learn how to use the library.

My friend doesn't get to figure it out for herself.

It keeps them dependent.

They don't learn for themselves.

They don't stand on their own two feet.

My manager never has to take responsibility for his mistakes, if I'm always fixing them for him.

_____

_____

6) Before you offer help, ask first if it is wanted. Practice that daily.

7) The next time you offer help, notice your motives. Are you expecting love, approval, or acceptance? Write down what you discovered.

_____

_____

8a) Practice using these sentences, modifying them to your needs:
Can I offer you a suggestion?

Would you like my assistance or advice?

Try solving it yourself first, then call me if you get stuck.

I have an idea about that, but let's see if you can come up with one.

b) What else could you say?

_____

_____

9a) If you have taken on a problem that really belongs to your child, spouse, or co-workers, give it back to them.

Examples:

I see that I've taken over trying to plan your party. It's really your party; you should be the one organizing it. If you have a job for me let me know.

I realize I've been taking your job away from you by going on sales calls. I trust you to do a good job and ask for help when you need it. I won't go unless you ask me to.

If I do your research for your paper, I'm not helping you in the long run. I'll take you to the library but I won't do it for you.

FURTHER READING
AXLINE, Virginia M.
Dibs in Search of Self (New York, Ballantine books, 1964).

BEATTIE, Melody.
Codependent No More (New York, Harper/Hazelden, 1987).

BLAKE, Dr Karen.
Born to Please: Compliant Women and Controlling Men (New York, St Martin's Press, 1988).

LEMAN, Dr Kevin.
The Pleasers (New York, Dell, 1987).

CHAPTER 13

Not Needing to be Perfect

GOALS

• To recognize the need to be perfect

• To realize that human beings are imperfect

• To begin to allow yourself to be human, to make mistakes, to fail

• To consider evaluating things based on what is needed and appropriate, rather than comparing them with being perfect

For this discussion, I define the need to be perfect as striving for something impossible, never winning, always falling short. A man receiving a 95 percent evaluation deemed himself a failure because he did not receive 100 percent. An actress who did not get a part punished herself by practicing until she dropped from exhaustion. Another man so feared that he would not do a perfect job, he never began anything. Striving to do your best can be exciting and invigorating and healthy; always needing to be perfect can create stress and sometimes stress-related health problems.

This chapter helps you recognize the need to be perfect and its cost. It offers you more healthy and satisfying choices.

WHAT SURVIVORS MISSED
Pitfalls of Being Perfect

Accomplishment oriented people can take their achieving too far, demanding of themselves the perfect performance, the perfect body, the perfect job, the perfect children, and the perfect relationship. These people drive themselves to perfection, never meeting unattainable standards. They never enjoy the satisfaction of accomplishments because they always fall short of achieving their impossible goals.

Because people who need to be perfect often over-achieve, bosses do not see anything wrong. On the contrary, employers usually love perfectionists because they produce high-quality work. But friends and spouses may see the stress and exhaustion. However, perfect people do not always reveal their problems. That would mean they were not perfect. They secretly fear someone will find out they are not perfect. Keeping up this front means that friends as well as the 'perfect' person can have difficulty knowing anything is wrong.

Trying to Be Perfect in an Abusive Household
The perfectionist who comes from an abusive family often believes: *If I am not perfect, something dreadful will happen.* And often it does. Trying to take control of an uncontrollable situation, this child decides that being perfect would make things better.

Irv S.
'I felt if I were perfect everything would turn out all right. But, of course, it never did. Dad still hit Mom and me. I thought if I were good enough it would stop. I could never figure out Dad's system for punishing us. I kept trying to be perfect, but it did not make any difference.'

OLD PATTERNS
Some children learn to strive for perfection from their parents. When parents model being perfect, their children learn those habits. The drive to be perfect becomes part of the child's personal style. When a parent becomes abusive, the perfectionism goes 'hay-wire'. Dad forced the children to sweep the kitchen floor six times to get it right. Mom forced her six-year old to sit at the dinner table two extra hours until he ate with correct table manners. Needless to say, one person grew up cleaning compulsively; the other never cleans at all.

Four Attempts at Control
In an abusive family, being perfect becomes a Survival Strategy, a feeble attempt to control the abuse. The child – trying to control the situation – decides to be perfect and good, hoping to make a difference. This type of child believes one or more of the following:

1 If I am good and perfect, it will change things.

2 If I'm perfect, I'll conceal that I'm imperfect and therefore bad.

3 If I'm perfect enough, I'll avoid mistakes, criticism and punishment.

4 If I'm perfect I won't get punished.

All four can drive the perfect person to reach towards his or her unattainable standards. And these beliefs create problems. Let us explore each one in turn.

1 Being the good child

Without realizing its implications, parents can put incredible pressure on their children when they demand their kids be good examples or models. Dad saying: 'Other kids look up to you. You need to be a shining star'. One client heard those instructions as *I can't be upset, look sloppy, or mess up*. And he still demands that of himself as an adult.

Edwin K.
'My brother began drinking when he was 14. He was awfully angry and out of control. I became everything he wasn't. I danced, sang, played the clarinet, and always smiled. I tried to make my parents happy, although I was unhappy inside. Now my friends think things are just fine with me. I don't let my bad feelings show. And its hard for me to ask for help.'

2 Perfect to conceal being imperfect

Margerita R.
'I thought if I were perfect that would make up for what was wrong with me. I studied very hard for grades at school; I did extra credit projects. But that never impressed my father. And I still felt bad about myself. In adult relationships, when I get close to someone, I have a dreadful fear they will see my flaws.'

Margerita keeps the perfect façade together so no one will find out that she is imperfect, or more precisely, that something is wrong with her. Of course, all human beings are imperfect. But people who need to be perfect do not have room to be human.

3 Avoiding mistakes and criticism

The child who has been raised trying to meet unattainable standards can have a fear of making mistakes, or fear of failure, or fear of criticism:

Johanna I.
'I think ahead to what my boss might find wrong with my work, then I fix it. I dread his finding a mistake. He rarely does, but I'm in knots all the time.'

The perfect child then tries to avoid mistakes, failing, and criticism. This leaves very little room for fun, experimenting, trying something new, beginning without being an expert.

4 If I'm perfect I won't get punished

For these children being perfect is a feeble attempt to control their abuse.

Debra L.
'After I got slapped for looking like a slut, I'd go scrub my face so I could get it off. I was six years old. I tried so hard to be what they wanted, so hard to be perfect. Nothing worked.'

WHAT YOU CAN DO
Allow Your Feelings
Now let us put the focus back on to you. If you are someone who needs to be perfect you may be very upset reading this. You may think: *I'm bad because I'm not perfect.* This may lead you to feel angry at yourself, at this book, or at me. Allow yourself to have those feelings and thoughts.

Don't Compare
Another perfectionist's trap is comparing yourself with others. Some might think, 'I'm not as perfect as the people in this chapter', or *'Wanting* to be perfect means I'm not perfect'. Here are some suggestions for working with yourself:
1 Do not let those feelings stop you from growing and moving forward. Have the feelings and continue to grow.

2 Do not measure yourself against the people in this book or in your life and assess yourself as lacking or not perfect enough.

Remind Yourself: I'm Doing My Best
When you notice these thoughts, realize you cannot win. Stop and remind yourself: *I'm human and imperfect; I'm doing my best.* Continue examining your pattern using the concepts in this section.

Give Yourself Permission
When you make a mistake, that does not mean you *are* a mistake or you will be punished. Your behavior does not mean you are a failure or a bad person. Give yourself permission to make mistakes.

Grow Gently
You do not have to create a crisis – have your job, health, or relationships fall apart as these three women did – to recognize your pattern of perfectionism. You can begin to learn gently, gaining insights into yourself through other people's stories.

Ask Yourself: Do I Want To?
The drive for perfection became a set-up for burning out and being a 'work-a-holic'. Ask yourself, *Am I doing this because I want to do it perfectly or because I feel I have to?* This will help you to learn to discern between your choices that are driven and ones that are for enjoyment.

ADDITIONAL CASES
Roxanne

At 44, Roxanne dressed impeccably with matching shoes, purse, and just the right jewelry. She told me she would not buy beige shoes because she could not afford to buy the beige purse to match.

'Both my mother and father were perfectionists. Being perfect is part of my nature. When Dad was drinking, he exploded. I decided if I could just be perfect enough, Dad would not yell at me. Later in life, I tried to be perfect so people would not get mad at me.

'In school I got 'A's, I was the head of the class. But I never felt successful. Maybe I would feel happy for a second, but I'd raise my standard and then have more to do. I saw only my mistakes, not my accomplishments. I was never satisfied.

'Managing a large corporate department, I always received outstanding evaluations. But I never let up on myself. I lived in fear that I had forgotten something important. I stayed awake nights trying to predict and solve unforseen problems. I could not turn my mind off. I began to suffer from headaches and chronic fatigue. Finally, I had to take a year off and recover my health.

'I saw what being perfect was taking out of me. I began to let go. I saw the double bind I had put myself in. I realized others did not see the 'glaring errors' I saw; they did not even care. Now I can do something perfectly if I want to, not because I have to. People are more important to me than being perfect. A friend can stop by when my house is not clean. Before, I would just say, 'No, don't come'. When I notice I'm worrying over work, I can stop myself. I ask myself, 'Am I doing this because I enjoy doing it perfectly, or because I have to?' '

Juliette

At 24, this tall black woman was trying to become a model. Although she did not make lots of money, she coordinated all of her outfits – the pale green crepe blouse with the kitty-kit bow, the darker green skirt, the matching earrings and necklace. She told me how she learned to be perfect: 'When I was growing up in the 1970s the Black Power movement was at its peak. We were the first black family to move to our suburban Chicago neighborhood; I was the first black student in my grammar school; I was the first black piano student, and so on. We had the 'good life'. Mom and Dad told us we had to be the perfect family; we were an example. I became the perfect kid. I dressed right; I practiced the piano; I was a cheerleader.

'Behind this façade, Mom and Dad both beat us. My father called the cops 'pigs', but he beat me from the time I was eight until I graduated from high school. Once he beat Mom so badly she was hospitalized.

'I was the oldest of five, and I felt responsible; I had to set a perfect example. I felt I might be able to control the violence if I was perfect enough. He might not hit my younger sisters. I was terribly confused.

'As an adult I would just keep taking work from my boss, saying *Yes, I can do that*, when I had no idea how I would. I lied to cover my behind. I could not tell I was being overworked and abused. My boss finally fired me.

'I did everything I could, but I knew I could do more. I lived in dreadful fear of being found out and punished. I set myself up to be abused by three different bosses.

'I hit bottom. I was depressed and down on myself. In therapy, I began to see messing up with humor. I started having regard for myself and my growing. I let go of my huge expectations. I'm feeling good about myself. I don't need to prove or perform. But I can if I want to. I feel free. I just started back playing the piano, but this time my music is for me, not for a performance.'

Louise

Louise, 45, came into my office in overalls, a baggy, faded T-shirt, and old sneakers. She was 80 lbs overweight. She told me she had once weighed 110 lbs.

'Mom was the perfect mother and housekeeper. You could eat off her kitchen floor, although she said it wasn't clean enough. I think she overdid it to make up for Dad's drinking and craziness. We all walked on egg-shells, pretending that being perfect might make Dad less demanding and abusive. While he was watching the football game no one was allowed to talk, but he could talk on the phone so loud we could not hear.

'I learned her standards; I sang in the choir, got good grades and joined all the right school clubs. I dressed elegantly; I had a trim figure. Looking back, I felt an inner panic as if I had to hold up the sky or it would fall.

'When I was 21 I fell in love with the perfect man. I tried to be perfect for him. Then he tried to kill me. While I was hospitalized for six weeks, I realized my perfect world was falling apart. The next year I wore overalls and T-shirts, gained 50 lbs. I even worked the night shift so I would not have to see people. During uncontrollable rages, I threw ash trays, bowls, cups – never at people, always at the wall. All those years of anger were finally erupting. With a hospital therapist, I realized I had been so emotionally involved and so driven to please, I could not make good, objective judgments.

'I trained as a secretary; gradually I stopped beating myself up for making typos and I left bosses who did. I try to see what is appropriate and needed and not what is perfect. I don't need to prove I'm o.k. or talented; I know I am. The things I do are not earning me self-esteem points, but they satisfy me. I would love to have a perfect home and wardrobe again, but I know it's more important to feel my feelings, not to lie, to have supportive friendships. I shifted my values from pretence to what is really important.

SUMMARY

- Needing to be perfect means striving to meet unattainable standards and never winning.

- The abused child often believes *If I am perfect things will be better and I won't get punished.*

- He or she tries to control things by being good or avoiding mistakes.

- The demand to be perfect can lead to stress, health problems, and eventual burn out.

- Don't compare yourself to others.

- Tell yourself, *I'm doing my best.*

- Give yourself permission to make mistakes.

- Ask yourself, Am I doing this because I want to do it perfectly or because I feel I have to?

QUESTIONS AND ASSIGNMENTS

1) Do you feel you have to look perfect at all times?

Yes ____No ____

2) Do you think someone will yell at you if you do not behave perfectly?

Yes ____No ____

3a) There is a big difference between doing something bad and concluding you are bad because you did something bad. Survivors often think they are bad if their behavior is bad. Do you feel that if you are not perfect you are a bad person?

Yes ____No ____

b) Write down an example from your life.

Examples:

The dinner I made was a flop; I thought I was a bad wife.

My friend said I let her down; I thought I was a bad person.

_____

_____

4) What price do you pay for driving yourself to be perfect? Headaches, no sleep, loss of friends, pressure, no enjoyment?

_____

_____

5a) Write down your beliefs about being perfect.

Examples

If I'm not perfect I'll be punished.

If I'm not perfect people won't like me.

If I'm perfect Mom won't drink.

If I'm perfect Mom and Dad won't fight.

If I'm perfect people won't find out how flawed I am.

_____

_____

b) Rewrite each belief as a more freeing one.

Examples:

Getting punished as a child had nothing to do with my being perfect.

People like me for me, not because of my perfect behavior.

Mom's drinking has nothing to do with my being perfect.

Mom and Dad fight whether I'm perfect or not.

I'm a good person, including my flaws.

_____

6a) Mistakes are opportunities to learn. When you make a mistake it does not mean that *you are* a mistake. The more freedom you give yourself to make mistakes, the more you can learn. Close your eyes and visualize yourself making a mistake. See yourself apologizing or cleaning it up. Now mentally ask, 'What did I learn from this?' Notice that you are not getting punished. You may feel afraid at first. You are safe.

Examples:

I saw myself making a mistake at work. I felt foolish and afraid. In my mind, my manager just said, 'Well, you won't do that again'. I won't either. But no one yelled or sent me to my room.

I saw my husband discovering I had not written down a check in the checkbook. He told me he was angry, but I survived. I'll remember next time.

I saw myself taking home the wrong brief for my trial the next day. I called my partner at home, explained, went over and made a copy off his copy. I didn't die; I just figured out a way to fix it.

b) Write down your experience and what you learned from your mistake.

7a) When you feel driven to do something perfectly ask yourself, 'Am I doing this because I want to or because I have to?'

Examples:

I could have retyped my paper at 2 a.m. and had it look better, but I would have lost sleep before my final exam. So I went to bed.

I wanted my daughter to keep her dress clean, perfect . . . but she was having so much fun. I just threw it in the wash when she came home.

b) Write, 'Am I doing this because I want to or because I have to?' on an index card. Put it on the mirror or desk to remind yourself.

FURTHER READING

DOWLING, Colette.
Perfect Women: Hidden Fears of Inadequacy and the Drive to Perform (Summit Books, 1988).

FANNING, Tony and Robbie.
Get It All Done and Still Be Human (New York, Ballantine Books, 1979).

WEISNER, Dr Hendrie and LOBSENZ, Norma M.
Nobody's Perfect: How to Give and Criticize and Get Results (New York, Warner Books, 1981).

SECTION FIVE

Relating Positively to Others

You have already broken many abusive patterns. This section assists in breaking two destructive habits: being addicted to danger and lying. Chapter 14 helps you break the attraction to dangerous forms of excitement. Chapter 15 talks about lying, its impact on you and relationships, and the benefits of telling the truth. When you free yourself from these habits, you can build positive relationships with others. Chapter 16 helps you develop friendships based on mutual respect and caring, rather than abuse and co-dependence.

CHAPTER 14

Managing Your Addictive Nature

GOALS
- To learn if you have an addictive nature

- To take responsibility for it

- To discuss the addiction to danger and to work

- To explore ways to connect with yourself so your need for an addiction lessens

My 'guestimate' is that most people who are alcoholics, drug addicts, sex or gambling addicts, were abused. I have no way of proving that, but the people recovering from major addictions that I have met have all had an abusive past. They used their addiction as a Survival Strategy to cover up their pain. People with severe addictions such as alcohol, drugs or sex should, as I have mentioned, join a 12-step program. I discuss less toxic addictions – people who binge on their emotions, who are addicted to unhealthy relationships, being perfect or suffering or sex – in other chapters.

Here I examine the addictive nature underneath these addictions. Often, after an addict stops drinking or using, he or she just becomes addicted to something else – work, shopping, food. Jacquelyn Small calls these 'soft addictions' – addictions that are legal, less toxic and take longer to do their damage. Sometimes these people have dual or multiple addictions. These survivors have an addictive nature. Once they break themselves of their more lethal addictions, they refocus their addictive nature on something not as deadly. So their compulsive nature drives them to find another addiction.

In this chapter, I discuss two addictions – danger and work. These may not be yours, but you will probably see yourself in the examples. And you can use the tools for managing your addictive nature no matter what your addiction.

WHAT SURVIVORS MISSED

Whether learned or inherited, addictions often run in families. If you have an addiction, your parents and/or siblings probably do too. You may want to make a list of your extended family members and write down their addictions next to their names. This will give you a very personal picture of how addictions as well as abuse is generational.

So, as a survivor, you probably had many models for addictive behavior. And you learned to avoid pain, suppress feelings and remain unconscious. Addictions then help keep you from connecting with your true self. This may have been useful in an abusive family, but this breeds mental and physical problems later in life.

OLD PATTERNS

Now let us look at two addictions that society holds as less harmless than alcohol or drugs. Unfortunately, they are also socially acceptable. The person addicted to danger can be viewed as a risk-taker and adventurer. The workaholic is often a valued employee. But these addictions may be subtly dangerous and limiting your growth.

1 Addiction to Danger

Survivors who are addicted to danger are often unconscious about their own personal safety. They did not learn how to judge situations and people as safe or unsafe. Riding on a roller coaster has safety precautions. Driving 100 mph while drinking does not. These people risk their mental and physical well-being for the 'high' they get from danger. Their addiction to danger overrides their common sense. Because they find the danger exciting, even addictive, they purposely seek out dangerous situations and people.

Ross J.

While growing up, Ross's family had violent fights. Cups of hot coffee went hurling across the kitchen. As a child, Ross walked up to his father and took the cup, the knife, the hammer out of his father's hand just before Dad was about to throw it. As an adult, he once walked into a bar and walked between two drunks fighting. He stopped the fight but had no idea of the danger to himself. At 29, Ross still gets thrills from dangerous situations.

'My friends and I wanted to see how much action we could pack into one night. We drove fast with nine guys in the car. We switched drivers while the car was going full speed. We drank beer and smoked pot. We were hooked on excitement. Five years ago, we crashed a car and killed one of my buddies.'

Ross stopped driving recklessly only after his buddy was killed. But he took up hang-gliding. In therapy he began to see his need for excitement could be separated from his endangering himself. People who put themselves in dangerous situations jeopardize their safety. Such people could be physically hurt while they are seeking that dangerous thrill. The key to overcoming this addiction is to learn the difference between dangerous and exciting. Excitement is the result of action, stimulation, movement. On the other hand, danger is excitement that can result in harm or injury. You can find activities that are exciting but not perilous.

2 Addiction to Work

This addiction is far too common in our achievement-oriented culture. The workaholic is obsessed with getting ahead, doing more than his co-worker, beating the competition. This person takes winning too seriously, thinks about work and performance all the time, never allows himself off-duty time. He feels his self-worth is on the line with each failure or success. His life revolves around work excluding family, friends and fun.

Unfortunately, certain employers seek out the willing workaholics. For example, a law firm hires a new attorney paying him or her a high salary but adding, 'We own you now. That means unlimited overtime, taking work home and working weekends. If you want to be a partner someday, that's what's required.'

Now, what is the difference between just working hard and being a workaholic? The workaholic is driven to overwork; he or she has no choice about it. The hard worker can choose to put in 18 hours a day on a special project, but can then let go and relax when he has finished the job. He or she integrates relationships and other interests into a balanced life.

Chuck T.

At 38, Chuck was a recovering alcholic and worked in a large law firm heading the computer department. He put in at least 12 hours daily. He had designed their computer system and soon began consulting at other law firms. Even though he earned good money, he had no time to spend or enjoy it. His wife and little girl rarely saw him. Coming from a dysfunctional and abusive family, Chuck never learned to express his emotions. After he gave up alcohol, work became his drug, his way of avoiding his anger and deep fear of failure. He escaped into his work rather than facing his fear of intimacy and people. If he was not talking about computerizing the legal profession, he was not talking at all. Only when his wife threatened to leave him, did he agree to see a therapist.

WHAT YOU CAN DO
Intervene in Your Addiction to Danger
Many survivors who are addicted to danger know the risk but endanger themselves anyway. To break up their addiction to danger takes four steps:

1 Recognize the danger
If you do not see danger clearly, ask a trusted friend to evaluate a situation or person for you. Then train yourself to see what your friend sees.

2 Decide the danger is too costly a risk
The next step requires that you see the cost when you flirt with danger. You do not need to have your life threatened or be hospitalized to recognize potential danger. You can decide reading about others. You can decide to stop endangering yourself while reading this book.

3 Remove yourself from the danger
Then when dangerous situations arise or you are with dangerous people you can remove yourself or call for help.

4 Seek excitement that minimizes danger
You can find jobs and activities that offer excitement without risking your safety. The exercises at the end of the chapter will help you implement these four steps.

Intervene in Your Workaholic Behavior
1 Recognize your addiction to work
To begin handling your addiction you must recognize you have one first. If you feel driven to work and feel little choice about it, you are probably addicted. Your friends and family have probably complained about your long hours.

2 Realize the cost is too great
Ask yourself what does working so much cost you?

3 Be willing to confront what you are avoiding
Overworking can be a way of avoiding feelings, confronting fears, or people, or yourself.

4 Learn to relax
Take time – even just a few moments – each day to relax and breathe deeply. Enjoy the blue sky, the grass or a tree.

5 Ask yourself: do I have to or do I choose to?
When you are going to put in extra hours, ask yourself: do I have to do this, or am I choosing to do this?

Connect With Yourself
To connect with yourself, begin by feeling your emotions, consciously breathing and sensing what is happening in your body. When you are getting compulsive about something, stop and take 5 long, slow breaths. Ask yourself what am I feeling emotionally and in my body? You can train yourself to interrupt your compulsive thinking.

SUMMARY
- Certain adult survivors have an addictive nature.

- After they have stopped drinking or using drugs, they become addicted to less toxic things: work, shopping, sugar.

- People who are addicted to work or danger can break their habit.

- People can learn the difference between excitement and danger.

- They can interrupt their compulsive thinking by breathing and staying in touch with themselves.

QUESTIONS AND ASSIGNMENTS
1a) List the things you are and have been addicted to.

Examples:

Time

French fries

5'2" blondes that are mean

Shining my shoes

Being on time

Alcohol

_____

_____

_____

b) List the names of your immediate and extended family. Next to their names list their addictions.

Example:

Mom – compulsively neat, suffering, addicted to food and sugar.

Dad – alcohol, cigarettes, perfectionist

Curt – alcohol, time, workaholic

Aunt Franny – alcohol, rage-aholic, cigarettes

Uncle Bert – cigars, coffee, sugar

Cousin Barb – Being on time, compulsively clean, workaholic

_____

_____

_____

_____

_____

2) Do you find you need danger daily or else you do not feel alive?

Yes ____No ____

3a) If you need excitement in your life, consider separating the danger from excitement. Try skiing, water-skiing, racket ball, squash, ballooning, para-sailing, roller coaster riding. Find activities that are safe yet exciting.

b) Make a list of activities you can do that are exciting but not dangerous.

_____

_____

_____

4a) If you are a person who has been attracted to dangerous relationships, ask yourself; are you ready to change?

Yes ____No ____

b) What does the danger cost you? Write it here.

Examples:

My boyfriend drives his car too fast. I'm juiced, but we have been close to car crashes many times.

My friends live so close to the edge, they don't have any time to just hang out and be. I don't have any peace of mind.

---

c) Start a friendship or relationship that has positive, non-dangerous qualities. Write down what is positive about this person.

Examples:

My friend Susan lets me finish a sentence. She cares about me.

I feel safe.

This person is predictable.

I know I'll be taken care of.

---

d) Know that you may feel bored or uninterested because this relationship lacks danger and familiarity. When that happens write down your experience.

Example:

I know Susan is nice, but she is so bland and good.

I feel safe, but bored.

I know exactly what is going to happen, but it feels like something is wrong.

I feel disoriented.

---

e) Realize you may crave the danger, but that is not going to give a satisfying relationship. Write down what you do want.

Examples:

I want someone who I can depend on — someone nice. I see that the men I have been attracted to cannot give that to me. I have to start looking for other things.

I am attracted to this person but I know his crazy life-style would just get me in trouble again.

_____

_____

5) Do your friends and family complain that you work too much?

Yes _____ No _____

6) Do you feel driven to work, even when your boss does not ask you?

Yes _____ No _____

7) What does being a workaholic cost you?

Examples:
   Friends

   My relationship with my son

   Fun

   Stomach aches and tight jaws

   Headaches

   Sleepless nights

   Happiness

_____

_____

_____

8) If you were not working, what would you have to face?

Examples:
   Fear of people

   A failing marriage

   Being alone

   Not being good enough

_____

_____

9) One time this week, consciously decide to stop working and do something else, e.g. go home at 9 p.m. instead of 10 p.m.

10) Centering and focusing on your breathing look deceptively simple. However, doing this exercise 10 minutes twice daily can help you break compulsive thinking and feel more calm and centered.

Sit comfortably with your feet flat on the floor uncrossed and hands resting comfortably on your lap uncrossed. Close your eyes and take a long, deep breath. As you breathe out, put your hand on your stomach and let the exhalation push your hand out. Breathe in and follow the air rushing into your lungs. As you breathe out, let the air push your hand out as your stomach expands. Continue focusing your attention on your breathing and follow your breath in and out easily and gently for 10 minutes. If your mind wanders, bring your attention back to your breathing.

FURTHER READING

BEATTIE, Melody.
   Codependent No More (New York, Harper/Hazelden, 1987).

HAYES, Jody.
   Smart Love: A Codependence Recovery Program Based on Relationship Addictions Support Groups (Los Angeles: Tarcher, 1989).

NAKKEN, Craig.
   The Addictive Personality: Roots, Rituals and Recovery (Center City, Minn.: Hazelden Foundation, 1988).

PADUS, Emrika.
   Your Emotions and Your Health (Chapter 41, 'From Compulsion to Free Choice') (Emmaus, Penn.: Rodale Press, 1986).

SMALL Jacquelyn.
   The Therapist of the Future: Transformers (Marina del Rey, Cal.: DeVorss & Company, 1982).

CHAPTER 15

Telling the Truth

GOALS
- To help you realize you may still lie because you fear punishment
- To assist you in seeing you may lie to bolster your self-esteem
- To help you recognize what lying costs
- To suggest telling the truth as a new habit

Some survivors learned to lie to minimize their abuse. They may still lie because they fear punishment or to bolster weak self-esteem. But lying has a cost; people do not trust a person who lies. And that person loses self-respect.

WHAT SURVIVORS MISSED
Telling the Truth Can Still Look Dangerous
People from abusive homes may have been conditioned to fear telling the truth. Their parents did not encourage honesty by making it safe. Adult survivors can still be deathly afraid of telling the truth.

Nathan M.
Several years ago, Nathan, who managed a purchasing department, left me a message cancelling our regular session. The message said he had a death in the family. When I called his office to reschedule our appointment, the secretary told me he was home ill. I called home and reached an obviously sick man. I began the conversation, 'You sound terrible!'

I was about to catch this otherwise very responsible man in a lie. I wanted him to know he was still safe. Rather than saying, 'Why did you lie?' I said, 'All you had to do was tell me you were sick. Are you all right?'

'Yes. I'm O.K. I didn't think you'd believe me if I told you I was sick.'

I said, 'Why not?'

'Well, my mother never believed me when I was sick. She said I was faking. She'd send me to school with a fever; the nurse would send me home; then I'd get punished for getting my mom in trouble with the school. It's easier to lie to you.'

I continued, 'You don't have to lie to me. I won't punish you. I want you to feel comfortable telling me anything. And you are even safe when you lie to me.'

The words seemed obvious to me, but not to him. When he recovered and came in for his next session, we explored how lying protected him. He saw his whole pattern. And – over the next weeks – that perhaps he did not need that protection now. The adults in his life never rewarded him for telling the truth, rather he was punished for it.

OLD PATTERNS
Parents Who Don't Want to Hear the Truth
Some children learned to lie because their parents did not want to hear the truth. Children learn this very early. Such adults do not want to admit the truth to themselves so they cannot acknowledge it to their children.

Rick J.
'I knew my mother did not want to know how I really felt. She wanted to know I was happy. So that's what I told her. Now when my boss asks if things are under control, I always say Yes. And they rarely are.'

Sylvia C.
'I told my mother Dad was coming into my bed at night. She slapped me and told me not to talk about my father that way. I quit telling her. I didn't tell anyone I was molested until I called an abuse hotline last month.'

Rick and Sylvia learned to tell adults what would appease them, not what happened or what was really going on. By the time they grew up, their lying habit was firmly in place.

Exaggerating to Bolster Low Self-Esteem
Here, the adult survivor whose self-esteem is low elaborates on the truth, attempting to increase self-esteem. But, of course, the lying ultimately undermines self-esteem.

Shanna C.
'I let friends think I'd been a faculty member at a university when I

taught a summer workshop on campus. I told a woman I wanted to impress I was in an auto accident, but I survived. I really just dented the fender. I said I had a rare disease, when the doctor was treating me for a rash. I figured she'd feel sorry for me and like me.'

This woman felt she had to embellish her history so people would like her. Just being herself was not good enough. This sets up relationships based on deception. The survivor who is exaggerating is usually well-aware of his lying, and that lowers self-worth. So the lying to increase self-esteem backfires, leaving the person feeling worse.

What Lying Costs
Lying may still look like a good idea from time to time; however, it has consequences.

Eroding Self-Image
Here is a simple example of what happened when Robert, who already suffered from low self-esteem, lied.

Robert C.
'I knew I shouldn't use the office phone to make personal long distance calls. Even though I told my boss I wouldn't, I did it anyway. I was careless and my boss overheard me. I felt terrible about myself.'

Punishing Yourself
Sometimes people feel so badly that they have lied that they punish themselves.

Janie S.
'I told my department manager I was sick, when I just needed a day off. Immediately I noticed I wanted ice cream, lots of it. I had to go clean it up with her, or I know I would have binged. I've been doing well in Overeaters Anonymous for 2 years; my lies risk too much.'

Undermining Trust
But lying also does damage to relationships. People learn quickly not to trust a person who lies. The liar cannot be counted on. Most people presume that a liar will just as eaily lie again.

Howard P.
'I took a vacation day on a business trip without telling my wife. She found out. Now she's suspicious when I travel.'

Emotionally Pressuring Yourself
When a person who believes lying is bad does indeed lie, he or she falls short of personal standards. And when the person violates those standards, he or she suffers. Lying puts the person

who lies under emotional pressure. Will people find out? Will I have to lie again? What will people think of me?

Sally L.
'I told my mother we were not coming for Christmas dinner because we were going to Frank's parents. Then I had to tell Dad the same lie. Then I had to tell Frank not to mention it. Then I worried my mother-in-law would tell my mother we were having a quiet Christmas at home. The aggravation was not worth it.'

When you lie, people begin to question your honesty and integrity. They anticipate other lies. You can only rebuild broken trust by telling the truth.

WHAT YOU CAN DO
Appreciate How Lying Served You
For abused people, lying helped them survive. If you are one of those people, appreciate how it has served you.

Confront Your Fear of Telling the Truth
Understand why you may be afraid to tell the truth. The child who lied to stay safe does not need to now.

Recognize the Cost
It may look scary, but lying has consequences on the job, in your home, and relationships. It erodes self-esteem, damages trust, and creates needless worry. Sometimes people even punish themselves.

Acknowledge the Benefits of Telling the Truth
When you do tell the truth, you feel good about yourself. You are establishing yourself as a person people can count on to tell the truth. You can stop worrying, just as Jennifer did.

Jennifer D.
'I made a list of the lies I'd told. Then I started communicating the truth to those people I'd lied to. The stuff I lied about was minor, but it occupied my mind. After I finished each conversation, I felt less worried, more peaceful. There's more room for me.'

When you honestly reveal your mistakes, people usually respond positively. Confronting your fears, you are building a new reality that you will not be abused. You are building inner strength. Others trust you and know they can count on you. Knowing that about yourself gives you pride and a sense of competence.

ADDITIONAL CASES
Mel G.
Mel, 52, entangled herself in a web of lies at work. To help his

therapist understand, he related how lying was woven into everyday life.

'When I was in high school, the teacher asked each of us who was coming back next year. I told her our family was moving. And we were. We'd sold our house and were moving to the next town. When I got home, my parents were outraged. Why did you tell her that? We don't want anyone to know 'that kind of stuff'. I was beaten for telling the truth. Throughout my childhood my parents implied or overtly suggested that telling the truth was not such a good idea.

'When I started working, I told little lies to get out of tight spots. As part of one job, I managed a $200 petty cash fund. I 'borrowed' that money many times and paid it back a month or two later. At another job, I had a very abusive boss. I knew I had to get out of there. I let him think I embezzled $3,000, so he had to fire me. I lost friends and colleagues did not trust me. I did not take any money, but I felt I had to lie to create an escape. It never occurred to me that I could just walk away. It cost me friends, reputation, and my own self-respect.

'After that I realized I had to take a hard look at my values and how I was not living up to them. I examined my behavior for a couple of months, and finally, I took a stand to tell the truth. At times it's hard, but I do it anyway.

Patricia K.
'My step-father hit me regularly. One evening at dinner he decked me across the dining room table. The chair broke underneath me and I hit my jaw on the foor. The next day the school counselor noticed the bruise. I told her the story and others like it. She called the police. The officer took my statement and told me if I wanted to press charges I would have to testify against my step-father. I would break up our family if I told the truth about him. I just couldn't do that.'

Now Patricia is 24 and looking for her first job.

'In the Life Skills I didn't think I had a lying problem. But over several weeks I find it so frightening to tell interviewers just what I've done. I want to make up things. I fear that if I just tell the truth something will happen. Recognizing what happened with the police, I am less anxious. When I see interviewers responding positively to my credentials, I know the fear is from my past. I'm letting go of it.'

Mel and Patricia saw the consequences of lying and retrained themselves to tell the truth. Communicating honestly takes courage and practice, but they gained self-respect. People around them can count on them to be honest.

SUMMARY

- Adult survivors sometimes lie to avoid punishment, feel safe, or keep things under control.

- People can exaggerate the truth to make themselves more interesting and attempt to increase self-esteem.

- Telling the truth can look dangerous.

- When people lie they usually punish themselves in some way.

- Others cannot count on a person who lies.

- Telling the truth promotes closeness and trust with others and inner strength and pride in yourself.

QUESTIONS AND ASSIGNMENTS

1a) Did you get punished severely for telling the truth?

Yes _____ No _____

b) Write down an example.

Examples:
   I told Mom I stole five dollars from her purse. I gave it back, but she grounded me for six months.

   I pretended I was sick. When I told my parents, they spanked me and made me go to my room after school for two weeks.

_____

_____

2) Do you regularly exaggerate stories so people will like you?

Yes _____ No _____

3a) Do you lie because you fear punishment?

Yes _____ No _____

b) What are you afraid will happen?

Examples:
   I'll get the strap.

   I'll get yelled at.

I'll get fired.

My friend won't talk to me.

---

c) Is that a real fear any more?

Yes _____ No _____

4a) Do you leave out critical details so people do not know the whole truth?

Yes _____ No _____

b) Name a time when you did that.

Examples:

I told my husband I went shopping; I didn't tell him how much money I spent.

I told my daughter Daddy was going on a trip. I didn't tell her we were getting divorced and he wasn't coming back.

5a) Go back and tell the truth to someone you lied to. What happened?

Examples:

I told my co-worker I lied about finishing a job. He said he knew anyway. I was relieved.

I cleaned up a lie I'd told my wife. I went out with Max, but I had told her I went to the gym. She was mad, but we got closer as a result.

---

b) How do you feel about yourself now?

Example:

I was scared to death, but I feel good about me when I tell the truth.

I hate myself when I lie. I felt like a weight's been lifted when I cleaned it up.

6) When you see yourself getting ready to lie, practice telling the truth.

FURTHER READING

BRINK, Carol.
The Bad Times of Irma Baumlein (New York: MacMillan Publishing Co., Inc., 1972).

LEVY, Elizabeth.
Lizzie Lies a Lot (New York: Delacorte Press, 1976).

CHAPTER 16

Making Friends

GOALS

- To discover and appreciate reasons for isolating oneself

- To recognize the elements of positive, mutually supportive friendship

- To learn the skills needed to make friends

- To encourage people to reach out and make new friends

WHAT SURVIVORS MISSED
Supportive Friends

Having supportive friends offers many benefits. Friends provide pleasure, enrichment and companionship. People learn new ideas from friends. In the book *Your Emotions and Your Health*, studies confirm that people who have support networks are more impervious to stress and disease. [1] In other words, having friends not only enriches life but promotes health. Even people living alone who have friends to rely on are less likely to develop stress-related conditions and illness.

For the adult survivor, especially one who functioned mainly alone, reliving past trauma can create ongoing tension and stress. With a friend to talk to, the survivor can release some of that stress. He or she not only has support through difficult times, but a friend to enjoy the good times.

OLD PATTERNS
Isolating Can Perpetuate Abuse

People from abusive families often missed out on the benefits of friends. Instead, the adults may have isolated themselves from other people. Such abusive parents even tell their children to stay away from people. By keeping the family away from others, the adults control the environment. The family has no way to compare their toxic situation to a non-abusive one. The children have no positive outside frame of reference to indicate something might be wrong at home. No friend or relative looks in on the home to offer support, information, or a different perspective.

Danielle T.

This young woman had no friends or contact with other families as a little girl. She thought all fathers initiated their daughters into sex.

'I never went over to a friend's house until I was 16. My mother finally let me stay at my girlfriend's. I was shocked that her father was so nice. He didn't yell; they finished dinner without a fight. That was my first clue that something was not right at my house. I eventually did tell my friend about my father molesting me. She was my first real friend and confidante.'

Colleen F.

A woman coming to a battered women's shelter told the counselor: 'The minute we began dating, he wanted me to give up my other friends. When we got married, we moved away from my mother and brothers. It was just far enough that I couldn't see them regularly. I gave up my friends. He wanted me to be totally his. I had a baby and no car so I was trapped at home. A friend brought me to the shelter.'

These two women had no friends to provide outside information and assistance. Danielle did not even know she was being abused, so she could not ask for help. Visiting a girlfriend's house shifted her frame of reference, so she could recognize her abusive family. Colleen was physicaly trapped at home, so she could not get away. Eventually a friend did help both of these women.

Breaking the Isolation

Some children from such homes grow up determined to make friends and break out of the isolation, while others – perhaps due to fear – continue to isolate themselves. They often live alone, have few friends, and rely on no one but themselves. They simply continue the family's isolating pattern. That way, people will not hurt or disappoint them. These children lack friendship skills and any of the benefits that accompany having supportive friends.

Samantha P.

'We had neighbors; we never talked to them. Mother and Dad had no friends; we never had people over to the house. The house was such a mess! I couldn't bring a friend home. Now I live alone. I'm very self-sufficient, but I don't have any friends. I'm lonely, but I don't know what to do about it.'

She realized her lifestyle was efficient but lacking in human contact. In her Life Skills class, this woman began making friends. In addition to accomplishing things each day, she looked forward to seeing people and sharing with them. Many positive friendships develop in the Life Skills groups. People develop confidence, practice reaching out, and learn they can discriminate between healthy and unhealthy friendships. The new friends provide the survivor with information as well as a support network.

WHAT YOU CAN DO
Building Healthy Friendships
Perhaps after reading this section, you have decided you need to make more friends. To develop friends, you need to meet people. That means:

Reach Out
- Say hello to a new person.

- Speak with your neighbor.

- Call someone you want to get to know and make plans.

- Go to a gathering or function to meet people.

Get Together
After you have met people, what do you do next? Friends talk to each other, offer support and companionship, do things together, share common interests. Consider reaching out and asking people to do things.

Select Good Friends
But what kind of people make good friends? What are the qualities of a good friend? You can count on a good friend to be there when you need him or her. When you are developing and nurturing friendships, you show interest and caring and respect for your friend. And you are entitled to respect, attention, and caring from them.

Demand Respect
If a person is not showing you respect, interest, and caring, perhaps you should re-evaluate the friendship. Ask yourself these questions:
1) Do you feel good about yourself when you are with your friend?

2) Does your friend treat you with kindness and respect?

3) If your friend is not respectful and you mention it, does your friend apologize?

If your friend consistently disrespects you and does not change, you may be subjecting yourself to abuse. Consider ending the friendship. If you cannot, ask yourself, 'What am I getting out of this abuse?' You are worthy of relationships based on mutual caring and concern.

Friendship Pitfalls

As I have said, in a dysfunctional family the self-involved parent meets his or her needs, not the child's. This gives no modelling for healthy relating, for mutual caring and support. As a result the adult survivor often repeats negative patterns in adult friendships. So you can watch for and change your friendship patterns. Let me describe some friendship pitfalls and how to handle them.

1 Being overly loyal

An adult survivor can be loyal to the friend without looking to see if the loyalty is warranted or appropriate. For example, declaring, 'I know my friend would never let you down!' Here the overly loyal person pledges allegiance without finding out if the friend did indeed let the person down.

To avoid this pitfall, do not offer your loyalty blindly. Look at each situation to see what is appropriate. 'I asked my friend if he was telling the truth. He said he had lied. I told him to clean it up. Before, I would have blindly assumed my friend was right.'

2 Lack of self-esteem

The survivor can believe: 'I'm not worth much, so I'm grateful if anyone is my friend'. That sets up a climate for the friend to abuse, use, or be unkind to the survivor. The survivor continues to accept the behavior because he thinks no one else would be his friend.

As you increase your self-esteem, you will begin to realize that you are worthy of having good friends. And that implies deserving and demanding respect. Consider taking a stand: *I deserve to have good friends that treat me with respect.*

3 I'll fix you: you fix me

These friendships revolve around a non-verbal agreement, 'I'll solve your problems so I don't have to deal with mine', a basic component of codependent relationships. Both friends avoid dealing with their issues and taking responsibility for their own lives. Sometimes a person takes on a friend in order to 'fix him up'. This is distinct from empowering the friend to solve his or her own problems.

To address this issue, ask yourself what problems belong to you.

If a friend begins to take on your problems, ask them to stop. If you see you are fixing the other person, stop. For instance: 'I told my friend I was having trouble with my relationship. She began telling me what I should do, where I should go for help. I simply told her we were working on it, and if I needed suggestions I would ask her.'

If you are an overhelper, you might say: 'I noticed myself making phone calls for my girlfriend without asking her first. I stopped. Then next time we talked, I asked her if she wanted my assistance.'

4 Being too needy

In this case, the survivor is lonely and feels desperate for companionship. The person clings to the friend, forcing the friend to move away just to get some breathing room. The friend's rejection can be very upsetting to the already needy and vulnerable person.

If you feel needy and tend to cling to friends, be aware that you may overdose them. Give them room by backing off before they have to push you away. Or tell them you can get clingy, and they can let you know when you are being needy. Talking about it will lighten up the issue for both of you. Remember, when friends tell you they need some space, they are not rejecting you. Here is how such a conversation might go: 'My husband just left me and I'm alone for the first time. I find I need to talk, but I know I'm taxing my friends. So I just said, 'Look, if I ever get too much for you, just tell me'.'

ADDITIONAL CASES

You may be someone who has placed a premium on being alone because it offered protection. Or you may have friends, but not satisfying ones. Or you may just want to develop more friends. Whatever the case, you may see yourself in the following people's stories. The exercises afterwards are designed to help you begin to develop nurturing friendships.

Alex B.

This 39-year-old librarian told a Life Skills class about his childhood: 'The louder the fighting, the more I retreated into my world of books. I did not have any friends; learning and books were my friends. I loved the adventures between the pages better than my own life. I did not need people. I've never married or had a serious relationship. It's not that I don't like people; I just decided it was easier to do without them.'

After a few weeks Alex reported, 'Now that I'm in this group, I might like friends if they were like you people.'

Alex began meeting with two group members regularly. The

three went to movies. Toward the group's end Alex shared: 'I had Hank and Rita over for dinner, and we read from my favorite short stories. We each took turns and laughed and talked in between. We had a great time. I think I have two new friends that aren't books. This is the first time I've reached out to people; I think I can do it again.'

Penny W.
'My mother and father both worked at the factory, but their salaries were not enough for the six kids. The church left bags of old clothes on our front steps. We'd grab for the ones that looked halfway presentable. We had clothes, but they were not washed or ironed, so we looked funny. The kids at school teased us. Nobody wanted to be our friends.'

Now at 40, Penny, having worked her way through school, has a good job working in a bank. She meets interesting people.

'I am still so grateful that anyone wants to be my friend. One friend was just plain mean to me. I know I should have said something.

'Now that I'm in the Life Skills, I am beginning to see I deserve friends – kind friends. I am practicing standing up for myself. My mean friend asked me to lunch again and I turned her down. I see that nice people want to be with me. I don't have to take whatever my friends dish out. I'm learning to choose good friends, not just anyone who'll pay attention to me.'

SUMMARY
- Friends and a support network promote healthy people.

- In some dysfunctional families adults and children isolate themselves.

- Limiting friends and outside contact can keep the abuse in place because people have no positive frame of reference.

- Some people grow up lacking friendship skills such as meeting new people, developing friendships, and nurturing these relationships.

- Some friendship pitfalls are inappropriate loyalty, lack of self-esteem, and solving the friend's problems for him.

QUESTIONS AND ASSIGNMENTS
1) Remember a friend from your childhood. What did you like about him or her?

Examples:
　We had so much fun.

　We could talk for hours.

　I could tell him anything.

　She was so happy.

_____

_____

_____

2a) Do you have friends that do mean things to you?

Yes _____No _____

Examples:
　Purposely exclude you in group conversations.

　Put you down.

　Stand you up.

　Talk behind your back.

　Break confidences.

b) What do you do about it? Nothing, talk to them, end the friendship?

_____

_____

c) If you need to, take a stand. Write it here.

Examples:
　I deserve friends that respect me.

　I have kind friends.

　I have friends that support me.

_____

3) Healthy friendships are based on mutual respect. Friends are interested in each other's lives. They show concern without using each other. To practice recognizing these qualities, read these stories and answer the questions that follow them.

Janice and *Beth* met for dinner. Janice talked the entire evening about herself. She interrupted Beth several times.

Is Janice interested in Beth's life?

Yes _____ No _____

What would you do if you were Beth? Circle your choice.

   a) Leave dinner.

   b) Talk to Janice.

   c) End the friendship.

   d) Say nothing.

   e) Do something mean to Janice.

John and *Bill* had been friends for years. Bill recently married and was promoted. At their regular card game, John was brusk and nasty.

Is John treating Bill well?

Yes _____ No _____

What would you do if you were Bill? Circle your choice.

   a) End the friendship.

   b) Talk to John.

   c) Ask a mutual friend to talk to John.

   d) End the regular card game.

   e) Pick a fight with John.

Kitty and *Maude* planned to spend an evening at Maude's watching a video. When Kitty arrived, Maude said she needed to talk about something that was upsetting her. Kitty insisted on watching the video. They watched the video. Is Kitty showing concern for Maude?

Yes _____ No _____

What would you do if you were Maude? Circle your choice.

   a) Ask Kitty to leave.

   b) Turn off the video.

   c) End the friendship.

   d) Throw a tantrum.

   e) Go into the other room and call another friend to talk.

4) Say 'Hello' to one new peson today. Write down who it was and what happened.

_____

5) Pick a place where you can meet new friends — Church, support groups, 12-step meetings, park, work, a party, community function, concert, plays. Plan to go there and meet one new person. Write down who you met and what happened.

_____

_____

6) Make a list of people you have met that you want to get to know better. Invite one to do something — have coffee, meet for lunch or dinner, telephone, visit, or plan an activity together. Write down your list and what you plan to do with each person.

FRIEND   PLAN

_____   _____

_____   _____

_____   _____

_____   _____

_____   _____

7a) What are your friendship pitfalls? Circle yours.

Being overly loyal.

Not feeling you deserve respect.

Getting into fix me/I'll fix you friendships.

Being too needy.

b) Write your action plan for handling your pitfall.

Examples:

I took a stand that I deserve kindness.

I'm going to watch out for friends who want to fix me.

I'll warn friends I can be needy.

FURTHER READING

LOWRY, Lois.
Anastasia's Chosen Career (New York: Dell Publishing, 1987).

NEWMAN, Mildred and BERKOWITZ, Bernard.
How to be Your Own Best Friend (New York: Ballantine, 1981).

PADUS, Emrika.
The Complete Guide to Your Emotions and Your Health (Emmaus Pa.: Rodale Press, 1986).

RAY, Sondra.
I Deserve Love (Millbrae, Cal.: Celestial Arts, 1987).

SECTION SIX

Building Healthy Sexual and Intimate Relationships

Building on what the reader has already learned, the next two chapters focus on developing intimacy and expressing sexuality appropriately. For most adult survivors, being close meant being abused. For the survivor of sexual abuse, sex meant being abused. When the survivor does begin to let people in, getting close or being sexual can trigger abusive memories. However, the more positive experiences a person develops, the less power the fear has over him or her.

As you begin work in these sensitive areas, go slowly. Understand that the very thing desired — closeness or sexuality — may bring up fear. You may need to stop, move away, release old feelings. Ask your friends and intimates to be patient and gentle. And be patient and gentle with yourself.

CHAPTER 17

Developing Intimacy

GOALS
- To define intimacy

- To help you discover what stops you from being intimate

- To give you criteria for assessing healthy intimate relationships

- To explore ways you can develop more intimacy

Now that we have looked at developing healthy friendships, let us consider relating more deeply, i.e., developing intimacy. Intimacy means close emotional contact, being present with another person. You cannot be intimate when you are controlling, manipulating, or dominating a person because you are preoccupied with that. You cannot be intimate if you fear people because you are focused on your fears. If you are concentrating on your thoughts or agenda, you will have difficulty being intimate.

WHAT SURVIVORS MISSED
People who grew up in a family that related intimately had the best instruction on how to be intimate. Their learning was braided into their everyday life. People whose families lacked intimate contact often fear intimacy as adults. And they lack the ability to develop intimate relationships.

Jessica T.
Jessica, a survivor of emotional abuse, describes her struggle to be emotionally intimate with a man. She wanted closeness but feared it.
    'On our first date I was scared. I was trying to impress him. When he talked, I was rehearsing what I'd say next. After I talked, I wondered if what I'd said was O.K. After he left me off, I realized, no way was I being intimate.

'On our fourth date, I was relaxed and starting to be just myself. I was with him when he talked. My mind was not chattering a mile a minute. When we looked at each other, I did not look away. I could stay with him. When he took my hand I was scared, but I didn't go numb or run away. I didn't pull away. I told him I was afraid of getting close. He did not make fun of me; he just said, 'Let's take our time'. I guess we're getting some intimacy.'

Jessica found a man who supported her as she reached out for more intimacy. Even though she was scared, she was committed to having more intimacy in her life. She learned to communicate her fears so they dissipated. She took her time getting close and her partner supported her by telling her they could go slowly. These actions help build closeness even though people are afraid.

OLD PATTERNS
Many survivors avoid intimacy altogether by keeping friendships superficial or just staying away from people. They are not sure being close looks like such a good idea. Frequently, adult survivors stay as far away from intimate relationships as possible. Or they dive into close relationships too quickly. They get too close too fast. Many survivors confuse intimacy and sex.

Fear of Intimacy
For the survivor, closeness can mean getting hurt or even danger. During childhood the survivor's intimates abused him or her. To make sure of not being abused, frequently a survivor has designed his or her life to stay as far away from people as possible. Although an effective strategy, this isolation brings extreme loneliness.

Phil B.
'I have loads of friends, but I've never had a close relationship I'd call intimate. I'm so scared of being hurt like my parents hurt me.'

Inappropriate Intimacy
Some adult survivors need intense intimacy immediately. They tell all about themselves to a person they just met. That frightens people, and often they move away rather than coming closer.

Charlene B.
One woman described herself at a party: 'I saw this cute guy. I went up to him and said Hi. Before he could tell me his name, I'd told him I was a recovering alcoholic and my father sexually molested me. He turned bright red and walked away very quickly. I see that I scared him off.'

Intimacy Does Not Necessarily Mean Sex
Lots of people confuse intimacy and sex. People can experience

intimacy during sex, but not necessarily. They can have mechanical sex without emotional closeness. People can perform sexually but not make intimate contact.

Intimacy can be more confronting than sex. For instance, survivor of sexual abuse either stays away from sex entirely or endures it. They endure it by distancing and by removing themselves. But after the abuse has been healed and they want to enjoy sex, they may be unable to allow closeness. They may long for it, but are afraid.

WHAT YOU CAN DO
Develop Intimate Friends
People develop intimacy in stages. It builds over time. The Trust and Friends Chapters describe beginning and intermediate levels of relating. People begin to know each other as acquaintances. They meet casually and perhaps agree to have coffee. If they like each other and do things together then they are buddies. If they begin to respect and trust each other, then they are friends. Only when safety, respect, and trust are in place can real intimacy grow. After friends establish trust and caring, they can move to deeper levels of sharing.

Tanya G.
This woman is describing various levels of relating and her decision to want something more.

'I met Heather at a workshop. We did one of the exercises together. We liked each other and decided to have lunch. We discovered that we were at a similar place in our lives. We had both divorced, left our home towns and moved to New York. We'd both gone back to school to finish degrees and get better jobs. Over the next year we met for dinner, a movie, or lunch once every week or two. We talked on the phone regularly.

'That summer we went on an automobile trip together. That car gave us plenty of time to tell each other long stories. I told her some things I wasn't so proud of, but I knew my secrets were safe with Heather. That let her tell me some stuff. We just became closer and closer. And we had so much fun. I trust her like I've never trusted anyone. We respect each other. We work things out. She is my first real intimate friend.

'Now I have a new boyfriend so I don't see Heather quite so much. But we talk on the phone. I don't have the intimacy with Max yet that I have with Heather. But I see that I learned what it was like with her. Now I can be patient and work on building it with Max.'

Intimacy does not happen all at once. People develop intimates.

Communicate Your Fears

To have closeness in your life, you need to interrelate with people even though you may be afraid. With some friends you will be able to tell them you are scared. Try telling your fears to your friend. Usually that brings people closer. Many times when you communicate your fears, they disappear or diminish. Practice checking out your fears to see if they are real.

Build Stamina for Intimacy

If being close is new for you, you may need to develop 'intimacy stamina'. You may find that you get scared or push people away when you get close to people. As a defense, some people become mean or hurtful after they have been close. Rather than feel their fear, these people lash out. If this is your pattern, try expressing your fear without being hurtful. If you need to move away, fine! Do that, but come back after your 'intimacy break'. Tell your friend what you were going through. That will create closeness again.

Create Intimate Friendships Before Sex

If you want to develop intimacy, begin by developing close, intimate friendship without sex first. If you usually sleep with a person after the first date, try dating the person for two or three months without sex. Let the friendship develop first. The following chapter on expressing sexuality gives more guidelines and suggestions.

People do not relate intimately all the time. They move from one level to another. After an intimate conversation, the mood shifts to talking about the weather. After people make small talk, then they share more deeply. No one level is better than the others. A balanced person has them all available and can shift from one to another.

ADDITIONAL CASES

Harry R.

'I spent a lovely, intimate evening over dinner with a woman I truly like. We had both been sharing very personal things. Then she brought out coffee. I began to criticize her. She'd put the dishes in the dishwasher wrong. She had cheap cups and saucers. I stopped myself in the middle and told her I was pushing away because I couldn't stand the intimacy. I said I was sorry and told her I needed to go outside for a few minutes. I did. Then I was fine again. I suggested we talk about lighter subjects for a while.

'She told me other men had done the pushing away bit before, but she never understood what happened. After a great date they would head for the hills never to be heard from again. She thanked me for being so honest and responsible. And for getting through it and sticking around.'

Hope H.

Hope's father was an emotionally abusive alcoholic. Hope learned to remove herself emotionally. Since Mom worked full-time, Hope parented her two younger sisters. At 31, Hope still kept people at a distance. In the Life Skills class, Hope began developing intimate relationships using the check list for healthy, intimate relationships found at the end of the chapter.

'I'm always on my guard. I don't trust people. I learned the only person I can count on is me. I'll get so close and then I want to protect myself. When men start getting interested in me, I go out one or two times; then I find an excuse to end it.'

After six months in the Life Skills, Hope and the other group members had shared their lives and secrets and socialized together. During one session Hope began: 'I just can't count on anyone. People are disappointments.'

Another group member retorted: 'You can count on us, but you won't let us in. I'm getting insulted. We respect you. You know you can express your feelings with us. We all want to be close to you, but you won't let us.'

I asked Hope if she would try something. She said yes. I asked her to look at each group member and just be with them and let in their love. She did. I asked: 'Do you trust these people? Can you count on them?'

'Yes! But just you people.'

'That's fine. It's a start. There are nine people you can count on. Do you want to be close with these people?'

'Yes. But what if they disappoint me?'

'They might. We are all human. But can you talk to them?'

'Yes.'

Hope began that night letting nine people closer. She layed the groundwork for developing intimate relationships.

SUMMARY

- Intimacy is emotional closeness and being with another person.

- Some survivors fear intimacy while others are too intimate too soon.

- Intimacy is more than sex, and often far more difficult.

- Intimacy does not necessarily mean sex.

- Some people push others away after being intimate.

- To learn to be intimate, develop close friends, communicate your fears, love yourself, and build your stamina for intimacy.

● You can learn certain criteria for evaluating healthy intimate relationships.

QUESTIONS AND ASSIGNMENTS

1) When you have shared deeply with a person, do you want to move away?

Yes _____ No _____

2) When you watch two characters in a movie being intimate, do you feel uncomfortable and want to get away?

Yes _____ No _____

3) When you talk to a person do you think about what you are saying rather than giving them your full attention?

Yes _____ No _____

4) When you are making love, do you think about performance or other things rather than being present, focusing on pleasure and the physical sensations?

Yes _____ No _____

5) After you are intimate, do you find yourself pushing away, saying hurtful things, or finding fault with the other person?

Yes _____ No _____

6) I have created this check list so you can evaluate your relationships to discover if they are healthy intimate relationships. Answer each question Yes or No. Regarding_____
(name a friend or family member):

Yes _____ No _____ 1) Can you express your feelings openly and safely with this person?

Yes _____ No _____ 2) Can you negotiate your differences fairly and cooperatively?

Yes _____ No _____ 3) Do you have mutual respect and genuine concern?

Yes _____ No _____ 4) Is there trust and honesty?

Yes _____ No _____ 5) Are your differences encouraged?

Yes ____No ____ 6) Can you express yourself without fear of shame or judgment?

Yes ____No ____ 7) Can you both get your needs met?

Yes ____No ____ 8) Do you both take responsibility for your actions including the impact your actions have on others?

Yes ____No ____ 9) Do you work to resolve problems?

Yes ____No ____10) Is there room for mistakes?

Yes ____No ____11) Are you both committed to learning missing Life Skills and practicing them?

7a) Ask a friend you feel safe with to do this exercise with you. Sit across from each other with knees barely touching. Take five minutes and just look into each other's eyes. If this is too long, start with two minutes and build up to five. Do not talk. Notice your thoughts and bring yourself back to just being with this person. Notice if you want to or do look away, and bring yourself back to just being there. Take another five minutes to talk over the experience. This exercise will build your 'intimacy stamina', your ability to be present with another person.

8a) Do this exercise with a safe friend. Each take 10 minutes to talk. The other person's job is just to listen and be present. Do not comment or ask questions. Switch after 10 minutes and let the other person talk. Then take another 10 minutes to review the exercise.

b) Write down your feelings when you are being present and when someone is being present with you.

_____

_____

_____

9a) As you build more closeness into your life, you will be afraid from time to time. This is normal. List your fears of being intimate. Identify what you are afraid of:

Examples:
  I'm afraid you'll leave.

  I'm afraid you'll use what you know against me.

I'm afraid you'll find out something terrible about me and won't want to be my friend.

_____

_____

_____

b) When one of your fears comes up, tell your intimate friend. What happened when you did?

_____

_____

10) If you are a person who gets intimate too fast, practice talking about lighter topics, small talk. Talk about the weather, sports, fashion, the news.

11) If you usually sleep with a person on the first date, try waiting for a month or two. Build a friendship that can lead to intimacy.

FURTHER READING

CROWTHER, C. Edwards.
  Intimacy: Strategies for Successful Relationships (New York: Dell Books, 1986).

LARSEN, Earnie.
  Stage II Relationships: Love Beyond Addiction (New York: Harper and Row, 1987).

CHAPTER 18

Expressing Sexuality Appropriately

Although I already mentioned that this book is not a substitute for good therapy, I highly recommend therapy if you have been sexually abused and are having difficulty. If you are experiencing a specific sexual dysfunction, seek the help of a qualified sex therapist. Most are treatable conditions. You can also read one of several fine books recently published detailing the complexities of sexual abuse. Other books cover treatment of sexual difficulties that can result from abuse. I do not discuss either here, but I have listed several excellent books under Further Reading.

However, I do explore survivor issues that effect your sexual expression. For instance, adult survivors of any abuse, not just sexual abuse, can have difficulty expressing their sexuality appropriately. They sometimes express their sexuality inappropriately, without always knowing they are upsetting or even frightening their partner. Some have eliminated any sexual activity from their lives, becoming celibate. Others feel guilt and shame. Still others become addicted to sex. An abused child can grow up confused about his or her sexual identity, about love and abuse, about the difference between sex and affection.

GOALS
- To help you learn what is appropriate, non-abusive sexual expression

- To discuss being overly seductive, sexual guilt and sex as an addiction

- To assist you in overcoming fear of being touched

- To outline your rights as a sexual being

- To offer guidelines for enjoying your sexuality

- To help you heal your sexual self

WHAT SURVIVORS MISSED
Learning Appropriate Sexual Expression
Appropriate, non-abusive sexual expression means that both people can freely express themselves sexually without threat or fear. One partner does not dominate, i.e. neither partner uses age, sex, or position to control the other. I define as sexually inappropriate the person who:
- Does not invite, but imposes his or her will on a partner

- Is overly seductive

- Forces a person to be sexual

Here are some examples. The boss demands sex with the secretary or she will lose her job. The father requires his daughter to submit to sex to validate himself. A teenage girl purposely brushes her breast against an adult man. A man forces his date to have sex with him. In these cases, the person equates sex and power, using sex to increase self-esteem.

When a person is sexually appropriate, he or she respects personal boundaries. A boss who is sexually appropriate may be attracted to his secretary; but he would never demand sex by threatening her with losing her job. The sexually appropriate father is not sexual with his daughter. A teenager does not sexually brush against an adult man. A man asks his date if she wants to have sex or makes sexual advances, giving her room to turn his invitation down.

If you are a survivor or the partner of a survivor, remember an abused person can interpret loving, sexual expression as inappropriate. Sexual behavior can trigger the survivor. A loving touch can evoke fear. A kiss can feel dirty. A strong hug can trigger fear of physical harm. That person may see the present event through a filter from the past. Such incidents can be painful and explosive. Partners willing to communicate can clear up such misunderstandings. The cases that appear later in the chapter illustrate this problem and how to work it out.

Being Overly Seductive
Children who were sexually abused can have a host of problems. Such children can develop overly seductive behavior that carries over into adulthood. Because sexually appropriate boundaries were never drawn, these survivors learned to seduce as an everyday way of relating. This way of expressing affection is too sexual, too friendly and they are oblivious to it. It makes others

uncomfortable and even fearful. A man rubs a woman's shoulders at a party a little too long and a little too intimately. A woman stares at a man's crotch not knowing she is embarrassing him. A person brings up sex in conversation long before the relationship is ready for it. They can be unaware of sexual boundaries and overstep them regularly. Many times these survivors do not know they are being sexually inappropriate. They have a blind spot. Chuck's story at the end of the chapter describes an overly seductive man and how he overcame it.

Confusing Sex and Affection

Other survivors confuse sex and affection. They ask for sex when they want a hug or love. They themselves do not have a clear boundary between sexual expression and just interacting. One woman, whose father sexually abused her, said: 'My father insisted on giving my sister and me baths when we were 11 and 12. He'd wipe my bottom too hard and play with my breasts. I hated it. That was the only physical contact I had with him. As a woman, I find the only way I relate to men is sexually. I'm rubbing or hugging or petting right away. Then I wonder why men treat me like a sex machine.'

Loving Touch
Need for good touch

Research shows that human beings as well as animals need to be touched, held and cuddled lovingly. In the 1950s researcher Harry Harlow took infant monkeys away from their mothers, depriving them of touch. When these monkeys became mothers they ignored their babies and sometimes abused them. To attempt to repair these monkeys, later experiments provided the deprived monkeys with a monkey therapist. The monkey therapist supplied touching, holding and stroking, and in some cases was successful.

Creating good touch

Perhaps when you were touched as a child you were punished or hurt. That may mean touch looks dangerous to you. Or perhaps you may have been deprived of loving touch.

To help people overcome their fear of touch, I use the tapping exercise described in Chapter 2. When I have conducted that exercise, many times at least one person did not want to be touched. I worked with one such participant by asking her to touch my hand several times. Then I asked her if I could touch her hand. Yes. I told her to remove my hand when it became uncomfortable. After a while I asked her if she could hug me. She did. Then, could I hug her? I did. Taking about 20 minutes, this process started giving her an experience of good touch.

If you fear being touched but desperately want loving touch in your life, what can you do? I developed some simple methods for you to begin letting in loving touch. Several exercises in Suggested Assignments assist you in building good, safe touch.

OLD PATTERNS
Lasting Effects of Internalizing the Abuse
The sexually abusive adult often pledges the victim to secrecy which, in turn, communicates to the child that the abuse is indeed wrong. Then the child often concludes, 'I am bad', internalizing the abuse. The person carries that sense of feeling 'bad' to adulthood. It continues to affect adult relationships long after the actual sexual abuse has ended.

Yolanda G.
'My dad was my pal. We played and laughed. One night he was tickling me; he held me down and kissed me on the lips. I was seven. It was different; I didn't like it. Then he started coming into my room and touching me. I lost my pal and my childhood. I felt confused and betrayed. And he told me this was our secret. I was never to tell. I knew I was bad.'

Yolanda told the Life Skills group about her father. She found that the group did not think she was bad. Slowly she began to shift her interpretation of what had happened. After months she related: 'I see now my father had a problem, not me. I'm not bad, something bad happened to me.'

If survivors still think they are bad, they easily become objects of abuse available for other people's pleasure, but not their own. When survivors let go of the belief that they are bad, they feel entitled to emotionally healthy sexual partners. Making this shift is necessary before survivors can express their sexuality in a healthy way.

Guilt
Guilt means feeling bad for doing something. Survivors, as well as people who have not been abused, often feel guilty about sex. Those who have survived sexual abuse can feel additonal guilt. For example, a little girl feels guilty because she liked the sexual feelings, attention and closeness, but knew somehow the sex was wrong. Or, a teenager feels guilty because she loved her father, but hated his molesting her. Then, when such children grow up and begin normal sexual exploration, they can feel additional confusion and guilt. These people can have difficulty enjoying normal sexual pleasure.

Sexual Addiction
Although more survivors have difficulty being sexual at all, some become addicted to sex. Some survivors of sexual abuse received

attention and affection during sex, so they continue to try to meet those needs through sex. The sex is often mechanical and lacking the intimacy they seek. Professionals estimate that the U.S. has one million prostitutes – men as well as women – many of whom are repeating their sexually abusive pasts.

Dr Partick Carnes, in *Out of the Shadows* states that the sex addict has no control over his or her sexual expression. An addict uses sex to alter his mood. It becomes an obsession, just as alcohol or drugs become an obsession to the substance abuser. The sex addict risks everything for another sexual high. Many have to lead double lives to cover up pornography, affairs and prostitution.

Maya G.

Maya, 29, was a successful New York City business woman married to a stable, kind successful businessman. She had been molested by a neighborhood man and her father from ages 7 to 11. The closer she and her husband got, the more uncomfortable and unworthy she felt. Maya was no longer attracted to him and started having affairs. On her frequent business trips she picked up men at conventions. She had stopped counting how many men she had slept with. Her life-style enabled her to keep her secret rendezvous well hidden from her husband.

In therapy, Maya began to discover her deep disdain for men. She revelled in her one-night stands because she could have sex and throw the men out. She was getting even. In therapy, she began seeing her pattern and realizing she was dissatisfied with herself and her dual life. She began attending Twelve-Step meetings and talking about her problems with other addicts. A year later she stopped the affairs.

Overattached, Sexually Abusive Mothers
Survivors who have had overattached mothers have another set of problems as children and adults.

Melanie F.

'She was obsessed with me. She washed me three times a day, watched while I was on the toilet. She always managed to let her hand stray across my breast.'

This alcoholic mother suffocated her daughter emotionally. The result: at 30, my client was still trying to separate from her mother, was confused about her sexual identity, and had difficulty with boundaries and intimacy.

These survivors usually have psychotic or alcoholic mothers – often far more damaging than an alcoholic father because the household stability usually depends on the mother. A stable mother can partially protect her children from an alcoholic father.

The overly-attached mother's intrusiveness begins to feel inces-tuous to the daughter. The abuse is often not a specific event, but woven into a dysfunctional web. When this child grows up she can have problems differentiating herself from others. She is on the fence about everything and everyone – and sometimes about her sexuality. She can doubt her femininity and attractiveness.

Men Molesting Girls
Most sexual abuse takes place between men and girls or women. Whether fondling or penetration or any form of sexual inapprop-riateness, the person can be traumatized. Here, Roya describes some typical sexual problems she had for years after her abuse.

Roya G.
'My step-father came into my bedroom every morning before he went to work, put his hand under the covers, and touched me. I wanted to scream, I hated him, but he was my father. I had nightmares and recurring yeast infections. I could not have orgasms for years.'

Men Abusing Boys
Even though the vast majority of sexual abuse takes place between heterosexuals, sexual abuse between men and boys does occur. In some cases, society's abusive attitudes towards gays compound the abuse.

Men who were sexually abused report being abused by their teachers, coaches, therapists or older friends. Such male survivors sometimes do not consider what happened to them abuse. It may have provided them comfort, excitement or an emotional outlet. However, this survivor can have all the problems associated with sexual abuse: difficulty having intimacy, trust problems, bound-ary confusion, blind spots and so on. This survivor may try to have the experience over and over again to validate his masculinity.

Selecting the Safer Sexual Partner
People have many reasons for choosing a gay lifestyle. Frequently gay people report that they knew they were gay from the time they were very little. Although researchers have many theories, they do not know why certain people turn to homosexuality. However, I have interviewed a type of adult survivor who consciously chose homosexuality as a response to abuse.

Arlene T.
'I had an uncle as well as my grandfather who molested all my sisters, girl cousins, and me. I figured all men were weak, wimps, and perverts. Why would I want to be in an intimate relationship with one? Now do you understand why I am gay?'

This is not to say that all gay people have been abused. But I have observed gay clients who clearly chose their preference based on selecting the 'safer' sex. I do not try to change people's sexual preference; I help them heal and resolve the abuse. I am offering this observation not as a conclusion or judgment about homosexuality.

WHAT YOU CAN DO
Claim Your Rights as a Sexual Being
Perhaps you never considered that, as a sexual being, you have rights:

1) You have the right to say no, not to want sex at all. From time to time, this is a normal response, even if you were not abused.

2) You have the right to receive affection without sex if that is what you need and ask for.

3) You have the right to sex without abuse.

4) You have the right to enjoy pleasurable sensations. You do not have to put up with sex because you think you have to meet your partner's demands.

5) You have the right to safe sex. You may feel that stopping to use a condom might break the mood, but you have a right to protect yourself.

Use Certain Guidelines for Enjoying Your Sexuality
1) Do what feels right and safe to you. Go at your own speed.

2) When you find a person you are considering as a lover, use a reality check. Ask a friend whose judgment you trust about your prospective lover.

3) If you were sexually abused, sex will probably be a trigger to you. If you cry or scream or get upset, you are probably reacting to events from the past. Your reactions will diminish over time. Ask for what you need, to be held or left alone for a few minutes.

4) When you invite a person to be sexual with you, give your partner room to decline.

5) You may want kissing, petting or sex initially and then feel uncomfortable. If that happens, ask your partner to stop or slow down. You can continue or stop altogether. Communicate what you are feeling.

6) Select a lover who is patient, understanding, willing to let you go at your pace.

7) Go slowly, stop if needed.

8) Softness and tenderness may be very hard to deal with for a while. You may feel fear at first, but you will get used to feeling good.

9) Choose a partner whom you trust and feel safe with and who respects you.

Here are some people who have put these guidelines into practice.

ADDITIONAL CASES
Chuck D. and Cheryl R.
Chuck and Cheryl agreed to be sharing partners in a Life Skills class. They were both very sexually attractive people. And Chuck was notorious for picking up women. I thought Cheryl, having been sexually abused so badly, might not like his overtures. So I whispered to Chuck, 'Do NOT come on sexually to her'.

I said it with a great big smile. He knew exactly what I was talking about.

Two days later Cheryl called me: 'I have been in bed since our first class. I cannot stop throwing up.'

'What's been happening?'

'Well, Chuck asked if he could take me out for coffee after class. And he stared at me. He told me how attracted he was to me. He put his hand on my knee and stroked my leg . . . and I had to run to the Ladies Room. I got sick. I went home. I have been sick ever since. Since my uncle raped me when I was 18, I really haven't let a man close to me. I think Chuck's behavior triggered all my fears about sex and men. I want to talk to Chuck myself and see if we can straighten this out.'

I was furious with Chuck but I wanted Chuck and Cheryl to work this out if they could without my intervention. Cheryl finally called: 'I called him and he apologized. He had no idea what he had done. I told him it had brought up all my buried fears. Now, I can get to work on what I have been so afraid of.'

She was an inspiration! I was relieved! Then, I called Chuck. Now that I had cooled down, I could tell him clearly how angry I was. I wanted to know what had made him do that after I had asked him not to.

'I didn't do anything wrong! I wasn't coming on to her! Honest!'

I knew from Cheryl's account exactly what he had said and done. It sounded very sexual to me. I told him that.

'But I didn't think it was!'

Now, I was stumped. I did not think he was lying. Then, it

occurred to me: maybe he genuinely did not know. Maybe he had a blind spot.

'You didn't know that your remarks were sexual.'

'NO!'

Now, we had a different problem. Chuck's mom had been an alcoholic. She used to stand in the hall in her black lace underwear and lure him. She would have him come into the bathroom and rub her back while she was in the tub. He hated it and his mom, but he also liked it, and he loved her.

I realized he had his wires crossed. He had his feelings about women confused. He could not just care about them without being sexual.

'Women tell me I'm a woman-chaser, a seducer. I don't know what they are talking about!'

I was seeing that he really did not know.

'You have a blind spot. If you are willing to tell on yourself, you could use the group to work on this.'

'I am!'

By the end of the Life Skills group six months later, Chuck was relating to women as friends and people. By getting feedback from the group, he learned what he did specifically that was seductive. Cheryl released her fears about men. She had her first boyfriend since high school. Both broke old patterns and began to establish new, more healthy ones.

Lee Ann G.

At 33 and in public relations, Lee Ann had had just a couple of relationships with men – both bad.

'My brother molested and abused me from six until I was 14. He made me have oral sex with him. I hated the sex, but I was more scared of his violence. One time he beat me until I couldn't move and threw me in a dark closet. He brainwashed me telling me I was stupid and ugly.

'My parents never knew; I kept it all together. I grew up believing men just wanted sex and didn't really care about me.

'As an adult, I'd push a man until he got verbally violent. Then I'd be nice and right about how awful he was. I couldn't show my feelings. I did not have sex with a man until I was 28. Then I'd do everything but intercourse. I hated it.

'I knew I had a problem. I've been working on it for four years. I had to heal my anger and pain with my brother. And I had to look at my own anger at all men. Then I met a wonderful man; we only went together eight months, but I could practice everything I'd learned. I felt good about myself, I was vulnerable with him, I learned to enjoy sex. Most important, he was patient, he let me go slowly, he was very understanding about what had happened to me.

'Just recently, I was attracted to a man who brought out the worst in me. I chose not to get into a relationship with him. Before, I would have gone for him. But I can see what's good for me and what's not. I had a choice. I also have good men friends, who like me for me and are kind and gentle.'

Lee Ann is still learning to express her sexuality. She worked on her own anger and unresolved feelings. She can see the potentially dangerous relationships ahead of time, and choose not to get involved. She can see the positive qualities she wants in a man and choose the good ones.

Jane C.

At 24, Jane works in a clothing store. Very attractive, she wears silk pants and blouses, designer earrings. When she came to my office, she told me: 'I began having flashbacks about my father molesting me while I was making love. I'd jump up in a cold sweat and clench my fists. My boyfriend freaked; he broke up with me. I thought: I'm making this up. My father loved me, he'd never do anything like that.

'At Christmas, I visited my older sister. I told her about my dreams. She told me he had molested her. She had always feared he had done it to me too. I was shocked, but also relieved. I was starting to think I was crazy. Then the torrent of feelings. I was angry and in such grief and very confused. Sometimes I had to take the day off and just stay in bed. But after two years of work I have sorted it out. I know I'm not alone. I have a new boyfriend. I was scared to tell him, but he was very understanding. Still I get afraid when he gets on top of me, but we just slow it down or stop for a few minutes. It passes.'

Connie T.

Connie's father died when she was 12. By the time she was 16 she was sleeping with different men. For Connie at 29, sex gave her the closeness and affection she did not have at home. As an adult, she'd slept with many men, most of whom she didn't remember, because she was drunk. Connie got herself to AA at 24, but she still needed Life Skills and therapy.

'I began to see I was running from one man to another. I had a terrible fear of being alone. But when I was with men, I didn't get what I wanted. I started listening to what I needed – sometimes to be close but no sex, sometimes just to talk, sometimes to say no. I also want a friend and a companion, not just a one-night stand. I stopped sleeping around. After a year, I'm developing men friends.'

SUMMARY

- Being sexually appropriate means sexually expressing yourself without dominating or threatening.

- You may be unaware that you are overly seductive.

- You may confuse sex and affection.

- If you are afraid of being touched, you overcome it.

- Feelings of betrayal, guilt and a sense that *I'm bad* can have an impact on your sexual relationships.

- You have rights as a sexual being.

- You can use guidelines to choose healthy sexual relationships.

QUESTIONS AND ASSIGNMENTS

1a) Do you have a hard time speaking up when someone is sexually inappropriate with you?_____

Examples:
A guy in the movies put his hand on my knee.

A man who just gave me a ride home tried to kiss me.

b) What would you say now?

Examples:
'Please take your hand away'.

'I don't want you to kiss me'.

2a) Do you have sex when you really just want affection and closeness?_____

b) Next time, practice asking for what you want.

Examples:
I'd like you just to hold me.

If we make love, I'd like you to sleep overnight and not leave right away.

What would you say?

3) When you need a hug, ask for one. Write down your feelings.

Example:
I felt great. I was clear and didn't try to manipulate anybody. I got what I wanted and nothing more.

_____

_____

4) As you are doing this exercise, if you feel uncomfortable at any time, stop. You are in charge of your own experience; if you don't like what is happening, stop. Allow your tears and other feelings just to be there.

Find 10 to 15 uninterrupted minutes. Lying down or sitting in a comfortable chair, close your eyes. Take a couple of long, slow deep breaths in and out. Let your body gently relax. Now imagine a beautiful ball of golden light just above your head. Let its healing and cleansing powers move through your body. See its golden glow filling your head and neck and shoulders. If the light seems stuck or you see a dark area just take a breath and as you breathe out see that area filling with light. Now fill your chest and abdomen with light . . . And now let it fill your legs. Let its healing power cleanse your thighs, calves and feet. Now gently put your hand over any area where you were beaten or molested. Ask out loud the light to cleanse these areas. (*Example* I ask the light to heal and cleanse my breasts, my buttocks and my female organs.) Now ask the light to heal your negative thoughts and feelings about yourself and others . . . Ask the light to heal and cleanse your very being . . . Give yourself a moment to feel your emotions.

This light has the power to give you its blessing. Feel the blessing and love of the Universe flood throughout your whole being.

Say out loud three times: 'I claim my power to decide what happens and doesn't happen to me. I'm in charge of my body and my life'.

Take a few moments to enjoy a sense of peace and power and healing . . . When you feel ready open your eyes.

5) Pick a gentle and loving friend. Sit opposite each other, knees just touching. Ask him or her to massage your hands with hand lotion in a non-sexual, loving manner for five minutes. Keep your eyes closed, don't talk. Take a few minutes to talk about it. Then rub your friend's hands. What happened?

_____

_____

6) Take a stand about sex. Here are some examples:
   I only have loving sex that feels good to me.

   I am in charge of my sexuality.

   I have the power to create a positive sex life for myself.

   I have the power to say no and not to have sex if I'm not ready or if it does not feel right to me.

Write your stand down. If you need to remind yourself, write it on a card for your desk, refrig or medicine chest.

---

7) When and if you are ready and want to, choose a lover who is patient and understanding. Have him or her read the Sexual Rights and Guidelines.

FURTHER READING

BARBACH, Dr Lonnie.
    For Each Other: Sharing Sexual Intimacy (New York: Signet Books, 1982),
    For Yourself: The Fulfillment of Female Sexuality (New York: Signet Books, 1975).

BASS, Ellen and DAVIS, Laura.
    Courage to Heal (New York: Harper and Row, 1988).

CARNES, Dr Patrick.
    Out of the Shadows: Understanding Sexual Addiction (Minneapolis: CompCare Publishers, 1983).

EARLE, Dr Ralph and GROW, Dr Gregory.
    Lonely All the Time: Recognizing, Understanding and Overcoming Sex Addiction for Addicts and Codependents (New York: Pocket Books, 1989).

TOWER, Cynthia Cosson.
    Secret Scars: A Guide for Survivors of Child Sexual Abuse (New York: Viking, 1988).

WOITITZ, Dr Janet B.
    Healing Your Sexual Self (Pompano Beach, Fla.: Health Communications, Inc., 1989).

ZILBERGELD, Bernie.
    Male Sexuality: Guide to Sexual Fulfillment (New York: Bantam, 1984).

SECTION SEVEN

Planning For the Future

With several previous skills, you needed to unlearn old habits before learning new ones. In this section, you may be learning skills you never learned at all – namely managing money and setting goals. Because you probably lived from day to day, you may not have had much energy or given much thought to the future. These last two skills give you an opportunity to begin designing your future. That may be uncomfortable, but can also be exciting. These skills allow you to have what you want in life.

However, adult survivors report two common barriers to having money and accomplishing goals:

1) Negative internal messages

2) Commitment to struggle

I have discussed these barriers with regard to self-blame, being used, having fun, and self-sabotage. Now let us see how they affect money and goals.

If you believe that you do not deserve money or good things, you will have trouble making money, going for the better job, feeling entitled to achieving your goals. You may come up against internalized messages like *I don't deserve it, I'm not worth much* or *I'm bad.* In both the Money and Goals Chapters, I address the *I don't deserve it* thinking.

As I have said, many survivors are also deeply committed to struggle. When life starts getting good, even easy, people can feel uncomfortable, frightened.

Be aware that you may be attached to struggle. When you begin making money or achieving, you may go back to needing to struggle. Just notice that this is what you are doing, and make a choice between struggle and having what you want. Consider the possibility that the struggle is over and you can live your life without it. If you need to, turn back to the Not Sabotaging Chapter and review it.

CHAPTER 19

Managing Money

GOALS
- To help you uncover abuse connected to money
- To help you examine your beliefs about money
- To teach you a simple method of monthly budgeting
- To put into practice positive money management

WHAT SURVIVORS MISSED
As a rule we do not teach our children how to manage money, so some people – abused or not – just don't know how to budget, spend wisely, or save. For some survivors, their parents used money as a tool to inflict emotional abuse. These people often have negative feelings about money or, at the very least, ambivalent feelings about money. In addition to a lack of skills, they have made negative decisions about themselves and money. If a person feels he does not deserve to make money, he will have a difficult time generating it.

OLD PATTERNS
Using Money as a Weapon
The cases below illustrate how adults braided money into abuse. Sometimes, a parent used the child's earned money for his or her own selfish purposes. Other times, money became a weapon just like a belt or a pan.

Nadine T.
'I worked two jobs all summer for college. My father put the money in a savings account. When I was leaving for college that fall, I got the passbook from his top dresser drawer. It read $1.37. When I confronted him, he denied it. But I know my alcoholic

father had used the money to buy booze. No one is ever going to control my money again.'

Cheryl V.
'My mother had verbally abused me all my growing up years. She had inherited money from her mother, so she never worked. When I married and had a family, we struggled for the first few years. She never offered to help us. After she died, I thought surely I would inherit the money. Her will stated that I had been a bad child, so she was giving all her money to a charity. I did not care about the money. What really hurt was that even from the grave she stuck it to me one more time.'

Needless to say, both these women were extremely angry about money. As they worked on their money skills, they realized that they were furious with their parents, not money. Money was just the weapon they happened to have in their hand. After examining their negative money beliefs, they began reprogramming their beliefs using affirmations.

Thinking You Don't Deserve It
As I have said, in an abusive household, many times the child received negative messages about him or herself such as *I don't deserve it* or *I'm not worth it*. This negative programming not only affects self-esteem but it spills over into the ability to generate money and feel worthy of achieving in life.

Sheila C.
A verbally abusive mother told her very capable daughter, Sheila, *You'll never amount to much.* Even though Sheila knew intellectually this was not true, the mother's programming had done its damage. The daughter still operated as if she were not worth much. Even with her college degree, she had difficulty feeling worthy of a well-paying job.

Equating Self-worth and Money
People often equate money with self-esteem. Our culture puts a tremendous premium on money. Those who have money have status. And people fall prey to evaluating themselves and others in terms of money. Your self-worth is an inner state that does not depend on how much money you earn. Money does not equal self-worth. Your value as a person does not increase because you have money. Conversely, you are not a failure if you do not have money. Money is just the exchange medium we use to buy and sell services and products.

Overspending
People try to bolster their self-esteem and fill emotional emptiness

by overspending. When overspending goes out of control, people can become spending addicts.

Sharon Y.
About 5'2" tall and maybe 100 lbs., Sharon had a passion for shopping. But she got into trouble when she could not stop the spending.

'Whenever I got the blues, I'd go shopping. Buying things made me feel better. Except, after years of trying to feel good about myself, I still didn't. And, when I didn't have money, I'd spend anyway. I ran up lots of credit card bills. I've been in Debtors Anonymous for two years now.

Underearning
Others who feel inadequate and not worth much can have a hard time earning money. They are underearners. Underearning means either not charging for your services, undercharging, or not going for the promotion. The belief that *I'm not worth much* can generate this behavior.

Ralph W.
When Ralph, now in his forties, graduated from NYU, he went to work for his father. But Dad did not pay him much, and Ralph never asked for what he was worth in the marketplace. Managing his own business, Ralph was careful about money, but not assertive. I knew from his caring manner and thoughtful eyes that he took care of his clients. But he did not take care of himself by charging adequately for his time.

'I can't bring myself to talk about money when a manager wants my services. After much agony, I finally blurt out a figure that is much too low. It's lower than my competitors. I get the job, but I know I could have easily charged more and still been fair.'

WHAT YOU CAN DO
Reprogram Negative Beliefs about Money
Parents – or whoever raised the child – may have openly communicated beliefs about money, or they may have indirectly indicated them. Whatever the case, the child assimilated these beliefs and most likely made them his own. If the family experienced a traumatic incident regarding money, this could have affected the child's beliefs and feelings about money later in life.

Parental beliefs shape a person's behavior and attitude. To illustrate, a mother who lived through the depression, believes the family should save money because you never know when it might be taken away. The father, who lost his job in the depression, believes he must keep the same job because you might not ever find another one. The child grows up believing money should be saved, not spent. He never enjoys money because he fears running out. A belief generates a certain behavior in these examples:

Parental Belief: Save for a rainy day.

Belief: Money should be saved because you will run out.

Behavior: I have trouble spending even when I have the money.

In the next illustration, the father, a minister, gave away money to the poor and needy. The son has a good job but has trouble accepting promotions he deserves.

Father's Belief: Having money is not being a good Christian.

Belief: Having money is bad.

Behavior: I have good jobs, but I feel guilty earning money for myself.

Track What You Spend

If you spend more than you earn, or go shopping to feel better even when you cannot afford it, you need to bring it under control. One way to do this is to write down everything you spend. Then you can see where your cash is going. You cannot ignore the outgoing funds. The exercise at the end of chapter will help you get started.

Start Budgeting

So many books have been written on budgeting, money, and finance that you may even find a money section in the book store. I have a few suggestions under Further Reading. But I have given you a very simple method in the exercises section. When you see how much money you earn each month and how much you spend, you can gain some control over your money. You can also easily see where it is going to and coming from.

Deserve to Earn Money

You deserve to have money in your life. You are worth it. Reprogramming your negative self-image takes time, but it can be done. Start now. Using the affirmations at the end of the chapter, you will see a difference in 21 days.

ADDITIONAL CASES

The following people have learned money skills and shifted negative beliefs to positive ones. They learned money management skills so they could take control of their finances and their lives.

Gwen O.

At 33, Gwen, a lanky six feet tall, sold computer time sharing. She knew nothing about money as a child, but taught herself money skills as an adult. Her panic attacks were serious at the time, but as she told me about them a year later she could laugh at herself.

'Mom and Dad saved lots of money but I could never figure out how they did it. I know they worried about money because they had lived through the Depression. Money was a well-kept secret at our house; we did not discuss it. Mom made a budget; she gave Dad an allowance, but I did not see the process. All I saw was Mom mumbling over the checkbook and Dad pacing.

'What I inherited was their worry. I was anxious and concerned about money. I'd shake when it came time to do my income tax. Thinking about it gave me a panic attack. I felt so much pressure and responsibility but had no practice managing even an allowance. I was afraid I'd screw up. I also believed money was beneath me, not spiritual.'

Gwen was not abused growing up, but married an emotionally abusive man. He controlled her and the money. Every other Friday, he would have his hand out asking for her paycheck. Then he would lecture her about how little she was earning.

'I married a man who felt entitled to everything. I felt entitled to nothing. Now that we are divorced, I have made myself learn to make a budget. It's even kind of fun. I still get nervous about taxes, but I'm much less anxious. I've read books on money and let my accountant teach me to plan and manage my money. I own a house. I'm even a little excited taking charge of my finances.'

When Gwen was a little girl, she did not recieve an allowance; she had no piggybank or savings account, so she could watch her small earnings grow. She did not work for money doing extra chores. Gwen had no training in earning, budgeting, or managing money. It was just there in Mom's wallet. When Gwen finally broke away from her husband, she had to learn money skills. Managing her own money reinforced her independence.

Chris A.

Chris, a short, stocky young man with lots of wiry brown hair, wrestled in high school and college. Now 22 and just graduating from school, Chris told about his ambivalent feelings regarding money.

'My mother controlled my money. I worked summers and part-time jobs from the time I was 12. She banked the money. When I was 18 and planning for college, I discovered she'd invested my money in her business inventory. It was gone. I was livid! We were sitting at our kitchen table when I shoved her off the chair and pinned her to the floor. I was screaming, she was sobbing, but I couldn't hear any of it. I could have killed her, I was so angry. But I stopped myself. I got off her and walked out of the house.

'Then, she disowned me. I had little to do with her after that. I applied for scholarships and got into a good school. I have earned my college money twice.

'My uncle gave me some money for graduation, but I worried about running out. I unnecessarily denied myself things I could afford. When I did have cash, I would not buy food because I didn't think I could afford it. I was still not clear how much I earned or spent.'

During the Life Skills class on money, we teach people how to make a budget and spending plan. They can actually see how much is coming in and going out, so money becomes less mysterious.

'I still felt fearful, but I stuck to my spending plan for a month. Then I saw exactly what I was earning and spending. I am getting a glimpse of money working for me rather than me being enslaved by money. I like the feeling.'

Betty K.
At 60, Betty had been a successful business owner, author, and producer. She wore her handsome steel-gray hair fashionably short. She loved to brag about her latest bargain from the garment district. As successful as she had been, she could not hold on to money. She made money; she lost it, then made money and lost it again. She revealed her story of codependence, abuse, and over-spending.

'My mother was over-attached to me; she sexually abused me from the time I was four until I was about 10. Although Mother said she was very independent, she lived off her second husband's money. We rode around in limos but I had no idea where the money came from. I had lovely things but never a sense of how you earned money or spent responsibly.

'As you might imagine, I had a distorted view of money. I developed a spending addiction. I bought myself nice things to alleviate the anxiety and deprivation. I made good money, but I was always on the financial edge. I was just repeating my chaotic and unstable homelife.

'I acted impulsively and sometimes too generously. I lent a friend $7,000 without looking to see if I could financially do that. I had no good business sense. After I repeated this pattern many times, I recognized I had a blind spot. I began remembering abusive incidents, and I saw how they related to money. I rigorously examined my money beliefs. I wrote out affirmations, reprogramming myself with more positive ones. I made myself learn about accounting, cash flow, and balance sheets. I'm not an expert, but I learned how to use them when I need them. I interviewed financial advisors asking their success rates. I'm finally developing money skills and solid financial responsibility.'

Betty took about three years to break her spending habits, change her beliefs, and learn new skills. She has stabilized her finances.

'I'm earning a good living and I have money. Financial stability – what a concept! I intend to keep it that way.'

SUMMARY
- Negative beliefs about money limit ability to earn and enjoy money.

- Some abusive parents used money as a weapon.

- People who believe they are not worth much can severely limit their ability to earn money.

- By tracking expenses and income, people can devise a simple budget.

- By living within that budget, people can begin to gain control over their money.

QUESTIONS AND ASSIGNMENTS
1) All of us can trace our money beliefs back to our parents or the adult who raised us.

Examples:
Dad: Money is the root of all evil.

Mom: Money is bad.

You: Money is dirty.

You cannot be good and have money.

If you have money you must be doing something wrong.

a) What did your father, or the person who raised you, believe about money?

_____

_____

b) What did your mother believe about money?

_____

_____

_____

c) What do you believe about money?

_____

_____

_____

d) What did you learn about yourself?

Example:

I remembered my mother telling me negative things about money. I listed them. Now that I see what they are, I can change my thinking.

_____

_____

2a) What is a positive belief you could reprogram yourself with? For each belief you write down, write an affirmation.

Examples:

Money is neither bad nor good.

I can be good and have money.

b) Write them on an index card and put them on your mirror. Say them out loud several times a day.

3a) Although many books describe more complex methods of budgeting, this exercise offers a simple one. The following worksheet is designed to help you estimate your monthly expenses and income. Then you can see if your expenses are less than what you earn each month. You can also see where you are spending your money. When you have annual expenses divide them by 12 for a monthly figure. For example, one man spends $600 on clothes twice a year. Clothes should be in the monthly budget at $100. For other items, average several months' bills. Over three months the phone bill was $25, $40 and $55. The average bill is $40 so write $40 under phone.

BUDGET WORKSHEET

Monthly Expenses

Rent _____

Utilities _____

Telephone _____

Food _____

Transportation _____

Clothes _____

Entertainment _____

Savings _____

Credit Cards _____

Medical _____

Insurance _____

Taxes _____

Other ——— _____

Other ——— _____

Other ——— _____

Total: _____

Monthly Income

_____

_____

_____

_____

Total: _____

The 'Other' category might include child support or loan payments. Examine your checks over the past few months and see what you write checks for. You may have a category called 'Cash'. This will give you other expenses categories. If you want to plan for a big expense – a vacation or car – set aside some money each month in a savings account. Write car or vacation savings on one of the 'Other' lines. Tracking your income and expenses, you can create a simple budget. Living within that budget you can begin to gain control over your money.

b) What were your feelings while doing your budget?

Examples:

I felt panic, but I sat down and did my budget. Once I started, I felt fine.

I feel I am going to have some control over my money and that feels wonderful.

_____

_____

_____

c) Try living within the budget you designed for one month. Budgeting gives you more control over your money.

4) Write down every penny you spend for one week. That means keeping track of how you spend the cash in your wallet, not the money you spend when you write checks.

	ITEM	AMOUNT
Monday	_____	_____
	_____	_____
	_____	_____
	_____	_____
	_____	_____
Tuesday	_____	_____
	_____	_____

Wednesday

Thursday

Friday

Saturday

Sunday   _____   _____

               _____   _____

               _____   _____

               _____   _____

               _____   _____

5a) Imagine you have a young niece or nephew who has just started a first job and who has come to you for advice about money. What would you tell them?

Examples:

     Do not use your credit cards unless you know when you can pay off the balance.

     Have enough in savings to see you through an emergency.

     Don't buy things unless you can pay for them.

     Put some money aside each month for savings.

     Enjoy your money; you don't have to be afraid of money.

_____

_____

_____

b) Practice living by these suggestions.

FURTHER READING

GILLIES, Jerry.
     Money Love (New York: Warner Books, 1978).

HILL, Napoleon.
     Think and Grow Rich (New York: Fawcett Books, 1960).

ROMAN, Sanaya and PACKER, Duane.
     Creating Money (H.J. Kramer, 1987).

SINETAR, Marsha.
     Do What You Love, The Money Will Follow (New York: Dell Books, 1989).

CHAPTER 20

Setting Goals

GOALS

- To practice setting goals, making plans of action, and completing tasks

- To assist you in setting weekly goals

- To teach a method for setting long-range goals

A goal is something you want to attain. This chapter focuses on setting goals as a part of daily living and using a To Do List. It helps you set weekly as well as long-range goals. It breaks down the process of setting goals, implementing a plan, and finishing it.

When you wrote your goals for reading this book in Chapter 1, you set goals. When you did the exercises and assignments, you broke those goals into specific actions and simple steps and then completed them. So you have been practicing setting and accomplishing goals all along. This final chapter helps you apply these to your life.

WHAT SURVIVORS MISSED

The Goal: Staying Alive

Some people who were abused never thought about long-range goals. They were so busy just living, they never had dreams – or forgot them. Surviving was the goal. Such survivors did not learn how to set daily or weekly goals. In fact, planning the future seems foreign to them.

Lonnie W.

Lonnie is such a case. In fact, he helped me see that certain abused people live day to day and they never learned to plan or consider the future. I suggested to him during a session: 'Why don't you set a weekly goal? Then do something each day toward that goal.'

This able-bodied man looked at me as if I were from Mars. He remarked: 'What goals? I don't have any goals. I just live from day to day.'

The man in front of me had no idea what I meant. He certainly understood the words, but he had no practice in setting a goal and creating an action plan. So I got out a piece of notebook paper and handed it to him. I suggested that he write down his weekly tasks:

Weekly Goals

1) Make 5 business calls

2) Do laundry

3) Vacuum apartment

4) Schedule dinner with friend

5) Pick up son

6) Shop for groceries

7) Buy birthday present

8) Attend computer class three times this week

We listed these small, weekly goals. Then we broke them down into daily tasks:

Monday

1) Attend class

2) Make one call

3) Shop for groceries

4) Buy present

Tuesday

1) Make one call

2) Schedule dinner

3) Pick up son

Wednesday

1) Attend class

2) Make one call

Thursday

1) Make one call

Friday

1) Attend class

2) Make one call

3) Do laundry

4) Vacuum apartment

I suggested that when he finish an item on his list, he draw a colored felt pen line through it. Next session he came in very excited. He had done much on his list; other things he had forgotten. That was fine. It was a start. He said: 'This was fun. And I knew where I was going and where I was along the way. I liked seeing my To Do List filling up with color as I lined out my tasks. I felt I was accomplishing something.'

I asked him, 'Was this a useful exercise?'

'Oh yes. I never learned to do this. I watched my friends set goals, but I didn't know how. At my house, people were always fighting. My dad would throw me against the wall. Mom would just watch. I was terribly depressed. We never planned for the future. My job was to stay alive.'

This man was indeed alive, functioning, and had a job. But clearly he had no training in setting goals.

WHAT YOU CAN DO
Master the Process
You have an idea how to make a To Do List and put it into a weekly calendar. Now let us break down the actual tasks and discover how to get things accomplished. Accomplishing things takes four steps:

1) Setting a goal

2) Creating an action plan

3) Implementing it

4) Finishing it

Mastering these steps will help you achieve the goals you set out. The questions at the end of the chapter help you practice these steps.

Let Yourself Have Your Dreams
If you have been concentrating on staying alive each day, you did not think much about the future.

Nat Y.
'I gave up my dreams because I thought I was taking away from someone else. I never had dreams about my future: we weren't allowed. Wanting things was bad.'

The abusive part of your life is over, so you *can* think about tomorrow. Maybe you had dreams and gave them up, or maybe you are considering them for the first time. Now that you are out of crisis and beginning to meet your needs, you can begin to design your future. You can consciously plan and choose what you want to do. And you deserve to have what you want. The exercises help you get started.

ADDITIONAL CASES

First, meet several people who have done that. Doug, Joann, and Charles tell how they began to realize their dreams.

Douglas V.

Doug, a 42-year-old artist in a faded blue work shirt and chinos and a mop of light brown hair, lived with his gay lover for five years. Although his childhood friends teased him for being gay, the severe abuse came from his parents. He told a Life Skills class: 'Since I was little, I loved to draw and paint. My mother opposed it; she said, "Men don't draw, that's for sissies". Once my father found my paints and threw them out. We had a huge fight, and I left home for a while.

'But when I got to high school, my art teacher encouraged me. She helped me prepare for the all-school art show. I had three paintings and two drawings in the show. I was in heaven. My parents came and said nothing. We just walked through the show silently. My teacher even came over and told them how talented she thought I was. They said nothing. I was crestfallen. We got home, and my father got drunk and beat me up. After that, I was terrified to draw or pick up a brush.

'During the last five years, I started working on myself in therapy and workshops. One counselor suggested I paint again. I shook all the way to the art supply store. It took me two weeks of just looking at the paints to open them. When I finally started painting, I cried. That lasted several months. I felt like I was meeting a long-lost friend I had not seen in years. I cried out all the resentment and anger and grief.

'Six months ago I started showing my work to people. Just last week I sold my first painting. Not only have I accomplished a life-long goal, but also I have my beloved art back.'

Douglas had given up his dream of being an artist. With support, he released the abuse associated with his art and he reconnected with his beloved painting. He is doing what he loves best and is successful at it.

Joann R.

At 23, Joann worked as a temporary secretary. Her pale face and shy manner got lost in her brightly colored dresses. The oldest of four, Joann shared: 'I have never had goals for myself . . . I mean like future goals. Goals are a luxury I have not been able to afford. My daily goals were to keep my brothers and sister safe, to finish high school early, and to get out of the house. No one talked about career or dreams. Our dreams were a peaceful evening with no fighting, or my dad falling asleep early so we would not get yelled at.

'In the Life Skills class, I looked at real goals for the first time. It's strange, but exciting. I have this list of things I want to do just because I want to. I feel like a kid in a candy store . . . and a little guilty, about what – I'm not sure.

'I want to buy a stereo, a house of my own, get married, be happy. I have several careers in mind. I have to do more research. And I might even go back to school. My plans are not definite, but what's important to me is that I can make them.'

As a child, Joann rarely had time for herself – let alone time to see long-term goals. She focused on meeting the daily crises. Now that time is over and she can plan her own life. She learned basic goal setting skills and is happily designing her life.

Charles C.
At 38, Charles, who had worked in New York's garment district for 16 years, never really set goals. He looked quite normal, even though he reported: 'I was born deformed. Before I was 12, I had had eight operations to correct the birth defects – including forming a proper eye socket. My alcoholic father beat me – sometimes as punishment, sometimes for no good reason. I think he felt guilty for having a deformed son. I could not play games or go outside. Every vacation or holiday meant more surgery and long recovery. I wasn't entitled to any goals. Mom said, 'Do for others, not yourself'.

'I put myself through college and got a job. I had a battle with alcohol myself, but stopped drinking. After a bad first marriage and some therapy, I just remarried a wonderful woman. I'm happy and can do regular activities. I can swim, drive, cook, laugh. I'm content with my life.

'I had no long-range goals. Just staying alive and having some quality of life has been enough for me. But, since the Life Skills, my wife and I have been making some plans. We plan vacations; we have set financial goals and talked about having a family. I still find it hard to say what I want, but I blurt it out. I just had never looked beyond tomorrow.'

Charles no longer has surgeries and survives beatings. He fills his life with simple activities that give him pleasure. For Charles that is heaven. And he found, through the goals exercises, that he could plan and ask more of life.

QUESTIONS AND ASSIGNMENTS

1a) Circle the part or parts of the goal setting process you have trouble with.

- Setting a goal
- Creating an action plan
- Implementing it
- Finishing the task

Examples:

I have lots of ideas, but I can't get started.

I create a plan, but I get bogged down.

I have too many things going at once.

I don't have any plan.

I can't finish anything.

_____

_____

b) Pick one step you would like to strengthen. Make yourself a small assignment to strengthen that area. Focus on a specific task. Then do it. This puts you into action instead of talking about it. If you still need work in this area, make another task for yourself. Write it down and do it.

Example:

I'll finish one thing.

I'll clean my house for 30 minutes.

I'll make a plan for looking for a new job.

_____

_____

2) Sit in a chair for 10 minutes. Close your eyes. Take a couple of deep breaths and relax. Imagine you are six years old and have all the possibilities in the world available to you. You have supportive parents and unlimited funds. What do you want to do when you grow up? Write down your experience and your dreams.

_____

_____

_____

_____

3a) What have you always dreamed about doing? You may want to think about this question and do the process over several days.

Examples:

I had a dream to be a singer.

I've always wanted to be a vet. I love animals. My parents told me the training costs too much.

I want to be a teacher.

_____

_____

_____

b) If you still want to actualize that dream, what is an action you can take now to start working on that goal?

Examples:

Find out about voice teachers.

Talk to a vet and see what it's like.

Look into teacher certification.

_____

_____

_____

4) These next exercises will help you generate some long-term goals. List five accomplishments.

Examples:

Being alive.

Getting my life together.

Typing 50 words per minute without errors.

Not doing to my children what was done to me.

Completing school.

Cooking.

Getting and holding down a good job.

_____

_____

_____

_____

_____

5) List five things that interest you. Choose from the following list and add your own.

Examples:

History	Interior design
Painting	Museums
Making money	Sports
Buying a house	Biography
Fashion	Ecology
Plants	Camping
Medicine	Meditation
Music	Friends
Cars	Dancing
Animals	Trains
Travel	Language
Bettering myself	Writing

_____

_____

_____

_____

_____

6) List five things you do well.

Examples:

Cook	Manage people
Drive	Listen
Sing	Help people
Write	Play with my kids
Dress well	Learn new things
Build models	

_____

_____

_____

_____

_____

7a) List your long-range goals. The lists from previous exercises may help you.

Examples:

I want to have raised two healthy, happy children.

I want to be happy.

I want to earn enough money to retire at 60.

I want to make some kind of contribution.

I want to become a manager.

I want to learn another language.

I want to earn $50,000 a year.

I want to go to India.

I want to learn to play the piano.

I want to own a house.

_____

_____

_____

_____

_____

_____

_____

Put the list away for a few days and then review it. See if you want to change anything. Many people obscure their everyday goals with long-term goals and get overwhelmed. Put your long-term goals on the shelf and just do what is in front of you to do.

b) Divide your list into one, five and ten year goals. Put an 'L' by the goals you want to have accomplished by the end of your life. Put a ten by your ten-year goals, a five by your five-year goals and so on.

c) Now rewrite your goals:

My Life-time Goals Are:

_____

_____

_____

_____

My Ten-year Goals Are:

_____

_____

_____

_____

My Five-year Goals Are:

_____

_____

_____

My One-year Goals Are:

FURTHER READING

BOLLES, Richard.
   What Color Is Your Parachute? (Ten Speed Press, 1988).

GAWAIN, Shakti.
   Living in the Light (San Rafael, Cal.: Whatever Publishing, 1986).

SINETAR, Marsha
   Do What You Love, The Money Will Follow (New York: Dell Books, 1989).

WINSTON, Stephanie.
   Getting Organized: The Easy Way to Put Your Life in Order (Norton, 1978).

PART III

Conclusion

Evaluating Your Life Skills Growth

You have completed the Life Skills. Congratulations. Now turn back to the Quiz in Chapter 2 of Part II and answer the Life Skills questions again. Take the Quiz before you continue reading.

Now bring out the first Life Skills Quiz you took. Compare your answers. Pay particular attention to the Life Skills you wanted to strengthen. Did you answer more questions *no* this time? Even though you are still working on certain skills, have you made progress? Take a moment to reflect on the difference between taking the Quiz the first time and just now. You may be in a variety of places. You may recognize that:

1 You Need to Continue Work on Certain Skills
Even after you have done the exercises you feel that certain skills still need strengthening. In that case, go back through the book again, focusing on those particular Life Skills chapters. You may find that, in reading the chapters a second time you gain a new insight or take a deeper look at the issue. You can use the book to refer to when you need a refresher in a particular skill. Or you may want to join a Life Skills group run by a professional.

2 You Want Therapy
You may have decided you need professional therapy. Ask a friend, or call your county mental health center listed in the phone book. Or call the CHILDHELP hotline. The 800 number is listed in the Resource Guide at the back of the book. When choosing a therapist, make sure he or she is familiar with adult survivor issues. Refer to Appendix B: How to Choose a Therapist.

3 You Did Not Learn a Life Skill
Perhaps you read a Life Skills chapter, attempted the exercises, and were confused or did not learn the skill. You may have a blind spot that you will have trouble seeing without outside help. Find a

trusted friend, professional, or support group. Ask that person to look over your work with you. Remember, nothing is wrong; you just cannot see what is missing.

4 You Would Like Support
You would like to talk to others who have gone through similar situations. You may want to join a Life Skills group run by a professional. The Resource Guide lists support groups for survivors and how to contact them.

5 You Want to Join a 12-step Program
In the opening chapter I stated that this book was for survivors who are not actively addicted. However, you may have discovered in reading this book that you are an alcoholic, drug addict, overeater, chronic debtor, or sex addict. If so, I strongly recommend you join a 12-step program for your addiction. ALANON offers meetings for family, children, and friends of alcoholics. They are based on the Alcoholics Anonymous model. Local chapters are listed in the phone book.

6 You are Satisfied with Your Growth
You have worked through the Life Skills and are happy with your movement and want to continue developing your skills. Review the skills when needed. Many Life Skills participants report they have incorporated the exercises into their lives.
They ask themselves regularly:
- What would be fun for me?

- What do I need?

- Who has the problem?

- Have I asked if my help is wanted?

And they take a Life Skills approach to problems.
- Identify the problem.

- Break it down into steps.

- Assign yourself a task.

- If you need help, find a support person or expert to ask.

You do not need to know all the answers, just how to find them. You may have worked on one skill or many. But hopefully you have seen you can learn missing skills. One survivor summed up her healing and Life Skills work.

Rosa G.
'After years of pain and working on myself, there came a day when I knew I was all right. I am no longer dealing with the abuse

issues; my war is over. I am dealing with the regular problems that regular people deal with – getting a job, renting an apartment, meeting men. I feel like a normal person. The more I use the skills, the more together and happier I feel. Rather than looking for what's wrong with me, I look for what is the problem, what steps can I take to solve it, and who do I need to support me. The skills are great tools for living, and I intend to keep using them.'

ONE LAST STORY

When adult survivors become more public about their abuse, that makes it easier for other survivors to talk about theirs and seek professional help. Every time one of us stands up and declares that I am healed, healing becomes more possible for all of us.

In that light, let me share briefly my story. My dad was a hidden alcoholic. At times he was emotionally abusive. Mom instructed us: 'Do not talk to your father when he comes home!' Mostly, she buffered us from his anger and unpredictable behavior. But when we ate dinner, Dad picked on my sister's table manners. She snapped back angrily; I got very quiet and afraid. One day, we came home from school and Mom had bought four TV trays. As I chopped the salad, she said, 'We are eating in front of the television tonight'. We never ate at the dining table again.

Dad always went to work regularly; he never crashed the car; he was a functioning, yet hidden alcoholic. The same man who gently awakened me every school morning would drive us home weaving down the street, scaring us all. I loved him; I was afraid of him; and I was confused. I learned to accommodate and adapt to his behavior so well.

I learned to blind myeslf to the truth as a child and continued doing that as an adult. When I fell in love with my now ex-husband, I saw that he did not communicate sometimes and he pushed me away at other times. But I did not confront him about it. I developed a blind spot. Sometimes I repressed my feelings, letting my resentments pile up over almost nine years. They came out in covertly hostile ways. I did not have the skills I do now. I did not see the possibility that I could have confronted someone and worked something out. These are all typical life skills problems. Today I react much differently since I have learned those missing Life Skills. I have been the first student in my own Life Skills program.

When we heal and learn Life Skills, we can be productive, relate positively, have non-abusive marriages and have abuse-free relationships with our children. That means two people who are married do not physically or emotionally abuse each other; they respect each other and work out their differences. That means raising our children without hitting them or putting them down, including a slap, a beating, a put-down, a sexual innuendo, a rape. These are all forms of family violence.

The only way we can heal abuse is to heal ourselves one at a time. Let us begin. We have the commitment and the techniques. And we know it is possible. We can end family violence in this generation.

EPILOG

You are a remarkable person because you have survived abuse. You may not feel remarkable, but hundreds of times I have marvelled at how a client has survived and survived well.

You may still feel pain, but, in healing yourself, you have had to tap hidden strengths. As you have grown and learned Life Skills, you probably have sensed that inner strength. Because you have survived abuse and are recovering from it, you have confronted what many people will never deal with in a lifetime. People like you, who are healing their abusive pasts, are extraordinary people.

Your journey towards wholeness has helped you discover who are you. Releasing past pain has given you a greater ability to feel your emotions and all of life. indeed, you are now beginning to connect with your true inner self. That is the self that knows you are OK, that you can survive anything. Whatever life has in store for you, your Higher Self knows you can land on your feet. That is your spiritual self.

Set aside a few moments each day when you can be still. Close your eyes and take a few deep breaths and contact that still place within yourself, that deep self. As you do this, you may gradually become aware of your connection to something greater than yourself. You may call it spirit, the Universe, God or whatever; that does not matter. What is important is the connection to your Higher self. When you have made that connection, you can start to create your own reality in your life. Visualize your day in the way that you would like it to be. See your week going just the way you would like it to. See yourself a year from now doing exactly what you would like to do, saying what you would like to be saying and feeling happy, in tune with yourself and life around you.

Our planet and our lives are going through rapid changes. To grow with these changes, people need to know who they are – strong yet flexible, spiritual yet grounded. We need to rely on our inner stability and resources and not on outer securities such as money, job or relationships.

Those of us who have survived hardships will do the best in these changing times. And we need to extend a helping hand to others who are in need, to teach what we have learned to those around us. The more we help each other and develop a support network, the easier these transition years will be.

POSTSCRIPT

I would love to hear your reaction to *Life Skills*, your story and how Life Skills has assisted you You can write me in care of Marshall Educational Health Solutions, Inc.

Jill Raiguel

Source Notes

Introduction
1 'The Laundry List' is published by Adult Children of Alcoholics.

PART I
CHAPTER 1 *Who This Book is For*
1 Woititz, Dr Janet, *Adult Children of Alcoholics*, Pompano Beach, Florida: Health Communications, Inc., 1983.

CHAPTER 4 *Distinguishing and Defining Abuse*
1 These definitions are taken from the brochure 'Parents Anonymous' published by Parents Anonymous of Texas, Inc.
2 Daro, Deborah, et al, *Reducing Child Abuse 20% by 1990: 1985-86 Baseline Data*. A working paper prepared by the National Committee for the Prevention of Child Abuse, Chicago, I11., 1988. p. 5.
3 Werner, Dr Emily and Smith Ruth S., *Vulnerable But Invincible: A Longitudinal Study of Resilient Children*, New York: McGraw-Hill, 1982.
4 Goleman, Daniel. 'The Sad Legacy of Abuse: The Search for Remedies', *The New York Times*, January 24, 1989, p. C6.
5 Garbarino, Dr James, et al, *The Psychologically Battered Child*, San Francisco: Jossey-Bass, Inc., 1986.

CHAPTER 6 *Four Abilities Which Empower the Life Skills Work*
1 The 'Taking a Stand' and 'Intervening in Your Internal Abuse' sections are based on interviews with David Cunningham, former Associate Director of the National Committee for the Prevention of Child Abuse and presently on staff at Werner Erhard and Associates. Werner Erhard popularized the notion, taking a stand, in his program called The Forum.
2 Lerner, Rockelle, 'Boundaries for Codependents', pamphlet, Center City, Minn.: Hazelden Foundation, 1988, p. 1.

PART II
CHAPTER 2 *Not Dissociating*
1 Moody, Raymond A., *Life After Life*, New York: Bantam Books, 1975.
2 Assignments #6, #7 and #8 were created especially for this book by Hannah Woods, Sensory Awareness teacher authorized by Charlotte Selver.

CHAPTER 3 *Expressing Emotions Appropriately*
1 Davidson, Dr Joy, *The Agony of It All: The Drive for Drama and Excitement in Women's Lives*, Los Angeles: Jeremy P. Tarcher, Inc., 1988.

CHAPTER 5 *Asking For What You Need*
1 Beattie, Melody, *Codependent No More*, New York: Harper/Hazelden, 1987.

CHAPTER 8 *Expressing Anger Safely*
1 This sentence comes from Dr Thomas Gordon's *P.E.T. in Action*, New York: Bantam Books, 1976.

CHAPTER 12 *Not Overhelping*
1 Wallenstein, Judith S. and Blakeless, Sandra, *Second Chances: Men, Women and Children a Decade After Divorce*, New York: Ticknor and Fields, 1989.

CHAPTER 16 *Making Friends*
1 Padus, Emrika, *Your Emotions and Your Health*, Emmaus Penn: Rodale Press, 1986, Chapter 8, pp. 80–86.

CHAPTER 17 *Developing Intimacy*
1 Larsen, Earnie, *Stage II Relationships: Love Beyond Addiction*, New York: Harper and Row, 1987.
2 Based on John Bradshaw's characteristics of a functional family from *The Family*, Deerfield Beach, Florida: Health Communications, Inc., 1988, pp. 58–59.

APPENDIX A

Resource Guide for Adult Survivors

ASSOCIATED COUNSELORS: SEXUAL OR PHYSICAL ABUSE RESOURCE GUIDE
Gives free referrals to appropriate therapists or resources.
2860 E. Flamingo
Las Vegas, NV 89121
800-843-7274

CHILD ABUSE PREVENTION NETWORK
Created by the Family Life Development Center at Cornell University, this links information about child abuse and prevention.
http://child.cornell.edu/

CHILDHELP USA - National Child Abuse Hot Line and Links Page
Crisis counseling, referrals and information.
Several links to other websites.
15757 N. 78th Street
Scottsdale, Arizona 85260
800-4ACHILD or www.childhelpusa.org/

CULT AWARENESS NETWORK
Volunteer phone meditation for families;
counseling, education and information.
800-556-3055 or www.cultawarenessnetwork.org

MASTERS & JOHNSON NATIONAL TREATMENT CENTER FOR TRAUMA BASED DISORDERS

Nationwide referrals for therapists and support groups for dissociative disorder and ritual abuse.
DelAmo Hospital, Torrance, CA
800-553-6255 or www.delamohospital.com

MINNESOTA CENTER AGAINST VIOLENCE AND ABUSE

Information, resources and a discussion forum.
Good web links
www.mincaca.umn.edu/

NATIONAL COMMITTEE TO PREVENT CHILD ABUSE

Literature, brochures and current research.
200 S. Michigan, 17th floor
Chicago, Ill. 60604-4357
312-663-3520
Fax 312-939-8962 or www.childabuse.com

NATIONAL COUNCIL ON ALCOHOL & DRUG DEPENDENCE

Provides information, referrals, prevention, educational presentations and materials.
1424 –4th Street, #205
Santa Monica, CA 90401
310-451-5881

NATIONAL DOMESTIC VIOLENCE HOT LINE

24-hour toll free Justice domestic violence hot line funded by Department of Justice
1-800-799-**SAFE** (1-800-799-7233)
or www.usdoj.gov/vawo/hotlfs.htm

PATHFINDERS CENTER

Provides network of therapists, referral sources, and treatment services.
800-989-4649

RADER TREATMENT PROGRAMS

In-patient treatment for eating disorders and adult survivors.
Phone counseling and assessment.
12099 Washington Blvd., Ste 204
Los Angeles, CA 90066
800-841-1515 or Fax: 310-391-6259
www.raderpro.com or E-mail: rader@raderpro.com

RECOVERY

An e-mail forum and support group for survivors of
childhood sexual abuse/incest and/or their significant
others, with emphasis on healing and recovery through the
sharing of experiences, mutual support and pointers to
recovery resources. To join, contact by e-mail:
recovery@wvnet.edu

VOICES IN ACTION -
VICTIMS OF INCEST CAN EMERGE SURVIVORS

Literature, annual conference, referrals.
Based in Chicago, Illinois
800-7VOICE8 (800)-786-4238) or www.voices-action.org

For local chapters of 12-Step Programs, we recommend that you
check the listings in your local telephone book.

APPENDIX B

Additional Reading

BIREDA, MARTHA R.
Love Addiction: A Guide to Emotional
Independence (Oakland: New Harbinger
Publications, Inc. 1990).

EISENBERG, HOWARD
The Recovery Book (New York: Workman
Publishing Co. 1992).

FRIEL, JOHN and LINDA
An Adult Children's Guide to What's "Normal"
(Deerfield, Fla: Health Communications, Inc.
1990).

GOLEMAN, DANIEL
Emotional Intelligence (New York: Bantam
Books, 1995).

ORMAN, SUZE
The Nine Steps to Financial Freedom (New
York: Crown, 1997).

ORNISH, DEAN, MD
Love and Survival: A Scientific Basis for the Healing
Power of Intimacy (New York:
HarperCollins, 1998).

SCOTT, GINI GRAHAM
Resolving Conflict Within Yourself and With Others
(Oakland: New Harbinger, Inc. 1990).

APPENDIX C

How to Choose a Therapist

You have the right to interview people when selecting a therapist. Use the first phone call and first session to interview him or her. Come to that session with your questions. You are a consumer and entitled to a quality product, so do not be afraid to ask questions. Here are some things to ask:

1) What are your credentials, background experience and fees?

2) Are you familiar with abuse issues? Have you been successful with others who are survivors?

3) Were you abused or the child of an alcoholic? If the therapist was, and has dealt with the issues, that makes the therapist sensitive to them.

4) Do you direct the sessions and feel you know what is best for me? Or will you work in partnership with me, believing that you should empower me to make my own decisions. If he or she is interested in working with you in a partnership, the therapist is empowering you to rely on yourself, not setting up co-dependence.

5) Do you feel the effects of abuse are permanent, and that I am damaged? Or do you feel that I can heal and retrain myself?

6) Before making a final decision, ask yourself:
   Do you have a good feeling about this person?
   Does the therapist seem compassionate, understanding and non-judgmental? Compassion and experience are far more important than academic degrees.

APPENDIX D

Suggestions for Counselors, Friends, Co-workers and Spouses of Survivors

1) Be patient.

2) Be loving and gentle.

3) Do not judge.

4) Listen.

5) Find a support group or counselor if you need one.

6) Do not overhelp, taking on the survivor's problems.

7) Do not minimize their feelings of what happened.

8) If your friend's problems get to be too much for the friendship, refer them to a professional.

9) Notice your negative judgments about your friend or family member which limit them, such as "She's damaged," or "Something will always be wrong with him."

10) Get support from friends for yourself.

11) If you get into an argument or fight with your friend or mate, their abusive past may get triggered. You probably have more control than they do. Stop the fight. Take a time out if needed. Then talk about it.

12) When you find that your friend's situation is overwhelming to you, set a limit. You do not have to be there 100 percent of the time.

13) Healthy sex or anger can trigger an abused person even if it is gentle and non-abusive.

14) If you find yourself being abusive, STOP. If you cannot break the pattern yourself, get help. There are many 24-hour hot lines. Some are listed in this book.

15) Do not make the survivor the "identified patient" or your pet improvement project.

16) Identify your own issues and life skills and work on them.

17) As the survivor brings up feelings and issues, your relationship may be disrupted. Old patterns and modes of communicating are changing for the better, but this can still be upsetting.

18) By now, you understand that some survivors did not learn some basic skills. So, gently instruct them, rather than teasing or calling them resistant or stupid.

19) Know that, with two committed people, you can develop new patterns and a healthy, satisfying relationship.

20) If your friend or mate has tried to make you into their abuser, gently remind them you are not "Dad," or "Mom" or an abuser.

21) Keep in mind that some survivors have an "exaggerated startle reflex," that is, they jump with fear if you innocently touch them.